CAN ANY MOTHER HELP ME?

Jenna Bailey is from Sturgeon County in Alberta, Canada. She studied History at Queen's University in Ontario, Canada, where she developed her love of reading letters from the past. This led her to the University of Sussex, where she did her Master's degree in Life History Research.

Further praise for *Can Any Mother Help Me?*:

'I read it in one gulp: amazing!' Rachel Cusk

'An engaging and informative book, often touching, occasionally hilarious, sometimes profoundly moving . . . The book is a celebration of the kind of real and enduring friendship that some lucky women still enjoy today.' Sue Gaisford, *Independent on Sunday*

'It is the wonderful intimacy and spontaneity of the writing – long, chatty letters to close friends – that make Bailey's selection so compelling. Here are hearts and lives opened, an important social history, the authentic voices of intelligent women speaking to us from a fascinating archive.' Val Hennessy, *Daily Mail*

'The epic centrepiece of this collection is an account by "Isis" of her unrequited obsession with the family doctor. It's extremely moving and beautifully written, like an Elizabeth Taylor novel condensed into thirty pages. Bailey has compiled this material with great skill and respect.' John O'Connell, *Time Out*, Book of the Week

CCC, 1938

Can Any Mother Help Me?

Jenna Bailey

faber and faber

First published in 2007
by Faber and Faber Limited
3 Queen Square London WC1N 3AU
This paperback edition first published in 2008

Typeset by Faber and Faber Limited
Printed in England by CPI Bookmarque, Croydon, CR0 4TD

A CIP record for this book
is available from the British Library

ISBN 978-0-571-23314-4

10 9 8 7 6 5 4 3 2

To my beautiful sister Emma, who is always with me
May 30, 1983–May 21, 2007

Contents

Illustrations

In Text

Plates

Ad Astra, A Priori, Lough, Elektra, Rosa and Accidia at a CCC gathering in London, 1977.
Angharad, Jenna, Accidia and Elektra in London, March 2006.

Preface

In 2003, I was researching at the Mass Observation Archive at the University of Sussex, looking for a subject for my Master's thesis. The Archive, started in 1970, specialises in material about everyday life in Britain. I was told about a collection of old magazines dating back to the first half of the twentieth century, written by women belonging to some sort of club. It felt like a good lead.

The collection was in pieces, but as I started to read it soon became clear that a group of women, calling themselves the Cooperative Correspondence Club – or CCC – had created a private magazine in an attempt to alleviate the boredom and limitations of their lives as wives and mothers. They wrote articles about the things that mattered most to them – children, work, love, politics – and commented on each other's work. The magazine lasted for an incredible fifty-five years, brought to an end only by the age and ill health of the contributors.

The material had been donated to the archive in 1998 by one of the members of the CCC but had not been made public as there were issues with copyright. Only eleven of the contributors' families had given consent. For my thesis I was able to use the writing from those eleven women, which for my purposes was plenty. I began reading, and before too long I found myself growing more and more fascinated by this extraordinary group of women, whose hearts and lives were laid out in their colourfully written accounts. Their stories, however, were incomplete because only a small percentage of the material had survived – the rest lost or destroyed over the decades.

And so the idea of writing a book about these women and their magazine started to form, and with the help of the Director of the Archive I began the difficult job of tracking down families to gain consent and fill in the gaps. I discovered that one of the CCC members, with the nom de plume Elektra, was alive and well, aged ninety-seven and living in London. Through her I heard at first hand about the magazine and all of the women whom I had met only on paper. After meeting Elektra, I next found Accidia in Dorset, Angharad in Wales and then Auricula in Suffolk. These women generously took me into their homes and spoke openly about their lives. With every new encounter, I was able to colour in more of their stories and piece together the events covered by the articles in the CCC.

Almost all of the other members of the club were no longer alive, so I endeavoured to interview their children. Over a decade had passed since the last edition of the magazine, so some of them were difficult to locate. Eventually I was able to trace a member from nearly every family, most of whom were happy to share their memories of both their mother and the club. I trekked around England to meet and stay with these 'children', mostly now in their seventies. My visits were both encouraging and fruitful, as the energy and enthusiasm shared by CCC women was evident in their offspring. As an unexpected bonus, some of them had CCC articles that they had kept in their own homes. Through these interviews, I was able to fill in most of the blanks and gather enough material for the book really to take shape. I hope that what follows in some way fulfils the dream of Ad Astra, the magazine's lifelong editor, who wrote:

I have thought for the last few years that CCC ought not to perish as one by one we drop from the tree of life like ripe fruit in autumn. In a day dream I see a *book* explaining our origin, describing each member with indications of her life and interests, and recording CCC's life history.

Ad Astra, 1978

Introduction

A Cry for Help

96

Editorial.

Journey of the Magazines.

The magazine is taking a very long while to go its round these days. I think the delay is to a great extent due to postal difficulties but I hope all of you are doing your best to speed it on its way, especially as Ubique is waiting for it at the end and has not seen a number since July 2nd. What has happened to Number 44 I wonder? It went out on July 16 and had reached the end of A group by Aug 6, which wasn't bad going. The five members of B group (before it comes home & goes to Eire that is) have had it since then & it is not home yet and this is Oct 1 — five members, five weeks so far. Sent it off to C.M. by Seps so the delay is after that.

Stars for Number 43.

(This number set out July 2nd, reached the end of Group A on Aug 19, & came home on Sep 21st.)

		Returned snaps & envelopes for review.	At back.
Sviod	The Problem Solved	14.	
Younire	Photos of Samson Jock	12.	
Campo Alegre	Photos of Bridget & Stinley	10.	
Ad Astra	Women's Suffrage Triumphant	8.	
Younire	On running the CCC	8	
A priori	Day to Day	7.	
Campo Alegre	Festa de San João	6.	
Ubique	Snaps of the Family	3.	
Younire	Samson Jock Comes Home	2.	

Editorial written by Ad Astra, c. 1940.

Over the Teacups

COLBY

LETTERS for these columns should be WRITTEN ON ONE SIDE OF THE PAPER ONLY, and bear the writer's name, address and a pseudonym, and SHOULD NOT EXCEED 300 WORDS. The Editor does not hold herself responsible for advice given or opinions expressed in these columns

Going to Egypt

Nan writes : Will any mother or nurse who has lived in or near Ismailia, Egypt, with young children—mine are two and three years old—give me advice and particulars of the climate and food—is fresh milk procurable ? Life for the babes, servants, etc. ? I am most anxious to find out anything concerning children in that particular spot and any advice will be most gratefully received. This will be my first trip abroad, so I am quite an ignoramus !

Treating Constipation

Nos doh writes : A week or so ago a correspondent wrote for a cure for constipation for a child. I have found the following very good for a child of nearly three. For breakfast give the following dish. Overnight soak 1 table-spoonful of Quaker oats in 3 table-spoonful of cold water. In the morning add the juice of half a lemon, 1 table-spoonful of condensed milk and a grated apple (*skin*, core, etc., except the stalk), first cutting in half to see the centre is good. Prepare just before serving. Any other raw fruit may be used instead of apple. Let the child start lunch with raw fruit. If this is no use I should be glad to send the complete diet.
In this particular case it is for a child who does not digest starch.

Home Occupations

Ubique writes : Can any mother help me ? I live a very lonely life as I have no near neighbours. I cannot afford to buy a wireless, I adore reading, but with no library am very limited with books. I dislike needlework, though I have a lot to do ! I get so down and depressed after the children are in bed and I am alone in the house. I sew,

read, and write stories galore, but in spite of good resolutions, and the engaging company of cat and dog, I *do* brood, and "dig the dead." I have had a rotten time, and been cruelly hurt, both physically and mentally, but I know it is bad to brood and breed hard thoughts and resentments. Can any reader suggest an occupation that will intrigue me and exclude " thinking " and cost nothing ! A hard problem I admit.

Sunburn

Carron writes : In answer to "Twinkle toes," I do not think there is anything as good for sunburn as " Carron oil," it is far better than calomine lotion or anything else. My children have turned a lovely brown and had no redness, soreness or peeling. It should be well rubbed in and the part effected *not* touched with soap or water for two days. The oil is quite cheap and may be used anywhere on face or body with safety.
I have also made my children loose fitting gingham coats with long sleeves, for wear on beach or in garden when the sun is really strong, as this saves their arms and backs. Underneath they wear bathing dresses only.

Pandora writes : " Twinkle-toes " would find that her charge would avoid sunburn if she rubbed in the oil thoroughly about an hour before putting him outside. Unabsorbed oil on the *surface* of the skin simply prevents evaporation and causes him to fry. I have seen very bad sunburn resulting from this.
We have always found coconut oil much lighter and better, and more effective than olive oil.
A child will brown in the shade, under the light from the open sky as well as in
(*Continued on page 326.*)

Ubique's letter in 'Over the Teacups' in July, 1935.

A CRY FOR HELP 3

Ballingate, Ireland, 1935:

Can any mother help me? I live a very lonely life as I have no near neighbours. I cannot afford to buy a wireless. I adore reading, but with no library am very limited with books. I dislike needlework, though I have a lot to do! I get so down and depressed after the children are in bed and I am alone in the house. I sew, read and write stories galore, but in spite of good resolutions, and the engaging company of cat and dog, I do brood, and 'dig the dead'. I have had a rotten time, and been cruelly hurt, both physically and mentally, but I know it is bad to brood and breed hard thoughts and resentments. Can any reader suggest an occupation that will intrigue me and exclude 'thinking' and cost nothing! A hard problem, I admit.

This cry for help, written by a lonely mother using the nom de plume 'Ubique' (Latin for 'everywhere'), appeared in the July 1935 issue of the widely read British motherhood magazine *The Nursery World*. The letter, published in the 'Over the Teacups' column of the magazine, elicited a chain of responses from sympathetic mothers from many different walks of life living all over the United Kingdom. Fellow readers of *The Nursery World*, also writing under pseudonyms, were happy to offer Ubique suggestions to help her through her troubles. The majority of the responses echoed that of Sympathiser:

I am indeed sorry for 'Ubique' in her trouble . . . I wonder if 'Ubique' would care to correspond with readers. I should be very pleased to exchange letters with her, and this would give her fresh thoughts and would, I should think, cheer her up. Perhaps she will tell me if she cares for this idea.

Mother of Three, who wrote that 'letters are a wonderful help when one is lonely', even suggested that 'more fortunate new friends can enclose a stamped envelope, so that stamps need not be a strain'.

Ubique received letters from several women throughout the next couple of months and, in September of that year, she responded to *The Nursery World*: 'I feel I must thank all the kind people who have both written to me personally and via THE NURSERY WORLD. I'd love to write to them all personally, and correspond with lots of them, but even the stamps are 2d.' Instead, Ubique suggested that they form a correspondence magazine. This meant that each woman, writing under a nom de plume, would contribute an article on any subject and mail it to Ubique, who would assemble all of the articles and hand stitch them together in a decorative cover. She would mail the completed magazine to the first woman on a pre-arranged list, who had a set amount of time to read it and respond to the articles by commenting directly on the pages. That member would forward it on to the next woman, and so on, until the magazine had been fully circulated. There was only one copy of each magazine, and they would produce it fortnightly. The women decided to call themselves the Cooperative Correspondence Club (CCC) and proposed that the magazine be written exclusively for, and read exclusively by, the members of the club.

Like Ubique, most of the prospective members of the CCC were lonely and bored, and they welcomed the opportunity for connection and change that a correspondence magazine offered. One of the first women to answer Ubique's letter in 1935 was Janna, aged twenty-six. She regretted her decision to marry young, stating that 'there was so much else I wanted out of life, and in those days marriage often = housewifery, which I loathed. I didn't even, then, want children, and really had poor little [Julian] more because of boredom than anything else.' As Janna wrote, for women in the 1930s marriage typically meant being relegated to the home. During the inter-war years there was a great deal of emphasis on the family unit and on the traditional roles for men and women. The members of the CCC therefore belonged to a generation of women whose choices were limited as they were expected mainly to become housewives and mothers.

Ad Astra, another of the first women to join the magazine, was one of the members of the CCC who struggled with the lack of options available to women of her generation. In the 1920s, marriage bars were implemented that restricted women in public-service jobs and professional careers from working once they were married. The legislation differed slightly from field to field and was inconsistently implemented from the early 1920s until the Second World War. Though the rules varied somewhat, the premise was always the same: married women should not be working but should be in the home, and the man of the household should support the family. Teaching was one of the professions that was significantly affected by the bar, and Ad Astra, a passionate teacher, was one of the women who was forced to give up her career. She met her future husband, John, in 1927 but delayed marriage until 1930 because leaving her profession was such a difficult decision. Like her, many of the women who responded to Ubique were intelligent, university-educated women who were denied the opportunity to work. Once married and confined to the home, many of these women found that they were not ideally suited for life as a housewife and mother. A Priori, a mother of three who joined the magazine in 1937, explained that 'many of us, plunged into motherhood from being career girls, had a lot to learn about running a home'. Auricula, a latecomer to the magazine and mother of five, felt this way:

I had always wanted a family, although hopelessly incompetent. I had no idea how to look after myself, let alone a husband and a child. I had never cooked a meal or ironed a shirt in my life when I got married. Many was the time when my tears mingled with the soap suds as I tried to get white collars clean – in the end I scrubbed them with Vim.

Not only were some of the CCC women housewives by circumstance rather than by choice, but this occasionally was the case with motherhood as well, for at the time birth control was not readily available for women. Ubique specifically recruited A Priori to join the CCC after reading an article that she had written in *The Nursery World* under the name 'Mother in Spite of Herself'. In later years, when A Priori discussed the choice of name with her fellow club members, she explained that 'My point was quite a valid one, I think, that in those days before the pill many of us were mothers by accident.'

The women of the CCC were not simply a part of a generation that had to cope with the pressure of conforming to the roles of housewife and mother, they were also expected to conduct themselves the 'right' way within those roles. A high standard of housekeeping became the norm in the 1930s, and women's days were spent completing 'elaborate household routines and tasks'. While the majority of the women who joined the CCC were middle class and had paid domestic help, the amount of work required to run a household was so extensive that the women were still overrun with duties.

Changes in health care and medicine created an awareness that, through proper hygiene and feeding, the risk of infant deaths could be lowered. This was good news, but it placed even greater stress and time commitments on mothers. They wanted to know exactly how to care for their children, and they began to – and were expected to – faithfully seek out and follow the advice of experts such as Truby King. King was the most widely known authority at the time on proper care and hygiene for children. His methods essentially 'turned motherhood into a "craft" that could be learned and a baby into something that could be controlled'. The women of the CCC, like many other mothers in the 1930s, relied heavily on his advice. King's suggested regimen of rigid schedules and routines made the daily lives of CCC women even more taxing. In later years, A Priori reflected that:

Sitting up all night holding the hand of a crying baby didn't leave one a lot of energy for all the myriad of other jobs which had to be done. Of course, I have learned a lot about babies since then and would never leave a baby to cry or keep to rigid feeding times as Truby King advocated. Still we tried to do our best and TK was the latest thing . . .

Along with the changing physical aspects of child rearing, there was also a new emphasis on the psychology of raising children. Experts in the field began to emphasise the importance of strict schedules and routines that would improve a 'child's character'. While these changing practices in childcare resulted in some benefits, when combined with elaborate housekeeping standards they made the daily routine of the women in the CCC much more demanding.

This period as a mother and wife was particularly difficult for many women in the CCC because they lived in isolated areas and lacked any kind of support network. Waveney, a mother of four boys at the time she joined the CCC in the late 1930s, lived in a small village outside Bristol, far from her family, who lived in the north of England. Yonire, a member of the CCC from 1936, had moved down from Edinburgh's high society to her new husband's sheep farm on the Scottish borders, where she had the first of her five sons. This distance from one's family was often intentional, because during the interwar years middle-class families began to remove themselves from the traditional familial support networks that past generations had relied upon. Now, middle-class women were taking on greater responsibility for their home and children by cutting the strong ties with their parents. This was often accomplished by moving a great distance away so that parents and in-laws could not be involved in raising the children. For instance, Angharad married in 1945 and moved from Wales to Lancaster because her husband 'thought we should not settle too near our parents until we'd got ourselves established as a separate unit'. She explains that by the time she joined the CCC in the early 1950s, 'I didn't have a lot of people, I couldn't go and talk to my sisters because I was an only child. We had had a couple of years, miles from anywhere.' Many of the women in the CCC were in similar situations and longed for a support network.

Given these circumstances, the women of the CCC, like many mothers of the 1930s and 1940s, turned to women's magazines for help. These magazines became the main source of information on the latest techniques in both childcare and housework. Nearly all women's publications had articles by experts such as 'Woman Doctor', 'Psychologist' and 'Nursery Expert'. At this time *The Nursery World* was a weekly periodical published for mothers and children's nurses, and was the 'publication which everybody read'. Mothers counted on this magazine for child-rearing advice as well as tips on the more practical aspects of motherhood, such as the buying and selling of prams, cots and similar necessities. As many of these women were lacking companionship in their busy lives, the women's press also became a source for personal relationships through the 'problem page', interactive pages where women could write in and exchange experiences and information with other readers. These columns, such as *The Nursery World*'s 'Over the Teacups', where Ubique's letter was published, fostered a sense of community for women who wanted to connect with other women. It was in this spirit that the CCC came into being, as the future members of the club were already communicating with a larger readership in *The Nursery World* in an effort to escape their isolation and make connections with other mothers.

Specifically because the women hoped that the magazine would act as an antidote to their boredom and intellectual starvation, the original members, numbering between ten and fifteen, decided that they would try to create as diverse a membership as possible. This way the magazine would expose the women to a variety of lifestyles and experiences and make it more interesting to read. They aimed for a membership of around twenty-four women, and in their first years of existence they recruited mainly through advertisements in the *The Nursery World*. Occasionally another member recommended someone, but this happened infrequently as the CCC members preferred that everyone be relatively unconnected in their daily lives. One exception to this, and an example of the CCC's effort to diversify its membership, occurred when Ad Astra invited her friend Elektra to join in late 1938, specifically because she was Jewish. Some of the women in the magazine were writing anti-Semitic comments, and Ad Astra wanted her to provide the group with a different perspective. Elektra explained that she started in the CCC as:

. . . a sort of guinea pig being prodded and having to defend all these wicked things that people were writing . . . And so it was very painful, really horrible, and I hated it but I thought this is something I must do. And I consulted a rabbi and he said, 'Look – if you are simply on the defensive – this will go on forever – go on the attack' – so that's what I did. And the anti-Semitism stopped.

In addition to Elektra, the group also comprised women from a wide range of other religious backgrounds. Barnie and Waveney were devoted to the Church of England, while Isis converted to Catholicism, Janna was an atheist and Sirod practised ontology.

Religion was only one of the areas where the CCC diversified. The women lived all over the United Kingdom, with Rusticana in Scotland, Ubique in Ireland, Angharad in Wales and the majority of the other members based all over England. The CCC members ranged from upper-middle-class ladies to those who were born in working-class families but who had advanced through education into the middle class. Cotton Goods, the one working-class member of the club, was an exception. The women also had opposing political affiliations. Elektra and Cotton Goods were ardent Labour supporters, which contrasted with Roberta's Conservative background and A Priori's Liberal sympathies. There was a great disparity of lifestyle amongst the members. Waveney and Barnie were soldiers' wives, while Janna and Accidia were pacifists married to conscientious objectors. Finally, the range of personalities and characters was vast, with shy, conservative members like Country Mouse, eccentric extroverts like Roberta, and quick-witted, opinionated women like A Priori.

It was generally understood that you could only be a member of the CCC if you were a mother. In 1940, Rosa nominated a potential new member who had no children, and the women discussed the possibility of including her:

I shall be most interested to see if CCC as a whole wants new members or not. To me, it does not seem the right time to add to our number, as the postal delays are so great, but I am terribly tempted to make a suggestion nevertheless, but after the flop that Jennifer was, I hesitate to try again!

I have a friend near me who would I think be an asset, and if there is any feeling in favour of new blood perhaps she might be considered. She is 30, a Scot and graduate of Aberdeen, a linguist and musician and keen Labour party member, expresses herself with force and eloquence and *writes legibly*. She has a satirical and somewhat cynical sense of humour, married 4 years, no children – Perhaps she is not sufficiently different from our established intelligentsia to be acceptable . . .

Must one be a mother to be a CCC member? *We did say so.*
That had not occurred to me before. *(Ad Astra)*

Ad Astra then wrote:

Will members please sign here if they think Rosa's friend would make a good new member? I see several members do not feel the need of a new member just now, and of course one of the original ideas of CCC was that all members should be mothers and discuss their children in its pages, but she sounds good. So I leave it to you *all* to decide.

The women voted and, though it was not unanimous, they decided not to let the woman into the club, one member making it clear that no one should join who had no children.

This was one of the basic principles behind the magazine, and it seems to have been the only 'official' reason to deny a woman entrance into the club. However, the women also expected members to be able to bring something new to the magazine, be it through their upbringing, social status or geographical location. While the CCC's differences strengthened the group by sparking new ideas and discussions, it also encouraged a degree of snobbery and elitism. When a new member was being considered, the group would take a vote on the individual's 'acceptability' and a majority decision would be reached. Accidia remembers that she was asked to fill in an application form and hand in a curriculum vitae after she responded to an advertisement in *The Nursery World* to join the CCC in 1951. In her application she wrote 'briefly about going to Cambridge and what my life was like now, that I enjoyed reading, I didn't want to talk about children all the time, I didn't want to talk about cooking, I wasn't very domestic, that kind of thing, and I would value the friendship'. The original members then voted on her 'suitability' for the club, and Accidia was asked to join. In general, they were quite selective and only added women whom they deemed interesting enough. In the early years, the subtle pressure to maintain a certain standard after joining the club came in the form of a 'star system'. The members would allocate stars to women who had contributed articles that they felt were particularly well written, interesting or engaging. Some members would then donate a prize to the person who had gathered the most stars at the end of circulation. This only lasted a few years, however, and was discontinued once the women became better acquainted.

During the first ten years of the CCC, membership fluctuated slightly, with a few members joining but later dropping out. One of the more notable withdrawals was, according to A Priori, 'a queer woman called Roxanne, a doctor's wife, who took offence at everything anybody said to her. Her theme song was "My husband will not allow me to be insulted!" In the end she departed in a blazing row.' A more significant dropout took place in 1937, when Rusticana left the CCC after an argument (the cause of which is not remembered by surviving members). After leaving, Rusticana started her own correspondence magazine run along identical lines to the CCC. Her mag was called Phoenix, as it was going to 'rise out of the ashes of the crumbling CCC'. Phoenix flourished and continues to exist today. Several members of the CCC, including Cornelia, Cotton Goods and Yonire, decided to join both Phoenix and the CCC, and this was accepted by the other members of the club. A Priori wrote about this division just after Rusticana's defection and cautioned other members: 'I should want those members of CCC who have joined Rusticana's Club to promise no less support to CCC than they have given in the past. I myself refused the temptation, and it was a big one, and I am not going to run a Club, half of whose members give it only divided and half-hearted allegiance.' Following these and a few other dropouts, the CCC women decided to recruit again in the early 1950s. They added four younger members, Accidia, Stevie, Auricula and Angharad, to the group. This was the last time they admitted new members.

Shortly after the magazine began, the women decided that the role of editor, initially filled by Ubique, should be held by a new member each year. The editor was responsible for administrative details, such as posting advertisements for new members. Despite the fact that it required a lot of work, there was initially some jockeying for the position. Robina followed Ubique as editor, and then A Priori assumed the role in 1938, though not without some controversy. Although the details are scant, the following article written by A Priori demonstrates that there was a certain amount of tension amongst the members about how the editor should behave and what the editor's role should be:

I do not believe that CCC can survive if the Editor is *nothing* but an accommodation address. There are ways in which she can stimulate interest and smooth out difficulties, and also encourage new members, where suitable and approved by the Club as a whole . . . .

I am against censorship and feel that grown-up people

should be able to argue and take hard blows without getting tearful, sentimental or spiteful. I might possibly ask a member to reconsider an offensive article, but my ideas of offensiveness are wide.

Hear! Hear! A very clear statement of policy. (Soldier's Wife)

In 1939, Ad Astra took over from A Priori. This was also supposed to be a one-year position, but with the onset of the Second World War, the members agreed that Ad Astra, with her attention to detail and organisational skills, was ideally suited for the job and should continue. She carried on as editor of the CCC until its last few years in the late 1980s.

Despite the title of editor, Ad Astra did not edit the work submitted by the members. Instead, her job was largely an administrative one. She wrote an editorial at the beginning of every magazine and dealt with collecting and compiling the writing, often placing it in a hand-embroidered or otherwise decorative linen cover. She would send out an edition of the magazine on the 1st and again on the 15th of the month. Rather than waiting for one magazine to complete its circulation, Ad Astra would mail the next magazine so that they were constantly circulating.

There was a certain degree of prestige that came with the position of editor. Although it required commitment and work, it also meant that Ad Astra had both authority and control. She was the one who would 'crack the whip' when members were late with submissions or when a member was not contributing enough to the magazine (the general rule being that you had to submit at least one article a month). Her methods instilled a slight feeling of obligation in the women, as at the end of the year she would tally everyone's articles and write the results in the magazine so the group would know how often each woman had contributed in that calendar year. In 1977, Accidia reflected on the number of letters she had submitted:

> . . . if I don't write something tonight, I shall fail in my reso-
> lution to improve my record – Not that I have any hopes of
> being able to compete with the goodies like AA and Yonire
> who clock up to 24/24 annually. I am always surprised, when
> I read AA's annual figures, to find that I have sent fewer con-
> tributions than I thought I had. I conclude that I must *think*
> contributions when I am driving or doing housework, but fail
> to *write* them.

Ad Astra's personality was well suited to this position and some of the women saw her as a sort of head-
mistress of the group.

Although she did not edit the women's submissions,
there was an element of Ad Astra's work that related
directly to the content: coordination. As she was
responsible for compiling the writing, Ad Astra had the
opportunity to arrange the material as she saw fit.
Therefore, while she did not censor anyone's work,
when she saw something that was potentially offensive
she would often attempt to facilitate a discussion about
the submission. It would seem that, as editor, Ad Astra
did not feel that she could be as open as the rest of the
members. When the magazine was in its last decade,
her health was deteriorating and she found it difficult
to write for the CCC. After Sirod referred to her as a
'coordinator', she wrote to the others saying that 'if
anyone takes over the job and goes into it gaily assuming she can say what she likes and remain friends with
all members without any consideration of a's positions,
b's politics, c's family interests, I warn her from experience she has a surprise in store'.

While Ad Astra may have felt constrained in her role
as editor, in general the women of the CCC felt comfortable about writing candidly. This was mainly because
the magazines were to be read exclusively by the women
in the club. The group's mentality was that 'what was

written in the magazine stayed in the magazine'. Children of CCC women vividly recall that the magazine was fiercely guarded and often hidden away by their mothers, not to be shared or viewed by any other member of the household. (Many of the children, now in their seventies, confess to 'sneaking a peek' at the mag, the temptation being too strong to resist.) Even though the women wrote under noms de plume, this was slightly irrelevant in terms of privacy as everyone had to exchange names and addresses so that they could send the mag along in the post. However, the pseudonyms did provide a sense of security and anonymity for the members, because any non-member who happened to read the magazine would not recognise the names.

The feeling of privacy meant that, amongst other subjects, the women were able to write about sexual matters, topics that were only just becoming acceptable for women to discuss when the club began. Evidently, some members were reluctant to include this material in the magazine and sexual content was actually banned at one point. Janna alluded to this in the following entry from 1938:

Please, Robina, don't accuse me of 'falling back' on recipes instead of writing about sex! You surely know that I am much more interested in 'serious' than 'household' articles, but the latter are all right for a change and some people appreciate recipes, and . . . so on – and it's nice to please as many as possible.

If anyone has any doubts please know once and for all that I am all in favour of complete outspokenness on any topic whatsoever, and I am perfectly willing to contribute any experiences, however intimate or precious, of my own if they have any direct bearing on the subject in hand or are likely to be of help. I see no point in going into unnecessary details merely for the sake of relating them; and I have already briefly told of our approach to sexual union, where we got our little knowledge, etc. I should certainly welcome a serious discussion of sex problems, as I think the pooling of experiences is the only way one can really learn (except by often unhappy experience) the intricacies of this most important art.

Why not let the ban be lifted and all 'risqué' articles be published together at the end of the journal, so that those who do not wish to read them can easily skip? . . .

What about it, editor? Janna.

Although the details of the ban Janna refers to are unknown, it did not remain in effect for very long. Despite some hesitancy amongst the members, the confidentiality offered by the CCC gave the women the opportunity to write articles that went beyond what would have been socially acceptable in the public realm at that time. The following article by Roberta on the relationship between orgasms and the sex of a child, written in 1938, broached topics that most certainly would have been considered taboo.

Sex Determination!
I honestly think I have hit on an idea! And I feel that if you will all (not unless you wish to, since it is rather intimate this time) help, we might get somewhere, after all aren't there 22 of us?

Sirod first set me thinking. She said that there existed a theory that supported the idea that when a *woman* has an orgasm, certain 'juices' are set free and likely to have some effect on the ovary. Now I feel that this idea . . . is pretty near to the truth. Look at it this way. If you are a person who is likely to always achieve an orgasm during conception, then you will stick to *one* sex, e.g. if your first is a girl, and all your other children are conceived with an orgasm, then you will always have girls. Should your first be a boy, and you have full satisfaction from the sex act, then you will follow with boys.

Supposing you do *not* have complete satisfaction, well, the same applies. If you start with boys, or girls, so you will go on. *Unless* one child is conceived in exactly the opposite conditions.

Can anyone follow?

I feel that people who sometimes have orgasms and sometimes not are far more likely to have boys and girls.

For instance, I myself have always enjoyed sex, and I have

two boys and so I always shall, I feel, unless I try at the end of the month, make myself thoroughly 'acid' and *not* have an orgasm.

There are a few examples which I feel *may* support my theory!

Ubique – (please may I use you?), you to my knowledge, did not experience orgasms during her marriage. She has four daughters. Then *A Priori* may say 'but I *do* enjoy my husband, and I have three girls'! – yes, that's why!

Your 'love' makes you have girls! Try once, and *not* love your husband, and eat and drink bicarbonate of soda, milk of magnesia etc. and I'll bet you'll have a son!

I have a friend who always 'loves' her husband, she has 3 children of the same sex. I can think of many other examples. Would readers with boys and girls be willing to state if they are the kind of person to sometimes enjoy, and sometimes not, intercourse? By *enjoyment* – I mean they have and can fulfil complete sex orgasm.

Will this shock anyone? I shall leave a blank page for anyone who is *willing* to reply and perhaps Robina will re-publish it.

I don't think of it all as disgusting or shocking – but intensely interesting, and naturally absorbing since we are all mothers – and all think of this as natural. Anyhow, I think it *is* thrilling this boy and girl question . . .

The whole point which I do not seem to have made clear is this. I *don't* think that an orgasm can make *all* boys, nor *all* girls, but in some women it promotes boys and in other girls . . .

Maybe this is all nonsense, but I have a 'hunch' about it.

P.S. I have discussed this subject today with a girl friend (A Priori knows her too) and she says she was told by her doctor that an orgasm was *not* necessary to produce these particular juices, that even when just excited they appear, but one can still apply 'my' theory, even so . . .

We both agree most strongly though that an acid system produces girls (plus my theory) and that an alkaline state – boys.

One need not give details – just state whether my 'theory' is true or not in your own particular case.

The CCC provided an outlet for thoughts that the

women might not want to discuss with people in their everyday lives. This applied to more than just sexual topics. In 1962, a man accosted Angharad when she was on her way home from work, but she managed to evade her attacker. Angharad did not want to share the story with anyone involved in her daily life for fear they would try to stop her from walking home at night. Instead, she explained the story to the CCC:

The remaining problem is whether to tell anybody? I have decided no. For one thing, if I told anyone at all, the first person would have to be Morien [Angharad's husband], and as he's only precariously recovered from a tendency to imagine me the object of strange men's libido at the drop of a hat, the last thing I want is to do or say anything that might revive that tendency . . . So I have kept mum, like Midas's barber, but since it was too intriguing an incident in an uneventful life I know I shall burst if I don't unburden myself some way or other so – isn't CCC a *useful* institution?

While the women in the club often confided in one another, they also wrote, at length, about current events, politics, religion and literature. Many of the members were well educated and had a passion for the written word, so the standard of writing was high. The women were forthright and honest in their articles and often challenged and debated with one another. This created trust amongst the members and also resulted in lively and engaging discussions. Accidia said that sitting down with the CCC was like having an 'intellectual coffee morning'. The combination of intellect and exuberance often resulted in clashes in the magazine. Although the subject of the following dispute is unclear, as the accompanying articles have not survived, the way in which Cotton Goods discusses her disagreement with Janna shows how direct some members could be. 'Cornelia, I grant I've been a little unfair to Janna and we understand each other better now,' she wrote. 'It's not *Janna* I get out of patience with, but her ideas. I was once as pigheaded an idealist, and oh the daft things I did in the name of idealism!'

A Priori, in particular, was relentlessly confrontational and rarely missed an opportunity to challenge one of her fellow club members. Her comments from an article written in 1949 provide a glimpse of how she typically approached a disagreement in the magazine:

Elektra, I can't bear the thought that you might be really cross with me; terrified, I rush in to pacify you, and no doubt, like most peacemakers, I shall only make you crosser than ever. . . . However, to proceed. I suppose what you want me to elucidate is why I said your article on religious teaching in schools was shallow, narrow-minded and ignorant? Well, then . . .

This open and argumentative environment was further encouraged by the unusual format of the magazine. The women constantly commented directly on each other's articles as the magazine circulated, and this made the conversations and discussions decidedly interactive and lively. The remarks frequently sparked debates in subsequent magazines, such as A Priori's response to Janna in 1949:

Janna, you ask me to explain various cryptic footnotes I have put in the magazine lately. Well, I have thought a good deal about such things, but I don't know if you would really like me to discuss the whole thing fully. But I will try to make some headlines and if you would like me to go more fully into those which concern your personal affairs, I will do so.

The fact that the mag only circulated once meant that each woman just saw the comments made by members who had received the magazine earlier in the schedule. In a discussion with Roberta, A Priori expressed her frustration with this system:

Roberta, I didn't say I disliked footnotes as such. I don't mind if people write, 'I don't agree' or 'rot' or 'hear hear' on what I write. What I did ask you to stop is very long footnotes that would really make an article and which people [before] you on the roster don't see and also footnotes which make it difficult to read the original article.

This was often a contentious issue amongst the members and so Ad Astra frequently rearranged the mailing list so that the order in which the women received the magazine was always changing. The constant circulation of the magazine meant that a member could ignore contributions or comments that did not interest her, or that she did not wish to acknowledge. The sheer volume of content and number of contributors meant that there was always a number of ongoing discussions, and members could choose to participate in them or not.

It was not long after the CCC began that some of the women arranged to meet in person. With the onset of war, several members sent their children to billet with CCC families living in safer areas. Both Barnie's and A Priori's children went to Devon to stay with Rusticana. In 1943, Waveney, Barnie, Robina and Sirod booked a schoolhouse in Ilfracombe for themselves and their children and lived together for over a month. Many other visits and exchanges took place throughout the war. Living through this time together truly solidified the friendships within the CCC.

Once the war came to an end they decided to have a yearly luncheon. The big event was typically held in London at Elektra's or in Essex at Ad Astra's large country home. The women continued this tradition for over forty years. It was usually the same group in attendance, as members like Country Mouse or Michaelmas rarely made an appearance. Other women were unable to attend because they lived farther away, in Scotland or Wales, and so they seldom had the opportunity to meet many of the other members. Throughout the rest of the year CCC women would pop in on one another when they were travelling and then report the details of the visit in the magazine. Many in the group also spoke on the phone to share family news or discuss the CCC.

Throughout the decades of writing and meeting, a wide range of friendships developed. A few women in the magazine barely knew each other. When reflecting on Country Mouse's death in 1976, Accidia commented that 'I never met her and did not feel I knew her very well; she did not seem to "come across".' Others developed extremely close friendships, like Accidia and Janna, who had similar political viewpoints and were kindred spirits. Accidia recalled seeing Janna at her first CCC luncheon:

The first time I went to this luncheon . . . I was extremely nervous . . . I walked up and down, I was nervous to go in . . . I sort of crept in . . . and across the room there was this woman, and we looked at each other . . . we never forgot this . . . there was a kind of glance or recognition between us, a sort of affinity straight away.

Overall, the women in the club were a constant presence in each other's lives. Collectively, their letters reveal how they changed as individuals, and as a group, how they evolved from young mothers to elderly women and how they faced life's joys and sorrows along the way. Their writing provides us with a window into the hearts, minds and souls of an exceptional, and yet ordinary, group of women whose lives spanned nearly the whole of the last century.

I

Nursery World

an old schoolfriend of Michaels in, who started last Sept.   He
went to the school Peter now attends and he said to me "We have
some dreadful boys in our class - they come from Dagenham.   They
get the cane an awful lot, but they don't care"   The teachers
are all certified and with a degree and the teaching is excellent
BUT the pace is dreadfully hard, and I have known both boys
from this school - and girls from the similar school - unable to
keep it up.

WAVENEY.   My boys were all "trained" from three days, and no
not complexes.   Michael wet the bed rather late, but apart
from that they were all exceptionally good of this matter, and
as the "babe" was old enough to comprehend that his bigger
brother stood to pass urine, he, too, desired to stand for this.
I have found the problem of the afternoon pramride, when it
is a long one, often complained of by mothers trying to train
the child over a year.   Mine was a deep "sol" pram certainly
with which I've accomplished the job in even the street without
anyone aware of what I was doing, I always kept a mug
in the well of the pram, and when necessary the child "tialed"
in this.   I can't myself agree with the N.W., that
children are best not trained until nearly a year.

UBIQUE says that I send her nearly frantic! I'm sorry!! I thought
I'd been most careful lately.   Well ROBERTA, my friends call me
placid, BUT your article entitled "Prison reform" makes me
!!!%%%???!!!%%%?? and see RED RED RED RED.
I can only say ?????? you don't know what xxx a lucky devil
you are and that is why you write so.   I consider I'm a
lucky devil too.   My husband earns something over £400 and
it takes all our ingenuity to keep our end up.   I've had two
very cross sleepless babies, and there have been times, when I've
been nearly demented.   We reckoned Michael slept the night, one
an average, one night in thirty.   Patrick "took him over"
every Saturday night, and no matter how he howled I never moved.
However ill I felt I daren't let Patrick take him over any other
night because he just can't do with bad nights and it wouldn't
help if he lost his job.   After Ted came to Town, I was
really extremely groggy for months, and for two months I was
without help.   I was really quite ill, had two children of 7 and
4 to attend to and a babe that cried all night again, and I can
tell you there have been nights and nights when I've thought I
just couldn't carry on and I still maintain I am most reasonable
and sensible and levelheaded.   YOU DON'T KNOW TO WHAT LENGTHS
A CROSS - A REALLY CROSS BABY - CAN SEND A MAN OR WOMAN - even
when she has a good husband, shelter and sufficent for all their
needs, so please do have a little imagination and think what it
must be like when there is no food for the children and no work
for the husband.   Please, oh please have a grain of sympathy

Written by Cornelia in 1938.

Have any of you got a really 'shy' child? If so, what do you do about it? I should be so grateful for any views and advice, as I am faced with the problem of an apparently permanently shy and self-conscious child.

Barnie, 1938

When the women of the CCC initially came together as a group, they agreed that the club did not exist simply to discuss each other's children. Even though all of the members were mothers, and had to be in order to join, the magazine's purpose was to offer women an alternative to, and, for some, an escape from, their role as a mother. It was understood amongst the women that the children would not be the focus of the magazine.

Despite this, children infiltrated every aspect of these women's lives and therefore certain discussions about child rearing and life with children were inevitable. This was particularly the case in the early years, when their children were still quite young, and CCC women would query the group for help with specific problems or concerns, such as when Barnie wrote about her son John in 1938. These types of worries were commonly expressed, and members of the group would discuss various options for the child in question.

Roberta and Accidia shared their different experiences of motherhood with the CCC in the following stories.

Roberta

Born into a middle-class family in Chislehurst, Kent, on October 11, 1912, Roberta was the third daughter in a family of four girls. A bit of a tomboy as a child, she was involved in sports throughout her adolescence, particularly hockey and riding. After leaving school around the age of sixteen, she worked as a teacher until she married her husband Walter in 1934. Walter was a Swiss-German who was working as a stockbroker in London while trying to improve his English. The couple stayed in Chislehurst once they were married and had their first son Nicholas in 1935, followed by Christopher in 1937.

During the Phoney War, Roberta, Walter and the two boys moved to a farm in Cornwall with Roberta's sister Marjorie and her son David. Once it became apparent that Britain was not going to be invaded, they returned to Kent and, after a few other moves, settled in their home Nether Fawke. Walter continued to work as a stockbroker and also served as an Air Raid Precautions (ARP) Warden. As it was wartime and he was a foreigner, Walter had to check in with the police weekly. Roberta, in the meantime, was occupied with the full-time job of motherhood and with the duties and tasks involved in running a household during wartime.

An outgoing and eccentric person, Roberta was famous amongst the CCC for her atrocious typing, which made many of her articles illegible and infuriated the group. Her zest for life is evident in her descriptive passages regarding the various stages of her pregnancies and the deliveries of her children.

She wrote to the women just after the birth of her third son in July of 1943.

The Arrival of My Third Son, Guy

I have got permission to slip this in August 1st issue as I can't get it to AA in time!

To begin with, I can't quite make out why I have not one awful pang that I have another boy! I heard them say, 'Oh she will be disappointed, she has two sons,' but I piped up, 'Well, I am not one bit, I knew it was a boy all the time'! And is he lovely? Well, I nearly cry every time I look at him, he is such a dear darling, but to begin at the beginning . . .

I had not felt too well on the 26th and even told Walter when he got home, laughingly, that if this was my first baby I would have gone to the nursing home, but KNOWING everything as I did, it was all wind! I even sent a note to AA and said I felt very dead beat that evening etc., anyhow I went to bed at 11 as usual and slept. At 2 a.m. I felt a bursting sensation and liquid streaming all over the place. I was so scared it was blood that I dared not look! I called to Walter who was in the dressing room and he ran in and then told me it was merely the waters which had broken! So he came into bed with me and we lay and talked etc. but the pains had started and were very sharp and low already. I phoned the doctor and nursing home to warn them. The doctor told me not to move at all as she did not want me to lose any more water, but I had to get around a bit. At first she wanted me to get an ambulance but I begged her to let me go quietly with Walter in his car before breakfast, to which she agreed.

Walter made me tea at 6 a.m. and somehow I directed the packing (but had still such a lot to get for myself!) I had not even a towel and one or two odds and ends but the baby was all right! The boys woke up with the commotion and I shuffled in to see them.

Both looked anxious and dear wee Chris was a bit down as I told him I could not go to his school concert after all as Charlie had decided to come! It was difficult as pains were coming so I had to rush outside their door and pretend to do something until it had passed. I have never had these sharp pains before, and never so low down and knife-edged, however, all adds to one's experience!

Reby was up and I said how sorry I was to leave her with so much to do, all Nick's packing and last minute supervising and points to get in (all jobs which I had intended to do for her before August 6th). But she cheerfully said she would cope and was so sweet and good. Heaven knows where I would be without her; she has all meals to think of too, plus all the shopping, house and washing for C and other things. I had written her a note a week ago to be left when I went off so at least I had prepared that little bit! (merely to thank her for her kindness and so on).

I arrived at the nursing home at 7.30 and could not even unpack by then. I merely put all my things on a chair and fell into dear Hodge's arms and was carted up stairs to the labour ward! Gosh it was sheer heaven having her around again. She has been perfectly wonderful and so kind and good to me, and above all I have her ALL to myself, the other baby has its own private nurse. Jennifer came to see me and examined me, saying I had severe pains but was not even half dilated yet, she would be back as another baby was en route too!

Well, the agony went on and I have never had these low awful tearing pains before, however, 12 o'clock came and Jennifer came back and said I could have gas if I liked. I tried it but it did not do enough good so I asked not to have it as it worried me and simply did not even dull my brain or head. I was too far 'gone' by then! The pains were splitting me to pieces yet still I was not bearing down and yet I felt that I should be. However, suddenly I gave a stifled scream and at last began more or less to bear down, but unlike those with Christopher, which were easy and not so painful, these were frightful, and after a bit I was given chloroform and oh thank God the blessed relief! Four held up my legs and as I was about to split in two, I thought, I was put right out! I came to later and felt a bit exhausted but the sun was shining in the window; this is my third July baby, my third son, my third heat-wave infant! And I heard the darling lad crying, I begged to see him and in he came unwashed and wrapped in a cloth or something and I thought he was lovely. I cried when I saw him, and thanked God for his being fit and well. It mattered not that he was a boy. I still can't imagine *why* I had not one pang of regret or one wishful moment of longing which would have been very natural. I think all the time nature has been kind and prepared me and therefore my subconscious mind knew and absorbed the fact, as it didn't with C because I used to dream after his birth that he was changed to a girl, not this time though! It is Guy and I am happy and contented!

He only weighed 6lbs 13oz but he was 10 days early by his *normal* birth date and even more by this 40 weeks business so it was not to be wondered at – but he is such a pet . . .

I have a lovely sunny room, airy yet cosy and Guy's cot is beside me all day so I can look at him from time to time, and oh how much I had forgotten, the feel of a new baby, the overpowering sweetness of their smell and just the fact that one has created this bundle. Love wells up in me every time I look at him, I know I am going to ruin him absolutely! . . .

The food here is lovely, not very much of it but

beautifully cooked and served even in wartime. I am appreciating it so much and oh the joy of being able to digest easily! Well, back to my tale of 'birth'. MUST one have after pains?

I have had these severely, and for hours. I was not free until 5.30 that afternoon of the 27th, then again I had three hours in the early morning of the 28th but after getting rid of lots of 'liver' I was fine and have been since! Did anyone else have this too? I believe it is quite normal. I had two injections and ergot and so on to help me. Anyhow I am now 100% fit and happy and well.

Walter came to see me on the 27th and was quite overcome with son no. 3. I said I could not face another birth like that so was he happy our family was finished? And he said *he* would not mind another or adopting a girl. I was very surprised and pleased as I felt he'd be sure to say that three sons to bring up was enough! The poor darling was worn out as he had been up all night with me and then had a heat wave in London to face minus all the staff but one and the stock exchange going like mad owing to the Italian news and so on. Then he went home, had some food and *biked* all those miles here to see me in the heat! However, he said yesterday that he slept like a log and felt better but was still working under pressure and had not a second. Yet he managed to remember all the odds and ends, which I had forgotten and asked him to buy, and to bring this typewriter! I have a pen but no ink and hate pencil and no one minds the typewriter so here goes!

I had stitches for the first time too, two I think, but they are coming out today. The reason was because Guy was born with his hand under his chin, and they could not move his arm in time. No, not under his chin, I mean by his cheek!

He is due for his feed in a moment. *A Priori*, even if Hariet IS Hariet I know now how little you will care or mind, for the exquisite joy of holding, having and caring for a baby again is the LOVELIEST thing in the world. I am absolutely happy and only wish I could have made mother as happy by giving her a granddaughter, but fate means otherwise and now Pat will have to have the girl. Actually I imagine that one day I SHALL have number four (but he too will be a boy!?) but at the moment I have *much* to be grateful for, and my heart IS full of gratitude and everything that the baby is here, well and strong, alive and so adorable that I would not change one bit of him for the world.

Pregnant again in the autumn of 1944, Roberta wrote about some of the health problems she was dealing with as a result.

Autumn 1944

No Amanda?

Roberta – I do hope things are better when you see this – my Love. (Yonire)

. . . I have felt so deadly ill and sick that words cannot describe what I feel like, and how to keep going I have not known! But I had to do so of course. My tummy is like a ball of sick fire. When a plain dry biscuit is sent down he is at once up in arms and does his best to throw it out, but unfortunately does not succeed. I wish he did. He then lets the food sulk and churn round and round hurting, getting more rancid and sick and he does nothing to help it at all. Then it is passed on and my intestines begin the fun of playing up so that they make a dull aching pain. By the time more bits of food are being sent to my tummy he begins his game all over again so that all in all, for every hour of the day and night, I am sick and in pain and feel absolutely like Hell and look a thousand, yellow and grey and ill. I have been dieted, no success. I have had every known medicine, no result. I have been given the stuff to sip during a meal which is normally given off from the tummy glands to digest the food, as the doctor thought that my whole digestive organ had shut down, but after high hopes, nothing doing. Now I have my last chance, I am having injections every other day for 10 days. Walter is going to give them to me. They are some kind of Hormone. If these fail, I am to see a specialist who will come down from town to see me at my doctor's and he may say that the baby must be removed, for my own doctor says no one could continue with this for nearly seven more months. I feel like Hell all round and am praying the injections will do the trick, though I am so at the end of my tether that anything to release me from this will be welcome.

I was ill before Nicki came and was in a nursing home when he was five months on the way and I was not cured either, but I was fit and young then and willpower got me through the worst and I was not as ill as I am now. The reason why this has got me so badly is because of the following. I feel my health is at its lowest ebb with me not realising it until now. No holidays of any kind since war began, Guy is only one year old, then weeks and weeks of flying bombs and nervous upsets, broken nights for weeks, which all seem to have brought one's health to a low level. So one way and another I am not surprised that I feel so deadly ill. Of course in peace time too one had a far wider choice of food, but that is not really the point.

I am just wondering if I shall really have to say goodbye to Amanda, also how shall I manage my family if I have to go into a nursing home in

Sevenoaks? Oh hell, well, I shall pray and hope that the last hope, the injections, will do the trick. I feel so strongly that it is Amanda this time and if I have to part with this baby, will I ever have the courage to start again, remembering this time? No use trying to look ahead, I must wait and see what next week brings forth. By the way, I do not believe that because I was sick with Nicki I shall surely have another son!

Oh just one other thing, my left ovaries are very inflamed, I wonder why? Natural form of pregnancy?

LATER – Had 1st injection – no reaction so far – oh if I only *knew* how I'd feel this time in 10 days –

Despite her difficulties, Roberta remained with child and wrote again in April of the following year, near the completion of her nine months.

April 1945

High Blood Pressure

'Your blood pressure is too high, and you really MUST try and rest more and put up your feet' . . . fatal!

Just before Easter Christopher went down with a temperature of 103° and swollen glands. Nothing more to indicate the nature of his illness. Crossing my fingers I prayed it would pass off in time for him to enter the nursing home on the 3rd for his arranged tonsil operation (it could not be managed during my second week as I had hoped).

Easter Saturday Reby was off all day, and I had my sister and her husband whom I have not seen for seven years (he had just returned from India) and David coming for tea and supper. I had been looking forward so much to having them and had arranged the meals, flowers, etc., all in readiness. In the morning Nicki retired to bed with a temperature of 102° and swollen glands! However, I was determined to have my day, so Marjorie and Roy and David came and we did have a most enjoyable and happy day. The boys were very good and quiet and Guy was terribly happy to have visitors as he always is (he loves nothing more than friends for tea). Well, the weekend passed and the boys were no better and no worse. The day before Chris was to have his operation, the doctor came and said of course the op must be put off, and lo and behold he was covered with spots and looked too awful, closed eyes, bad breathing and Measles was with us. I have since heard that only three boys from the Beacon escaped! Not only has that school had it, but it has been raging in Sevenoaks. It took five days to develop his spots and true symptoms. Then the next day Nicki was all out too . . . So it went on and I nursed them carefully. They had M and B day and night, to keep away complications. Their temperatures rose to nearly 105° but finally all was well, and after 10 days from the start they got up for tea.

Yesterday, to be exact, they did get up for tea. Meantime, what on earth was happening to my tummy? The doctor called and gave me an examination, said baby very, very ready to be born, and had I pains? Yes, I said, I had, all day long, but not the right kind, only windy achy ones. Not so sure, she said, you look like labour at any moment, wire your mother.

Oh did I forget to add that Reby by this time was again away for the weekend? Her boyfriend has arrived from Canada and the marriage is arranged for next Wednesday with two days off for a 'honeymoon' prior to his sailing, oh yes, this came at the same time! I was coping with the two boys, Guy and the house and feeling like death but thank God for a most helpful and truly kind husband. Well, to continue. Later in the day I had a slight show, labour I felt sure was coming, phoned nursing home and doctor, who said I must quietly go in that evening. By nine o'clock I felt a bit better and no more show of any kind, so asked if I might stay. Meanwhile I phoned my sister, who very kindly said I was to have the boys sent to her. I got permission from the doctor to wrap them up with hot bottles etc., and Walter got permission to take them by car, and so Sunday dawned. I forgot to say that Isis rang me up the previous evening when I told her I was just off to the nursing home, being in labour I thought! It was lovely to have spoken to her and I appreciated her phoning me from her home very much. I look forward to reading all her news in CCC! . . .

Later. I must go into nursing home tomorrow the 9th in any case to have tummy pains investigated. May be liver, Jaundice, and I certainly look as yellow as a lemon. I dread it as I want to stay here to nurse Guy and the baby may not come just yet, ah well . . .

And finally, the long-awaited fourth child.

April 10, 1945

The Arrival of Our Daughter!

I will begin right at the beginning please! 'High Blood Pressure' has indeed ended in intense joy.

As I explained, I was ordered into the home on the 9th, so in the afternoon, having settled my last little job for the family, finishing up Guy's washing and so forth, I packed my cases and entered the Ormiston at 5.30 p.m. Reby was away still that day and so we just got someone to mind Guy (who was in bed!) whilst Walter brought me along.

My room looked charming, full of sunshine, bed all made, hot bottle, wireless set by the bed (the bed is by enormous windows overlooking lovely ground and hills beyond). The sight of the neat cosy room cheered me up a lot. I said goodbye to Walter and slowly

unpacked, leaving the baby things to sister. I still had
the nagging pain and was glad to get into bed.
Naturally I did not sleep at all well, in fact not after 3
a.m. In any case at 4 a.m. I was given castor oil! At 9
a.m. a hot enema, strange to say I enjoyed being well
cleaned out. It took away that 'full' and windy feeling
quite a bit, but *the* pain was still there! The doctor
came at 11.30 a.m. I was not in labour, I was sure. It
was then decided to rupture the membranes at 2 p.m.
that day. She felt I had gone on long enough, above all,
did she know that every day spent in the home I was
worrying about Nether Fawke and felt it was a case of
'wasting' another day. So I went without lunch and
naturally thought I would be given gas or something.
At 2 p.m. I walked into the operating theatre (not
labour ward) and was there met by 2 nurses, doctor,
boiling instruments and the rest and was told that *no*
anaesthetic would be given owing to my liver condition.

I don't know anyone I climbed on to the
who has had it done table and had my legs
without anaesthetic! strapped up and then,
(Roberta)

*I don't think they ever give
one an anaesthetic – I
didn't with Jockie – it felt
like being disembowelled –
and I know 2 other people
who didn't. (Yonire)*

well, if you haven't had this done to
you in cold blood, I won't say anything about it. It all sounds so *sim-
ple*, 'Rupture the Membranes'. Oh, but what has to be
done to you in order to do it! The two nurses held my
hands and I am proud to say I did not murmur once!
The final thing was to have the neck of the womb etc.
(feeling raw and tender after its stretching and bleeding) packed with gauze. That done, the operation was
complete. The doctor stood by me and said, 'You *are*
a good brave girl. Thank you,' and I confess a tear or
two rolled down my cheek! However, I managed to
slowly walk back to my room, supported by the
nurses and en route had my first pain!

I lay in my own bed feeling wretched, so sore, raw

and uncomfortable and with real hard pains every 5 minutes. Naturally, I tried to relax, but under the circumstances it was not easy, and the pains were advanced ones.

At 3.30 p.m. I went up to the labour ward. This took ages, as the pains were so fast, strong and close I could barely walk a few steps. However, once there, I felt 'safe'! (Doctor Jennifer was at her clinic until 4.30.) At 4 p.m. I told sister she must let the doctor know, I was getting on fast. Pains, hard, hard long ones every 3 minutes. The packing had bit by bit been taken way and by 4.30 p.m. I knew the baby was very near. Ten minutes later Dr Jennifer walked in and I felt at peace with her there. She instructed me how to use the gas and air apparatus and asked me to begin it. As I did so, my first bearing down pain came. Later came the head, and popped back, it felt marvellous! I was instructed carefully what to do all the time, and I did it. 'The head appeared then – now push *hard* with the next pain.' I did so, and the head was born (no bursting feeling at all). Doctor said to sister – 'What lovely dark hair – *and* it looks like a girl!' We waited a little. 'Now with the next pain *don't* push, but pant. I want to deliver the shoulders.' I did as I was told and the little body slid out. 'It's a girl too.' I leaped as if shot and turned round to see my new daughter lying on the bed, the second she was born, attached to me, and looking *perfect*! Little plump body, pale all over, not one bit red, masses of *short* black, black hair. 'Are you *sure* it's a girl?' I kept saying, not believing my own happy eye! The cord was cut and I held her for a second, floating with delirious happiness, a girl! And I *never* for a moment expected her! I lay on my back and the afterbirth came away without pain at all. I needed no stitches. I lay in Paradise, when bound up. The doctor said again, 'You *were* a good girl, thank you for being so helpful,' and *I* thanked her! (She has, actually, been marvellous to me, and the boys during their Measles, phoning each evening and taking such a lot of trouble.)

We both said how *true* was Dick Read's book, and she said I had indeed experienced a 'Dick Read' birth. What is more, it is quite true that during the *whole* labour I kept his words imprinted in my mind and was not once afraid. I knew *what* was happening and it was a birth that was truly wonderful (naturally it being a girl added glamour, I expect, if one must be strictly fair!).

I simply do not agree that labour is painless! I find that ridiculous, *but* everything he writes and encourages is indeed on the *right line* and helps more than anything in the world. I am utterly grateful to him.

Sister then came in with the bath, and to complete my great joy I saw my newborn bathed before my eyes, the first baby I have seen bathed at birth.   *I saw T. bathed*
Suzanne Verity was then weighed, $7\frac{1}{2}$ lbs,   *at birth. (Isis)*
after all that! I thought she would be about 5 lbs, owing to my rushing around prior to birth. Sister had nearly dressed her and found she had left her nightie downstairs, so gave her to me to hold. My infant eyed me up and down and then quietly sucked her fist! . . .

I forgot to add that at 8.30 p.m. last night Walter was allowed to see me for a little and his new daughter! Of course he is just beside himself with pleasure and can't grasp that she *is* a girl after all. We call her 'he' all the time! He looked a little tired, he'd looked after Guy all the afternoon and had been worried about me, not quite knowing what *was* happening. He knew I was to have the waters broken at 2 p.m., but had no idea labour might commence so rapidly.

Now I await his today's visit. Guy's measles we

can't fathom! On Sunday he had temp. of nearly 104°. Mon., Tues., Wed., completely normal! Eating as he's never eaten before (breakfast, lunch, tea and *supper*!) and NO RASH! Dr says he may get the rash yet but so far all points to a very mild attack. Thank God (or it may develop? Really a curious affair).

That evening Walter told me Guy had only 2 spots and was not ill with it anyway. (Ad Astra) But Roberta wrote later (13th) that Guy was 'full out' with spots, so there's no doubt he's really got it. (Ad Astra)

I am thankful the weather is so lovely as Walter did want to do a lot outside and he does love the sun and *if* Guy is well, it is so easy to have him in the garden. Hateful to be stuck indoors with a half ill toddler!

Reby had married today! I managed to arrange to have a wedding spray made up for her as a surprise and left her her wedding present and a letter. I hope all went well for her. Her husband goes back to his ship tonight, but has 3 days and nights off at the weekend, when she will join him. Then he sails on Monday or Tuesday and she comes back to me. Meanwhile a friend has 'lent' her char for Friday and Monday, so that will help a lot, though I do feel that I have a husband in a million! So willing, so cheerful, under all these circumstances.

Want to finish for post – here's Walter.

Roberta – I'm so <u>terribly</u> glad about all this – after all that. Love and blessings. (Yonire)

Suzanne was Roberta and Walter's last child. The family remained in Kent until the early 1950s.

Accidia

When Accidia joined the CCC in 1951 and chose her pseudonym, she had been reading about nuns suffering from accidie, a form of depression. Apparently, special friendships amongst nuns in a convent were discouraged and this caused the women great loneliness, which increased their feelings of accidie. This depression resonated strongly with Accidia, who at this time in her life was a mother of four and pregnant with her fifth, 'living in the sticks' and in a somewhat unsatisfactory marriage. Thus, she adapted the word slightly to form her nom de plume, Accidia.

Born in 1918, Accidia spent her childhood in Bristol. In 1937, at the age of nineteen and after a fairly standard childhood and adolescence, Accidia left home for Girton College, Cambridge. She first read English, then Modern Languages (French).

Throughout her adolescence, Accidia had developed an interest in pacifism and attended some International Voluntary Service for Peace work camps when she was in sixth form. In 1940, when she graduated from Cambridge, she decided to become more involved with the pacifist movement. She was teaching at a school in Llandudno in North Wales but spent her summers volunteering in a house for conscientious objectors. A rather primitive dwelling without any electricity, Esthwaite Lodge, located opposite Esthwaite Lake in the Lake District, was occupied by forty men and ten women. The men did forestry work, and the women were responsible for the domestic tasks for the group.

Accidia's decision to become involved with pacifism was difficult for her mother and caused tension in her family. Accidia's brother John, who had been the favoured child of the two, fought in the Second World War and was killed in 1940. To their mother's distress, John did not die in active service but rather was killed by a bomb when he was on forty-eight-hour leave, and therefore, in their mother's eyes, died without glory. The death of her son, particularly in this way, was a loss from which Accidia's mother never recovered. Accidia's involvement with pacifism was thus a contentious issue for her mother and made coping with John's death even more difficult.

Despite her mother's vehement disapproval, after two summers Accidia decided to move to Esthwaite Lodge permanently. It was here that she met her future husband John, who was the leader of the house and nine years her senior. The pair married in the spirit of wartime in 1941 at the Friends' Meeting House at Hawkshead near Windermere, a ceremony that Accidia's mother felt unable to attend. John and Accidia remained at Esthwaite House until 1942, when, due to pressure from John's mother to live nearby, they moved to Lancashire, where John worked in the local sawmill.

Initially the two moved to Wennington, a village about twelve miles outside Lancaster, where Accidia worked full-time as a teacher at Wennington School, a progressive school largely run by conscientious objectors. Here she gave birth to her first child, Phyllida, in 1943. The pair remained in Wennington, with John commuting to the sawmill, until his possessive mother convinced him that it would be more practical if they moved to the village of Caton, which was closer to her and the sawmill. Thus, after a year John and Accidia relocated to Caton and Accidia entered into one of the lonelier times in her life. As John was a conscientious objector, the people of the village ostracised her and refused to speak to her for the eighteen months that they lived there. During this time, Accidia continued to *work at Wennington School, mainly as a way of pre-serving her sanity. She would cycle the twelve miles to Wennington twice a week, with Phyllida in the basket of her bicycle.*

Meanwhile, John started to suffer from depression and had a nervous breakdown. He was given a psychiatrist's exemption from war work and the family decided to move down to Cornwall, where John was offered employment with the Workers' Educational Association. Accidia and John remained in Cornwall from 1944 until 1947, and here Accidia gave birth to their second child, Adrian, in 1946.

Another job change took the family up to Yorkshire, where John worked in the Adult Education Department at Leeds University. He organised and gave lectures in political science throughout the region and was frequently away as a result. Accidia, meanwhile, gave birth to Althea in autumn 1947 and Humfrey in 1949. While the first two years in Yorkshire were spent living in town, the family then moved to the countryside, and Accidia was left with four children, no transportation and very few adult companions. It was at this point, in November of 1951, after the birth of her fifth child, that she joined the CCC. The despondency caused by her loneliness was expressed clearly in her early submissions to the magazine.

In this short extract, written in 1951, Accidia was suffering from isolation in the countryside and the absence of contemporaries. Most of the CCC women were no longer young mothers, and so Accidia occasionally deferred to them as she knew that they had already been through similar phases. She was always quite aware that she was a new member of the group and that the majority of these women had already been writing to each other for over fifteen years.

Remaining at home with the children day after day, seeing very few people, I gradually feel my self-confidence ebbing and a devastating shyness descending until it would be an effort to speak to a stray cat. Whether caused by glands or geographical position, the effect is unpleasant, and far from being the serene and smoothly sailing Accidia depicted by one of CCC's members I become agitated, a prey to migraine and a natterer and curser. I seem to have missed Roberta's remarks on blowing hot and cold but can well imagine what she meant. John loathes what he calls my 'hardboiled virgin' mood but I am convinced *I think I'd like your* that if I did not occasionally withdraw *John! (Ad Astra)* myself mentally, and, as far as possible, physically from the family, I should go crazy.

She wrote the following discussion of different aspects of childbirth just after giving birth to her fifth child, Julian, on October 20, 1951.

No, Janna, I cannot truthfully say that I have enjoyed the birth of any of my babies. Three of them were vegetarian from conception and as I did my antenatal exercises most religiously (to the huge delight of the rest of the family who also 'grew babies' and did exercises) and adhered to a strict diet (based on Margaret Brady's book, which you probably know) I anticipated the perfect Dick Grantley Read confinement. I can only conclude that I am thoroughly bad at relaxing and that the undoubted pain which I feel from start to finish is entirely my own fault. I believe you have said that you still reflect with pleasure on the various stages of Julia's birth; I envy you this enjoyment; what I look back to with pleasure is that moment immediately after birth

when, before the cord has been cut, one sees the new
baby lying beside me and experiences that tremendous
thrill of excitement and joy. This time I was denied the
pleasure of holding Julian in my arms as he was
whisked away in his cot and did not reappear until
four hours later. Nor did the children have the joy of
seeing him 'all new' as no child visitors were allowed
in the Nursing Home. This removing of the babies
from their mothers except at feeding times is a practice
which I hope will soon be abandoned. I missed very
much indeed the joy of having the cot next to me and
hearing the occasional snuffle and irregular breathing,
but it was certainly a physical advantage to have nine
undisturbed nights before coming home. At the
moment I have the psychological satisfaction of hearing and seeing Julian at around 2.00 a.m. each day and
the physical dissatisfaction of a slight headache and
black rims under the eyes as a result! On the credit
side of the Maternity Home was undoubtedly the extra
rest, peace and leisure which could not have been
attained at home. Fortune smiled on me and spared me
the ward (7 beds) where the Light Programme drooled
almost from dawn till dusk, as it happened to be full,
and I and the next patient in time to me were put in a
small room where the wireless was mercifully out of
order. Apart from learning all about this patient's family and private affairs, and swapping tales of my children for tales of hers, I enjoyed the great luxury of
being able to read for several hours on end and at a
time of day when my brain was fresh and could take in
without effort what I was reading – a rare and delightful pleasure. It was also pleasant to be entirely freed
from responsibility – for oneself and for others. One
just lay in bed, was swabbed, given a tray of food at
regular intervals and left in peace; about the children,
though I had worried over the inadequacy of arrange-

ments during my absences before I came away, I found that I thought little and certainly felt no anxiety. In fact, I vegetated, reflected a certain amount, learned a great deal from my room-mate concerning working-class lives and working-class wives, and experienced once again that upsurge of life and idealism and enthusiasm which invariably follows the release from the apathy engendered by pregnancy – a pity that one so soon becomes cluttered up with domestic trivia and tends to become harassed and haggard during the months immediately following the birth of a new baby. Relieved of the inevitability of sink and duster and oven, one could be so much more creative in one's relationship with other people.

Now, at home again, the period of rest, recreation and reflection has slipped into its place in the past; the present is an adjustment to the old routine stretching its seams to incorporate an additional routine and the future . . .? Hard work in plenty, fatigue, exasperation at times but interspersed with those moments of sheer breath-taking happiness and delight that only the company of the very young can provide.

Congratulations, Accidia – every possible wish
for a happy Julian. (Rosa)
Well I am so glad to read this at last. (Sirod)

Just months after Julian's arrival, Accidia wrote about some of the more difficult aspects of her daily life with five children.

December, 1951

Ergs of Work

How much work can one reasonably expect from an able-bodied female? As futile a subject of debate as the mediaeval poser 'How many angels can dance on the point of a needle?'

When I read the *cris de coeur* of those seeking nannies via the advertisement column of *Nursery World*, who beseech aid with their 'one child, baby expected next year' and offer Bendix washer, TV, other help kept as tempting baits, I feel the flush of virtue mount to my cheek; this speedily fades to pallor as I listen to the account from a friend recently returned from Cyprus, of the work, including breaking stones for road repairing, done by women there.

Do *I* work hard? Do I work as hard as most women? Harder than many? Not hard at all? Years ago, in the early days of my scientific education which, alas, proceeded little further, we did an experiment in the measuring of work. An eager volunteer, who soon regretted her impetuous enthusiasm, was given a lidded cylinder, containing shot, to shake up and down without pause for, I think, one minute (it clearly seemed eternity to her). By some magic, which escapes me now, as then, one could calculate the number of ergs of work done. Perhaps if some such device could be evolved for the measuring of the amount of work done by the average woman, one could evaluate one's own prowess by the graph method.

People gasp on learning that I have five children and wonder how on earth I manage. Clearly they envisage either an efficient squad of family retainers or complete squalor. Actually we have neither. Two mornings a week a 22-year-old girl comes up from the village and lays about her with relative efficiency whilst I, an exile from the kitchen which cannot contain two (for purely physical, not temperamental, reasons), do as many of the numerous postponed small jobs as possible; for the rest of the week I 'do' for myself and this is when I feel that the score in ergs must be pretty high. We make our own electricity, 100 v DC, which means no washing machine, no vacuum and officially no nothing but the amber glow which passes for light. *Sub rosa* we run an electric kettle (30 minutes to boil, occasionally only 20 when the batteries have just been charged) and an electric iron. Cooking can be done in the Yorkist oven if we have enough fuel to heat it, but we almost never have since inefficient plumbing makes it necessary to heap on all we can spare in order to get a bare minimum of hot water. (One of the blisses of the Maternity Home was a piping hot bath every morning after the fifth – and a morning bath always seems such a luxury to a mother, I think; normally the early morning is a peak period of buttoning up trousers, fastening sandals, brushing hair, chivvying and chasing, dashing from porridge pan to cosset a sulky fire, shouting innumerable answers to innumerable questions of 'Mummy, where's my ____?' 'Mummy, A's doing so and so and I can't dress properly,' 'Mummy, B's locked the door and I can't get in to clean my teeth' . . . Lucky, lucky Daddy who dresses placidly and half-asleep, unconscious of the turmoil around him and unmolested by the throng![*]

Educationists frown on the shout; one should always go up to the child and *speak* to him. How I agree! But educationists *Bad training! My husband jolly well mucks in and <u>shares</u> the work. After all – they are his children (as far as we know). (Yonire)* can think out and write out their theories whilst sitting down and their legs and feet are not submitted to the trials and tribulations that mine are.)

Apart from the sheer ding-dong of washing up, sweeping, dusting, washing, cooking – the vicious circle – work presumably also includes running commentaries from 7.30 a.m. to 7.30 p.m. almost non-stop with one or other or all the children, not to mention drying one's hands five to ten times in the same number of minutes in order to cut paper, sharpen crayons, find scissors, thread needles etc. etc.: *'this very minute'* (a favourite expression of my eldest son), answering the phone with baby clasped to the breast and the 2-year-old clamouring to be potted and the laundry man knocking at the back door . . . Thomas Hood's 'Song of the Shirt' isn't in it.

Yet I thrive on it, and even Julian's refusal to regard night as the stop to busy fools does not unduly daunt me. True, the antenatal bloom has given way to the post-natal haggard and I feel like humming, 'Count your wrinkles, count them one by one,' every time I look into a mirror and I think a little wistfully of the bliss of the nine hours' unbroken sleep which might occasionally be mine next year, but all things considered, I can subscribe to the doctrine that 'hard work never killed anybody', even adding a rider to the effect that it has actually improved many of my acquaintance, including myself. May I therefore wish all members of CCC a hard-working and merry 1952, and at the same time thank everybody for so kindly welcoming the callow fledgling to the nest.

This woman is a gem! She reminds me of the younger AP plus something that is all her own. I'm so glad she is one of us. (Yonire) AP was not quite so multum-in-parvo *('pithy') though she was hard-hitting when she chose. (Ad Astra)*

Into the new year, Accidia shared with the CCC her endless list of tasks.

March 1952

Pox on't

Well, not quite *the* evil – merely the socially acceptable third or fourth cousin once removed, chickenpox. The score is one at the moment, Phyllida. Will each of the others go the full three weeks' incubatory period so that the dabbing on of calamine continues for another 12 weeks? Harrowing thought to be hastily ignored. 'Oh, they'll all get it!' says the family doctor with cheerful nonchalance. Maybe . . . it's very mild . . . better to get it over with . . . no complications or after-effects . . . yes, yes, yes I know, I know. But our dear sweet Julian has only twice in his 18 weeks of extra-uterine life failed to waken between 2.00 and 4.00 a.m. and I dream and long for a hibernation far more complete than that envisaged by AA, a hibernation of sweet sleep, undisturbed by 'Where's mummy?', 'Haven't you *any* money at all?', 'What did you do with those two small screws from the clock?', 'Where on earth are my slippers?' etc. etc., undisturbed even by the arrival of food, of literature, of music, undisturbed by any mortal thing. But, alas, the little ration of unbroken sleep, 4 or 5 hours perhaps, to which I have grown accustomed is now reduced to a series of cat-naps in between the merry trips to the adjoining bedroom to commiserate with the poor sufferer ('They tickle so, Mummy'), smooth the pillows, dab more of the lotion and utter a few words of sympathy before staggering drunkenly back for another brief period of merciful oblivion. If this has to be repeated for four more patients, heaven help my sanity!

I am not a good nurse by nature and perhaps fortunately for my family we are all usually in robust health. Routine during the day is now more or less completely askew. Domestic help is off because of the infection, and in addition to the usual and essential chores everyone is home for all meals, everyone except Phyllida is fighting fit and bursting with energy and all in all life's a sweat and the day just isn't long enough. However, I can think to myself how wonderful I am as I COPE and somehow fit in reading lessons, supervision of daily quota of sums, spelling, writing etc., crane my head around the door at the 1001st 'Look,

Mummy!', cook an adequate meal and get through the day without the thin thread of my patience eventually snapping. 'Well, dear, if you *will* have so many children . . .' says the soft voice of my mother and temporarily I feel inclined to echo it – only temporarily, though, because I do find children extraordinarily interesting and delightful beings. Of course, they're frequently maddening, infuriating, worrying, silly, exasperating, but not so frequently as adults, I think. And the simplicity, charm, spontaneity and *joie de vivre* of the very young is most refreshing. My ideal life would comprise 5 days' work with children, 1 day's social intercourse with the mature and intelligent, 1 day's complete isolation. At least, I should like to try such an apportioning of my time over a period, even if after all it did not prove ideal. Perhaps as one grows older, one prefers children in smaller doses.

Do most members of CCC feel thankful on the whole that their children now need less of their time and minute-by-minute attention? *Yes. (Ad Astra)*

At the moment I hate the thought of no more babies in the house – one's grandchildren would hardly be the same thing – yet when I read in CCC *I think grandchildren* what people are doing in addition to *will be lovely, I'm just* their domestic duties I realise that one *waiting for mine.* can probably become too inebriated *(Sirod)* with babies. And the more babies one has, the more one's life tends to lack a certain graciousness (though one hopes that this is only temporary). Elektra's charming house decoration schemes, Sirod's flower arrangements, for instance, are just pipe dreams here where fingerprints and the carelessly moved table or chair rule out pastel shades or subtle furnishings and where as like as not the jam jar full of wild flowers lands up on the floor – we are not complete savages I hope, but refinements seem to thrive best where children are older, where there are no children, or where there is money to provide sufficient hewers of wood and drawers of water. Perhaps Janna manages matters better, or perhaps I am a little greedy, wanting both the pagan delights of children and the 'civilised' delights of adults. What I need right now is some sleep (and 'a little less preoccupation with yourself' I can imagine some members of CCC muttering).

March 25th – Can now add Adrian, Althea and Humfrey as victims. Accidia   *Oh no! (Janna)*

Not AA. By god I think you're marvellous. Truly. (Ad Astra)
I do hope you'll get your sleep in full measure soon. (Cotton Goods)

Despite often feeling overworked, Accidia always longed for a large family and in 1954 she became pregnant again.

September 11, 1954

Longing for Lucilla

Desiring still to achieve that final daughter I thought the omens propitious this September. Statistically, there is stronger hope of bearing a female child after the age of 35 so at $36\frac{1}{2}$ chances should be good. I was in good health and an early summer baby would be delightful, while a winter pregnancy was to be pre-ferred to a summer one. The start was less satisfactory than in pregnancies one to [five], as I felt progressively sicker every day until by the end of the second month I was feeling very sick all the time when not actually asleep. Then I caught a flu type germ from Phyllida, who had been in bed for a week, and though I couldn't go to bed all the time, I fell into it whenever possible. After this, still feeling extremely unfit, I began to have unpleasant intuitions that I might mis-carry – probably I was nervous after last year's fiasco and I began to feel almost morbidly so, not without good reason as the next week shewed. Hateful feminine intuition, so correct! In a last-ditch stand, I am now condemned to bed for minimum one week, most probably three, and with, I feel (intuitively again), not much hope of success. Why I should go through five perfectly normal and boring pregnancies without hitch whatever I did (such as house removing during four of them) and then, out of the blue, start to miscarry beats me.

Emotionally, at the moment, I am in a suspended state, not daring to look forward (if I miscarry what utter melancholy at this time of year when everything is dead and dying, everything is grey and damp and dripping, and the wind forever moaning around the house!). If I don't miscarry I shall be in a state of wretched introspection all the time wondering whether I should get through the next six months without a hitch, wondering whether the confinement will be all right (John a widower? Myself on a chaise longue for the rest of my life? Hysterectomy and what-have-you, and turned into a hermaphrodite?), and whether the baby will be all right . . . *You wouldn't be. (Ad Astra)*

Now the moral of this is, as all sensible and older members of CCC would be quick to point out if their natural kindness did not check them, 'Enough is as good as a feast,' 'Why not be content with *five*, surely that is enough for any woman?', 'Why o'er reach yourself in heady ambition?' Or from AP perhaps, 'Why the hell don't you try something else instead of maternity for a refreshing change?' And from Cornelia, I think, 'Why not concentrate on your husband for a bit?'

I do hope all is well, Acc. Please let us know. Best of luck. (Sirod)
Much enjoyed. I do hope all goes well. (Waveney)
Alas! No it isn't. (Janna)
But so sorry. (Robina)

As is clear from Janna's comment, Accidia miscarried shortly after writing this article, one of several miscarriages that she had over the years. She did, however, have her longed-for last daughter Lucilla in September 1955.

When she wrote the following, Accidia had five children, aged from four to twelve, and her husband John was still organising and giving lectures in political science for adult education.

February 1, 1955

Carpe Diem

On the whole, I enormously enjoy my children. But there are times, as the four weeks immediately after Christmas this year, when a black accidie descends; I wake to a feeling of 'What the hell?' seeing the years' relentless passage, so little time, so little accomplished, and my life endlessly spent in tidying the muddles of others, cleaning the horrid little house, trying to fit a gallon-size family into a pint-pot establishment. The fields are grey and sodden, the sky ditto, the air murky and mild. Of my contemporaries I see nothing, hear nothing – since Christmas we calculate that John has spoken to over four hundred people – I to about four, and those would be dustman, fishman, police-man and the woman from one of the Harewood Estate lodges. The children bounce back from school with complaints that 'Elaine wouldn't play with me,' 'Y was bossy,' 'J had bagged the whole row of seats and wouldn't allow any of the A stream girls to sit down,' etc. etc. At the Univ. the clerks all have colds, make careless transcriptions or are insubordinate, while Profs X,Y, and Z deserve to be . . . I listen, make the necessary soothing or would-be helpful comments and have the modesty to give no indication that my own life at the moment seems a dull waste, a vale of (unshed) tears, an empty vessel, a froth of frustration . . . I refrain from shouting, 'For God's sake let's get away from here – I hate the north (only temporarily, CG), I am sick of Rawden Hill and this house, I am bored, bored, BORED.'

No, I just lie low and say nuffin – not from deep Christian conviction, not from psychological motives, not from a big-hearted consideration for other people's ears – and feelings, but simply because accidie has brought me so low that I can't be *bothered* to complain.

And how well that I didn't. Last week, when we were proposing to go over to Lancaster to celebrate my mother-in-law's 80th birthday, we had a phone call from my brother-in-law to say that his younger child, aged $5\frac{3}{4}$, had been taken off to the Isolation Hospital with suspected polio. A later phone call revealed that the diagnosis had been confirmed; polio in both legs and part of the abdomen, and that the child would be in hospital for a year at least. This bitter blow came completely out of the blue, the child having been off school with flu and no other cases of polio having been notified.

Once again, the lesson of *carpe diem* in regard to one's children is vividly brought home to me. Even without the swift descent of unexpected calamity which may leave one temporarily or permanently bereft of a child, the years of childhood pass incredibly swiftly (cliché number one) and I realise often that I don't perhaps enjoy my children as much as I should – the gorgeous sensuous thrill of Julian is easy enough to appreciate, but the older ones sometimes require more effort to enjoy, especially if I am tired. Althea, the restless, inconsequent chatterer, the incredibly slap-dash and untidy, the irritating and exasperating with yet an overwhelmingly generous heart and 'go with him twain' attitude to the poor or helpless – Phyllida, the lively, noisy, teasing mimic, occasionally now 'going over all adolescent', as she calls it, with the periodic pathetic plea, 'You *do* love me, don't you?' and the inevitable reassurance (despite the fact that I have just, after finishing the weekly washing, cleaned out the Hoover etc., found all her dirty clothes in a heap on her bedroom floor, disregarding my repeated requests that all dirty linen should be put in the appropriate place (Janna knows where this is!)) Adrian, gauche, even uncouth from sheer acute shyness in the presence of strangers, yet deeply affectionate, thoughtful, conscientious to a painful degree of slowness, methodical (as he undresses at night every garment is folded with extreme care and neatness), and with the type of mind that will probably turn to Egyptology or some relatively obscure oriental language known only to one other person in Great Britain; Humfrey, excitable, beautiful, intelligent, still near enough babyhood to enjoy sitting on my lap and being 'loved', yet independent enough to go off with the others.

This is like Jocky. (Yonire)

What should I feel if one of mine had been whisked off to hospital for perhaps a year or more? The rising grumble is stifled in my throat as I bend for the thousandth time to pick up a Dinky car tyre or collect the residue from a cutting-out session. Like all lessons, of course, the effect will wear off in time and, forgetful of what may be just around the corner, I shall from time to time indulge in those unprofitable reveries of what might have been in those years that I have misspent in domesticity. But, at the moment, I suffer in imagination with my sister-in-law, and at the same time, watch that I do not lose precious moments of enjoyment of my own five. *Carpe diem*, in fact – and eyes off all other roses but my children!

One of the reasons that Accidia found the stages of young motherhood difficult to cope with was because she felt neglected by her husband John. Although John was always a good provider, he did not meet Accidia's emotional needs, which added to her sense of isolation and loneliness.

2

Peace in Our Time?

Borealis. Is my morale 100% high? I only wish it were. I'll have to remember your words next time my innards start wobbling all over the place. This thought has helped me.

I had to laugh this week when the radio announcer said "The people of Lancashire have met this, the most recent attack on them, with characteristic courage & fortitude".

Well, anything less like a lot of bloomin' 'eroes would be hard to find that my fellow Lancastrians. I mentally looked around & saw hundreds of George Formbys, all looking "as soft as a ha'porth o' thray-cle" (treacle).

> **THOUGHT FOR THE WEEK**
>
> LET me not pray to be sheltered from dangers but to be fearless in facing them.
>
> Let me not look for allies in life's battle-field but to my own strength.
>
> Let me not crave in anxious fear to be saved but hope for the patience to win my freedom.
>
> Grant me that I may not be a coward, feeling your mercy in my success alone; but let me find the grasp of your hand in my failure.—SIR RABINDRANATH TAGORE, in "Fruit Gathering"

Characteristic Lancashire legs.

Written by Cotton Goods, c.1940.

I remember early one morning coming from that shelter towards the house to make breakfast. It was about 6.30 a.m. and the warning was still 'on'. The light was grey and search-lights still swept the sky. Suddenly there was gunfire close at hand and the searchlights all crossed together. I remember seeing the tiny plane caught in the beams and thinking, 'I've never seen one close like this before,' and stopping to look. I had CCC in my arm as I always took the currently collecting number to the shelter each night we went there. Then I saw the string of bombs leave the plane and I began to run to the house. I didn't get to it. The explosion was near and loud and I flung myself face down, CCC under me, on the edge of the lawn where it met York stone (which is very hard). The earth heaved under me and the light was white. It was really near.

Ad Astra

Although the women of the CCC were brought together by motherhood, it was their shared experience of the Second World War that solidified their friend-ships and created lifelong bonds.

Many of the women in the club were lonely and forced to cope without their husbands, who were either fighting in the war or involved in war work away from home. They were on their own, trying to raise young families, and the CCC acted as a wonderful support system, where 'you could write minor irritations about rationing and kids' school troubles' and any other concerns.

During the war, most of the CCC women moved at least once, and several of them sent their children away to boarding schools or to stay with families in safer areas of the country. Since the women were often on the move, they were frequently leaving friends and family and going to completely new towns. During all of this, the one thing that was constant, because it did not depend on location, was the CCC. The women maintained the magazine throughout the war and relied heavily upon one another for moral support, advice and companionship.

What is particularly fascinating about this phase in the magazine's history is that the women in the CCC held opposing political ideologies and yet they were able to discuss and debate without allowing it to affect their relationships. Ultimately, this shared experience of crisis and war actually brought them all significantly closer despite their extreme differences.

Although the women wrote prolifically throughout the war, very few issues of the magazine survived from that time. From the small number of articles that remain, the following selections from A Priori, Roberta, Waveney and Rosa shed light on daily life during the war.

A Priori

*Born in London on October 2, 1907, A Priori had a dif-
ficult childhood because her father was a bit of a gambler
and lost all of the family's money in a property development and then suffered from a nervous breakdown. A
Priori was incredibly bright and did well in school, but
when she was seventeen her father died, leaving the family with nothing but debts. A Priori had to go out and
join the workforce to earn money for herself and to help
her mother. The fact that she could not go to university
was something that she regretted for the rest of her life.*

*A Priori was employed at Ginn's educational book
firm in London for a few years and at the same time
worked towards a diploma in English literature at
London University. In 1930, she started at the* New
Statesman *in the advertising department, which appeal-
ed to her because of her left-wing political views, as well
as her interest in economics. While she was working at
the* New Statesman, *John Maynard Keynes asked her to
be his Personal Assistant, which she did for a year prior
to getting married. She admired Keynes greatly and
always spoke fondly of her time spent working with him.*

*In 1932, she met her future husband Lough in a
restaurant in Bloomsbury and married him soon afterwards. Lough had gone to Sandhurst under familial
pressure but found that army life did not suit him, so he
relinquished his commission and travelled and worked
his way around the world. Once he returned to
England he established a carpentry workshop and took
evening classes in wood carving. Lough was almost
penniless when A Priori met him, but they were in love
and made the best of it.*

The newlyweds remained in London, where Lough

found work making wooden door knockers and book ends for the company Heals in London. When A Priori gave birth to their first daughter, Jane, in February of 1934, they decided to move out of the city and relocated to Pishill Bank near Henley-on-Thames in Oxfordshire. Here Lough opened a furniture workshop but struggled to make a living. He started teaching to resolve the family's financial problems and was offered a job as woodwork master at Bottisham Village College in Cambridgeshire. By then they had their second daughter, Sally, who was born in 1935. They relocated to Swaffham Prior for a year and then to Swaffham Bulbeck, both villages in Cambridgeshire. Here they had their third daughter, Vicky, in 1938.

With money from Lough's family they were able to buy a house in Swaffham Bulbeck, a run-down, spacious Elizabethan home surrounded by countryside where the children could roam and play. A Priori kept goats, cats and dogs and gardened passionately to help feed her family.

In 1939, with the outbreak of war, Lough volunteered to repair aircraft at Marshall's Aerodrome in Cambridge. He also volunteered with the Auxiliary Fire Service (AFS) in the village. Early in 1940, A Priori sent Jane and Sally down to Rusticana's home in Salcombe, Devon, since it was thought that an invasion through East Anglia to London was quite likely. Barnie's children, Anne and John, had come from Lowestoft, Suffolk, to board at Rusticana's as well.

When A Priori submitted the following article to Ad Astra, Sally and Jane had returned from Rusticana's. Meanwhile, Ad Astra's children, Christopher (Kit) and Clare, ages five and seven, had been sent away to North Wales for fear of bombing. They were enrolled in A. S. Neill's progressive boarding school Summerhill, where they stayed for six months.

Dear Ad Astra,

This is just the usual open letter to let you know we
are still alive and flourishing – as I hope it leaves you
at present. I received no. 46 yesterday and took it in to
Cambridge this morning to post it off to Michaelmas.
It is late getting round, of course, but the delays were
rather less than I had anticipated. Recent numbers
have been so good, and such a comfort in these crazy
days. I have simply heaps to write about, but owing to
unexpected continued stay of lodgers, have had no
time at all to myself. Thank heaven they are out to
supper to-night so that I can snatch a few minutes for
CCC. If I have time to write any more before October
1st, I will send it off as I have before 'manuscript only.
Printed paper rate' for a penny. Do say, publicly, if this
is OK, as it might be useful to others if it is, and if it
isn't I must owe you a tidy sum by now.

*It has been quite OK. [N.B.
Anyone who wants to send this
way, AP sends only MSS, marks
envelope as she mentions, and
tucks flap in.] (Ad Astra)*

As the German radio has
boasted of the bombing of
Cambridge, I suppose there is
no harm in my referring to it.
And I can re-assure anyone who
is fond of it that none of its beautiful buildings have
been harmed, nor were any lives lost. Lough had been
standing by with his Fire Brigade most of the night,
this is in addition to his 12-hour day, and when the
third warning came at about 4 a.m. he was too
exhausted to hear it and I thought, 'Fire Brigade be
blowed, he must have *some* sleep,' so didn't wake
him. Of course, that would be the 'operative' raid. But
fortunately he got no call. Generally speaking we
don't get up when we get warnings, except that Lough
goes to see that his Fire Engine is ready for action, but
I stay in bed until I hear the bombs fall. I quite agree
that in theory one ought to take the children to the

comparative safety of the ground floor or dug-out, but when it comes to the point I just feel I'd rather die in bed. I do, however, think that a rural area like this one is very different from a town.

Lough is still working at his armaments job and I am glad to say that his real worth is coming to be appreciated (ahem!) and he seems likely to get more congenial work in which his skill can be used. There is also a possibility that the hours may be shortened as winter comes on, but unfortunately I believe they will still start at 7 a.m. This is by far the most grisly part of the whole proceeding and I most certainly do not get reconciled to rising at this unhallowed hour as time goes on. Anyone can have the dawn who likes it, give me my bed! 'Of all the crimes beneath the sun, say which in morning sleep was done?'

The children are not, after all, going to school in Cambridge as I felt I could not let them go on the bus alone in these dangerous times. I have been very fortunate to find a woman, who was a teacher before and since her marriage, to come and give them $2\frac{1}{2}$ hours every morning. Her husband has been called up and she has a little girl of her own of nearly three. She brings the child along, and she either plays with Vicky or joins in while her mother teaches Jane and Sally. The arrangement seems to work very well, though it has only been going four days so it is early to judge. They do handiwork of different kinds and she takes them up in the field and plays games with them, so they are not at work all that time. Jane told me today that she would like to do lessons in the afternoon as well, and I thought that a pretty good sign. I asked Mrs Hill if she would be willing to let them do writing on the Marian Richardson methods. Although she has never worked with them she said she was game to try, and I bought the books and now she is most enthusiastic. She worked as 'supply' under Miss Musther at Bottisham, so she has had experience of modern methods of teaching. I hope later on we might get one or two more children to join in.[*]

By the way, if you have any suitable first books, which Kit and Clare have now discarded, I wonder if you would lend them to us? We have Ballard's *First Number Book* and *Fundamental English*, *Book 1* and Beacon. By the way, for Campo Alegre, the Oxford Press do some first reading books at a penny each. They are called *First Steps for Tiny Folks*. There are heaps of them and they are quite interesting little simple stories. I quite agree, and so does Mrs Hill, that the Beacon readers are dull. She, also, doesn't think much of 'look and say' methods, which she says are mostly guesswork on the part of the child.

I did feel for you in parting with Kit and Clare. I don't know how we should have borne the absence of Jane and Sally at Rusticana's if we had not kept Vicky with us. I expect you have been glad these last few weeks that they have not been in Harrow. We shall all be most interested to hear how they get on. I wonder how they will re-act to the freedom to please themselves about lessons, particularly as they are advanced for their ages and have been used to the comparatively rigid discipline of the elementary school. Do let us know all about it . . .

Seriously, I don't think we need another member because when wartime pressure relaxes many of us may have time to write more, and then magazines may tend to get too long again. However, if anyone turned up that we badly wanted, I shouldn't oppose it.

I hope you are not finding it too difficult to cope

with CCC now that the war has really started. I was
so thankful to see it yesterday, with all its lovely
snaps. It does help me to keep sane – if I do!

Did you listen to Keynes the other evening? I was
surpised to hear him so optimistic and thought he *So was I!*
underestimated the inflationary tendency of the last *(Barnie)*
few months. Nevertheless, you notice that he
insisted that his own or some similar scheme will have
to be introduced before long. I want to reply to
Robina's article on Socialism when I have time. I
thought she raised some interesting points.

I do recommend those who are interested in World
government and our prospects of a sane peace to read
Harold Nicolson's book *Diplomacy*. In it he describes
the relations of governments to each other and the
manner of diplomatic intercourse. He points out the
great dangers of Hitler's method of dealing with foreign affairs as between the leaders of States, and the
lamentable results of such diplomacy in the past few
years. I believe the Pacifists are very keen on this idea
(they would be!). This book is a very sound and rea-
soned account of the working of foreign affairs. I am
wandering from my personal affairs and must go to
bed. It was nice to see Rose Dartle's face in the last
mag. I am so glad we still manage to keep a few snaps
in CCC. I do hope none of us has been really bombed.
Good luck to us all.

*Shortly after writing this, in October 1940, Lough
was sent to Kinloss aerodrome on the Moray Firth in
Scotland to repair bombers. In December, A Priori followed with Jane, Sally and Vicky, and the family
stayed there for a year, with the girls attending the village school in Findhorn. They moved back to
Swaffham Bulbeck in 1941, and Lough returned to
teaching, as it was a reserved occupation, and joined
the Home Guard. A Priori had their fourth child, a*

son, Piers, in 1943. She spent the war years working diligently to keep the family together by gardening, raising pigs, ducks and chickens, preserving eggs and bottling fruit.

Roberta

Roberta wrote the following piece in 1940 from her home in Kent. At this point she and Walter only had Nicholas and Christopher.

September 17, 1940

Sad Sunday

It is Sunday. A day which we all enjoy so well. Walter is home, the boys (now aged just 3 and 5) are occupied and happy and we as usual are all engaged in our own particular way of amusement and work. The sun has always shone for us on Sundays. We have had such a lovely summer, haven't we? Today is no different. We awoke at 8 a.m., pulled back the curtains and from our large bay windows beheld the view which holds us with fresh admiration daily. A mist was rolling back from the far-off hills and the sun was steadily working its way through. A fresh September morning, we agreed, very pleased.

Then we talked about our various 'plans' for the day. There was much to be done and seen to. The goat house to be swept and cleaned. A new feeding trough for the baby chicks to be made. The ducks' 'pond' to be cleaned out and refilled. A pile of logs waiting to be sawn. For me, there was idle, slack work, for it was Sunday. Beds to be made, a hasty dust around, the lunch to be prepared and started.

I snatched the papers and sauntered out into the sun with a lighted cigarette. I glanced through them, and paused and devoured the Book Supplement pages of *The Times*. Wrote several titles of books in my library list.

I looked at the sky, pure blue, shining between drifting pillows of clouds. Behind me came the sounds of sawing of wood and the boys' chattering voices, as they collected the fallen stumps and neatly piled them up in a convenient corner.

Over the quietness of the air and stillness came the sound of the siren. We didn't shift, as usual, until planes could be heard. Presently the air was humming with them. The boys went under the stairs to the 'shelter'. We waited and watched a bit. The clear patch of sky was crossed and re-crossed with white trails. The machine gunfire was a gentle, distant pop-pop. Nothing to worry about, we said, too far off. We came inside. Suddenly, a roaring – a hasty look and right over the house, so low that the noise was terrifying, were six planes, fighting like mad. We both ducked for the 'shelter', the noise of the machine gun was deafening, oh so deadly close.

A fearful noise, a moaning, a rush of wind and whirr of propellers, a crash, and then, afraid of how near it had fallen, we both went out to see, very cautiously as planes were still fighting hard overhead.

Yes, there she lay, a blaze of fire and smoke. She missed the oast house by inches. There, in the peaceful scene, lay a mass of twisted, tortured metal, pieces here and there, everywhere, trees torn down, iron railings of the field bent and buckled in her trail.

The all-clear sounded – the all-clear. We sat down to lunch, sober and quiet except for the boys, who let me say in all pride never once called out, cried or showed one spot of fear and simply longed to see the plane close.

As we sat at our dining-room table, the lovely, oh so lovely view still stretched before our grateful eyes but its beauty marred by the dull heavy smoke and smouldering ruins of once a plane.

A little fire engine ploughs its way to the scene and a few villagers walk over the fields. We see it all clearly. We are in the Grand Stand.

I didn't know the nationality of the plane, or its type, but I can't eat. A lump, a burning lump is inside me. I look at Walter, he turns away. He feels it too, then.

The afternoon goes by in a strange gloom. Another raid, but not here. After tea, I said I'd like to view the plane, I'd like to know whether it was German or English, not that it mattered, and I'd like to talk to Palmer (the special Constable, and our gardener). Perhaps, perhaps, they had all bailed out before the crash. Perhaps no one was hurt, except the plane. Walter took me.

We looked and looked at this incredible wreck, which was no more. I looked at the orchard by the tail of the plane. I looked and stared. A little mound, covered by a once white parachute, spattered with blood, patches of crimson here and there. Sickened, I asked Palmer, praying he would not confirm my thoughts, but yes, the German pilot of that bomber lay, in pieces, beneath his stained covering.

Palmer held out his hand, the pilot's Iron Cross. So he'd done something to 'earn' that, now he was dead. No longer a body, or a man, but pieces. I stared and stared as though to see beneath the stained silk. There lies, I thought, a man, who this morning had his breakfast, who slept last night, who spoke perhaps a few hours ago, now he is no more – no more, he'll *never* speak again, or look, or eat, or – well anything – he's dead.

He was someone's child, someone's brother perhaps, sweetheart, husband.

This is *war*, I said, this is *war*. No, God, no, I screamed inside myself. This is *wrong, wrong*. How can we get out of this net, this chaos, HOW? We are caught by the necks, we cannot be free, we cannot let go of that which our teeth has bitten into so deeply.

I said a prayer to myself. Walter said, 'Oh let's go, this is awful.' Crying, I walked home.

This is war, yes, this is war. This taking of lives in a deadly manner, this battering of slums, this burning of the helpless. What cruel monster has been let loose after 1,940 years of Christ's teaching of *Love*? WHAT? We do it to them because they do it to us. Bomber v. planes, British and German alike fall from the skies, sometimes carrying its burden to death with them. The other three from that bomber were alive and jumped by parachute and landed in a wood behind our house. One is badly shot and probably won't live. (29th Oct.: He has since died.)

The sun is setting. I am at the table in the dining room. Our glorious view, which covers so much, and stretches so far, is still there for me to behold. The cows and the sheep are still grazing placidly in their fields, smoke curls up from the gardener's cottage, away to the left. Yet the scar is still there. Soldiers guard it now. Soldiers with tents and guns ready to live there for days if necessary until this sad, lifeless mound of steel is conveyed elsewhere and the mound of flesh under its parachute? No one seems to know, it will be removed in good time.[*]

This is war. Hateful *Hitler's* war, now our war, because, oh Dear God, where will it end.

[*] *He was given a military funeral and now lies in our little graveyard. Local kids put flowers on his grave. (Roberta)*

Following the end of the war, Roberta, Walter and their four children moved to Brasted in Kent. In 1950, Roberta had to leave her family for several months as she was suffering from severe chest infections with symptoms quite similar to tuberculosis. She went to Switzerland to live in a convalescent home in the 'healthy Swiss' air. The two eldest boys, Chris and Nick, were away at boarding school, while Guy and Sue were cared for by Walter and the family's housekeeper and her husband, the gardener. Once she recuperated from her illness, Roberta returned home to Kent, and they remained there until 1952, when Walter was offered a job in Johannesburg as the head of the South African division of his bank. He moved in advance of the family, and Roberta prepared to follow with the four children once he had settled in. She first moved temporarily with the children to Davos, Switzerland, as she believed the Swiss air would benefit their health.

The move to South Africa never happened, however, as Walter soon informed Roberta that he had met another woman in Johannesburg and wanted a divorce.

Waveney

Waveney was born on September 16, 1909, in Gosforth, near Newcastle upon Tyne. She lived there until the age of ten, when her father, who had been the vicar of Stockton-on-Tees, moved to Darlington to be the vicar there. When Waveney was sixteen years old, she started a brief courtship with her father's curate, a handsome older gentleman. Though she was tempted by the flirtation, she knew that it was not the best choice for her and she asked her father if he would be willing to send her off to boarding school. Both parents were quite happy with this request, as they too knew the courtship was ill-fated and Waveney's mother thought it would be beneficial for her to lose her strong north-east accent. That same year, Waveney went to a finishing school for young ladies in London.

She returned to Darlington a year later and began to help her father with his work in the parish. As the eldest of four, she had familial responsibilities, particularly since her mother was a 'delicate' lady and couldn't handle much strain. Waveney took on some of her mother's duties and performed the tasks of a vicar's wife. She was still able to enjoy an active social life in addition to her duties in the parish, and she often attended dances and was involved with the tennis club and local drama groups.

It was through parish connections that Waveney met her future husband Maurice. He was the nephew of a wealthy parishioner, and once, while visiting his aunt, had attended a local dance, where the two met. It was love at first sight, but they could not be married immediately because Maurice was only a lieutenant in the army and had to wait until he turned thirty and reached the rank of captain before he was allowed to marry. Fortunately for Waveney, Maurice was ten years her senior and nearly thirty, so they only had to wait a year before they could marry, in December of 1929, just before Maurice received his captaincy.

In 1930, they moved to Camberley in Surrey, where Maurice gave lectures on tactics at Sandhurst Military Academy and where Waveney gave birth to their first son, Michael, in 1931. The following year they moved to Gravesend, Kent, and then to Yorkshire with the 61st Foot, Gloucestershire Regiment.

The family settled at Catterick Garrison, a large army camp in Yorkshire, from 1932 to 1934, and here they had their second son, John, in 1933. Then Maurice was posted to the Territorial Army depot in Bristol, so the family moved again, this time to a small village called Chew Magna just outside Bristol. Their third son, Ian, was born in 1936.

The following article was written in 1938 from Chew Magna. Maurice had just received orders that he would soon be posted to Plymouth with the Second Battalion of the Gloucestershire Regiment. At this point Waveney was about eight months pregnant. When she mentioned '"war" week' she was referring to the Munich Crisis.

1938

We have had our orders for Plymouth after New Year. It is a great relief not to be going off to Rangoon – but the world seems so unsettled at the moment that I sometimes wonder whether we shall ever get to Plymouth. I have a feeling that more troops will be ordered to Palestine and Egypt before long and that the Gloucesters including Maurice will be amongst them! If we only knew for certain about this the children and I would stay on here where we have this house (our own property) and all our friends and M and J's school near. To be landed down in Plymouth and saddled with a house there and the children entered for a new school and then to be told I am to be a grass-widow for several months would indeed be a blow. I have no relative or friend within hundreds of miles of Plymouth* and never having been so far West in my life I am not enamoured of the prospect of being stranded there without a husband. Of course, the Palestine bit may never materialise, but in these awful days – no one seems safe or settled for more than a day at a time.

*Rusticana – you'll be my nearest. (Waveney)

I just don't want to write of the 'war' week. It was a nightmare which I hope I'll never have to live through again. Maurice was under orders to mobilise and be off to a secret destination at 48 hours' notice. We had to sleep with the bedroom door open and ready to listen for the phone call which would come through, if overnight, to our private address. Bristol is a very bomb-able place, being a huge air-port, aeroplane factory works and important food port. There was one genuine air-raid scare – which everyone thought was official, and nanny and I spent a desperate evening cutting our brown paper strips and pasting up windows! The thought that if war came we should at once be separated and I having to carry on alone the family cares with next month's 'event' to look forward to was a tortuous thought. I had air-raid nightmares, I woke thinking I heard Julian screaming and I could not find him or get to him. I imagined myself in bed with the new baby a few days old and air raids overhead and the maids and nanny demented and distracted etc. Never do I remember such agony and tension of mind. Added to it all we all had *foul* colds and I felt literally like a chewed rag at the end of it.

Enough said on this vile topic: Please don't voice

sympathies or comments on this paragraph as all I want to do now is try to forget it.

Shortly after this, Waveney gave birth to their fourth son, Robin, in November 1938. The family did not relocate to Plymouth, but nearly a year later Maurice's battalion was sent there to prepare for embarkation to the Continent. Once war was declared the battalion was one of the first detachments to go to France. Now a major, Maurice remained there until a brief leave in April 1940. When he returned in May, the Germans were pushing into France and Belgium, and Maurice's battalion, which was part of the rear-guard action, was told to hold its position. He was captured on May 31, 1940, and taken prisoner.

In July, Waveney received a 'Missing Presumed Dead' telegram and did not hear news otherwise for six weeks. She told her children in later years that she gardened as ruthlessly in those six weeks as she'd ever done in her life. The following excerpt is a telegram that she sent to Sirod explaining that she had just received news of Maurice.

Chew Magna
July 20, 1940

The miracle has happened. I received yesterday an official printed p/c but addressed and signed in Maurice's writing – to the effect that he is sad, not wounded and in Germany. It is dated June 10th so had taken 6 weeks to come! There is no permanent address so I cannot write yet but will be allowed to do so later. It is all *such* a relief and I am glad in many ways that he is safely out of the next struggle. We hope to see you very soon as I am spending the whole of the school holidays in Bourton. Julian and Robin are already there with Nanny, and the boys and I fol-

low on Friday when their term ends unless circumstances compel us to go before. If we pass through
Cheltenham en route I will try to call – but plans are
still a little vague and uncertain. It is creepy here with
no children in the house. Yours, Waveney.

*Once Waveney knew that Maurice was alive, she decided
to take herself and her four boys to live with her father.
He was a rector now, and had moved to Bourton-on-the-
Water in Gloucestershire shortly before Waveney's
mother's death in 1936. Waveney's decision to move was
partly based on the fact that Bristol was a target in the
Blitz and was an unsafe area, and also on family
finances. Their income was limited following Maurice's
capture because, as a prisoner of war, he only received
basic army pay.*

*The following was written in her father's home, just
after he had given a Harvest Festival broadcast on a
religious radio programme that was produced weekly
by the BBC. She finally had an address for Maurice, but
their correspondence was much delayed and restricted.
However, Waveney was able to decipher his location in
Germany, as she and Maurice had developed a particular code for communicating prior to his departure in
case he was ever captured.*

September 28, 1940

Life, As I Sees It

I am having to make myself write this, not because I
don't want to, but because I am dead tired and Nanny
has been out all day and owing to present circumstances none of the boys are back at school. In any
case today is Saturday and a whole holiday. I have
heaps of things I want to say, mostly about ourselves
and recent doings. I'm afraid not perhaps of much
interest to other people. However, you are all so very

kind in your appreciation of these chatty but egotistical eulogies – so perhaps you will bear with me if I continue the story of the family . . . This instalment will explain in itself why I have had to leave the writing of it until the eve of publishing day and even risk getting it pushed out of this number after all. Oh! Editor dear – I HAVE tried so often during the past fortnight to get it written ere now.

I will begin the tale on September 14th, afternoon of the eve of my father's Harvest Festival Broadcast. London was being bombed and all the week this house had been like an estate agent's office and billeting post. It is not actually anything but a *neutral* area and therefore had not been previously populated with evacuees. But now day and night families with car loads of children and luggage were rolling up, imploring to be told of boarding houses, farms or rooms to accommodate them. We had three empty bedrooms on our top floor that week but were hanging on to them for a) two BBC engineers who were arriving that day to transform our kitchen into a transmitting station and b) Michael and John's headmaster and wife, who had wired that they must evacuate from Clevedon and wanted to look at a house in our direction. There was a contest going on between two other families (previously unknown to us) as to which of them secured those top-floor rooms the moment they were named by us as available! Here I must point out that whilst it is very nice to have those top-floor rooms at a time like this, we feel that they ought to be occupied, they are a drawback in other ways. For instance, there are no heating or cooking facilities or a WC on that floor, though there is a nice bathroom. It thus means that no less than 5 extra people can be put up there to live or sleep but all the extra work and cooking fall upon the shoulders of *one* cook in *one* kitchen; and she already

has more than enough to do. If only there was a kitch-
enette up there and a WC in the bathroom it would let
as a very nice little flat – but it isn't feasible for us to
put in all these improvements as of course it isn't our
own house and you can't ask the Church to pay up for
doing it. I don't think anyone could share the kitchen
and carry meals up to a sitting room three floors
higher. And what would one do if A wanted to bake
onions in the oven when B had a sweet soufflé in it?

I know that there ought to be give and take in these
matters – but other people round here have found
evacuees very trying in this respect. They look
strangely at them and then remark to their other evac-
uee friends, 'Just out to profiteer over me – that's all
she is.' Well, to return to my story, Daddy and I were
just going out for $\frac{1}{2}$ hour to look at the house M and
J's school proposed taking when a car bowled in at
the drive gate. 'Oh, it must be the BBC men,' I said.
But 'no', there were small heads in the back and loads
of luggage. The car drew up facing ours and out got
Norman, a cousin of mine (nephew of my mother's),
and his wife. 'Oh, Uncle R,' they begged, 'can you tell
us anywhere where we can sleep the night?' It tran-
spired that they had fled from Beckenham. For three
days they had tried to get away, but each time they
were ready to start the sirens went again and back to
the cellar they had to go. For three weeks they had
lived down there, not daring to let the children go further than the garden or end of the road. That morning
they got up at 5.45 a.m. as the 'all-clear' sounded and
pushed off in the car with their three little boys aged
8, $5\frac{1}{2}$ and 4 and a not too efficient nursemaid and
loads of luggage. They were across London by 8 a.m.
and at Aylesbury they began to search for somewhere
to go. They said the queues of people outside Agents'
Offices were ghastly and at each one was the notice

'Nothing to offer – Please do not call'. On they went
trying every small town or village they came to, sometimes leaving the main road to try some small hamlet
off the beaten track. They daren't stop for lunch, but
brought food and fed the children in the moving car
so as to waste no time. It was 5.30 p.m. when they
rolled in at our gate and these children had been in
that car for 10 hours!

We hauled them all out and put on a 2nd tea in the
dining room. We said of course they could pack in
here somehow for the weekend or longer and we left
them on their own for tea, whilst we went off to look
at the school house and hold a secret discussion as to
how we could cram them in and what beds we could
muster. The BBC men, we decided, would have to take
their chance in the already full guest houses. We
would phone friends and arrange for Mr and Mrs G
(the school pair) to be put up there. We had a camp
bed; there was even an old crib for the 4-year-old but
no proper mattress. Two children could sleep one at
each end of the same single bed perhaps. It must be
done somehow. Nanny was out and the cook was out
and only Olive (our jewel of a h. parlour maid, with
us since just before Maurice and I met) was in and
cooking our supper that evening. Drummond my ex-
film photographer and now RNVR brother was here
on a week's leave terminating the next day, and my
sister was due home to begin also a week's leave the
next day! Talk about a Hotel!

When we returned to the scene of action ¾ hour
later the children had shaken down together (7 boys all
under 9!) and a spirit of wild excitement prevailed.
They had none of them met before. The BBC engineers
and their van had arrived and two extraordinarily nice
friendly gentlemen were rigging up our one and only
kitchen into the transmitting station! We explained the

situation and they were very friendly and sympathetic about it all and refused to be perturbed by the 7 astounded pairs of boyish eyes watching them enviously for a moment and then dashing off again in the excitement of the moment. They congratulated Erica and I upon producing 7 sons between us! We found ourselves terribly short of sheets; ten had been washed that very same morning! However, we managed to dish out a top sheet for each newcomer and they had to lie on blankets. Fortunately we had plenty of the latter. I found a shakedown which made a crib-mattress and the four-year-old was put to bed in that. The nurse slept with him in a proper single bed. The two older boys were put in separate beds until they were asleep and then one was tucked into the foot-end of the other and thus were two other single beds available for their parents.

A final rehearsal of the Harvest Service was being held in the Church and relayed to the kitchen, where we could hear it just as it would be heard over the wireless the next day. It was amusing, between rushing about making beds, to slip down there and listen to Daddy reading or giving instructions one minute and then starting the choir off on a hymn whilst he came quickly across to hear how their singing was coming over! The BBC men were smiling and joking over the deliciously tempting aroma of steak and onions which was brewing beneath their noses on the kitchen fire. At last the seven babes were in bed, the rehearsal was over, the BBC men had departed for the night, and except for explaining things to Nanny and Irene, when they came in there was nothing more to do but wash the supper dishes and go to bed. There were 16 people under our roof that night! So much for poor Daddy on the last night which he had meant to spend in quiet final preparation for the morrow!

THE great day dawned. The service was at 9.25 a.m.

There were 17 for breakfast, as the verger came in, not having time to get home between the early service and 9.25 a.m. The 2 nannies and 7 children had theirs together in a small room and the five grownups in the dining room. Olive, Irene and Mr Milton the verger had theirs in the kitchen. The BBC men and another telephonist who appeared from somewhere were busy in the kitchen (which resembled the interior of a submarine by now) but no one minded and everyone was jolly and cheerful except the visiting nursemaid, who was dreadfully homesick and inclined to be unfriendly. The Rectory garden adjoins the Church, so as we dared not risk yelling children's voices spoiling the service and all the boys chose to go for a walk together rather than go to Church, we sent them off at 9.15 with the cousins' nanny for a walk. Robin remained monarch of all he surveyed and the spoiled pet of the BBC men. He got hold of their private telephone and called up Cheltenham by mistake but nobody minded or even scolded him! (Age 1 year 10 months!) The Church was filling fast! Daddy was running over his selection of prayers with a stop-watch as they took 2 minutes too long and he wasn't sure which to omit. I cleared the breakfast dishes through to the pantry and said the maids weren't to touch them and that Erica and I would do them later on. One or two visitors and officials from the BBC parked their cars in our drive and like Epaminandos I became all solemn-like and grave and conducted them into the now full and expectant church and congregation. Such an event had never been known in the district. And then the organ began to play. I felt in rather the same sort of dream as I did on my wedding-day; the sort of 'After all the preparations here we are this IS the real occasion and I feel that it is only a dream after all' feeling. The choir took their places, and the red light switched on and the Service began.

After it was all over and the distant passing visitors had light refreshments and departed, the BBC men dismantled the kitchen and mundane life began again. After lunch there was a further break-up of the party when my cousin went back to Beckenham, taking my brother as far as S. London with him and also the nursemaid, who by that time had made up her mind that she could never tolerate life here! It was decided that Erica and the three children should remain here until something in the nature of a furnished house, which she could share with a friend, turned up. Irene, the cook, announced that her young man was getting leave the next weekend and she would like to be married on Saturday. Rosalind my sister arrived the same Sunday evening after a perilous crossing of London, for her week's leave. Irene's marriage was not quite such a blow to us as it might have been as she is returning to us after the honeymoon, until the young man (in the RAF) is in a position to make a home.*

The cousins appeared to have colds, but it couldn't be helped, though it has been rather sickening for me to watch first Julian, then Robin and now John all get wretched colds from them, in Robin's case bringing back a semblance of the whooping cough, and rattling wheezy chest.

*Alas – She has decided to join him at P now, as soon as it can be arranged. Told us so today! Nov. 11th. Can anyone recommend a cook? (Waveney)

By the middle of the week we had a very nice house in view for them and last Monday they moved in. It was fun having them here but oh, the noise and racket it made. It would have been all right if my father was a business man who slammed the door after him at 10.00 a.m. and did not appear again until the children's bed-time. But of course he isn't. His office is his study, here right in the house, the first room at the top of the first flight of stairs. He was marvellously good and forbearing about everything but the continual scamper of feet and shouting of young voices and yelling and occasional squabbling was not conducive to his work. The younger cousins were not attractive children, they whined and whimpered at the slightest grievance. Their mother is much too sweet and gentle and reasoning with them all. The minute their father arrived back for the weekend they behaved far better. I must say I gave them full marks for being so little upset by their recent experiences and changes. They showed no signs of fear or terror and quite seemed to miss the sirens! . . .

Well, now it is Saturday September 30th. I left off writing this at midnight last night. It has been a hectic fortnight with such a houseful and no proper cook, but all of us muddling in and doing a bit here and there. My sister returned to her job a few days ago and Maurice's sister who came for 10 days also went away yesterday. We are once more, comparatively speaking, a small family.

Before I close and post this I must tell you that I have had two very delayed letters and two postcards from Maurice. They were all written in June and I did not get them until early September, but I suppose it is better than nothing. I am now longing frantically for the next mail. What is annoying is that Maurice writes one short letter (only 22 lines allowed) on a p/c each week but I get all four, by the same mail, about once in 5 weeks. I would so much rather have one each week. They are only allowed to write in pencil and he says nothing of the conditions under which they are living. He has heard *nothing* from me since May 12th (all my letters after that came back to me). I began writing to him in mid-August so perhaps by the middle of October he may begin to receive my letters. He is reduced to such questions as 'Are the hens still laying well?', 'How are Misty and her kittens?', etc. which shows how little they think it safe to say.

Unfortunately the plans for Michael and John's
school to move to this neighbourhood fell through but
I am determined not to let them go back to Clevedon
or Bristol district just now. Julian has begun lessons in
a little Froebel class with six other small children over
seven. I don't like the idea of sending them away to
board at a time like the present so I am afraid they are
just kicking up their heels and learning mostly nothing.
I have seen Sirod several times lately and envy her with
such nice schools so near at hand. Daphne is a charming natural little girl and Gili not nearly so plain as
Sirod used to say. John could do with a chapter to himself! Here, I have started another sheet which I never
meant to, so I must do something about filling it. I am
longing to know what has happened to Roberta,[*] Ad
Astra and Glen Heather's husband in all
these horrors. Also Cotton Goods – as
Lancashire too seems to have her share
of it. I do think of you all each night
and wonder which of us is getting it . . .

[*] *Oct. 29th. Still goes
daily to London but
often takes 2–4 hrs to
get home! He's very
cheerful tho'! (Roberta)*

I must away now to saw up some small logs for the
fires. The children have a bonfire going and are burning leaves and rubbish. It is rather a cold dull day,
after a phenomenally glorious September, fraught for
me with memories of Lyme Regis with Maurice at this
time last year. The Reg't crossed to France on October
1st last year and from that day to this Maurice and I
have only had 10 days together.

Thank you so many of you, for very kind letters
which have cheered me up a lot. I have had so little
time to answer them personally.

Love and best wishes is all I can say.

From Waveney

*Waveney – You and Rosa's letters make me feel
ashamed of doing so little – Good Luck to you. (Yonire)
Well, you have had a time! I am so glad
you've heard from Maurice. (Barnie)*

In many ways, this time in Waveney's life was a positive experience, as she was forced to cope on her own for several years and to sustain her family on limited finances. While this was particularly demanding, she emerged feeling stronger and more resourceful.

Maurice returned to England in April 1945 after being held as a POW in several different locations in Germany. When he returned he was very thin and had a heart condition that would plague him for the rest of his life.

The family continued to live in Bourton-on-the-Water with Waveney's father, whose health was failing. Following his death in 1947, the family returned to Chew Magna, with the boys continuing to attend various boarding schools. Maurice struggled with the transition to life at home. He had a particularly hard time coping with the changes that had taken place in England during his absence and, for years afterwards, would often speak of how things were 'before the war'. He returned to work in different administrative positions in the army. Waveney gave birth to Margaret, their fifth child, in 1947.

In addition to the difficulties Maurice had in re-adjusting to life after his experience as a POW, he was also frustrated with his work. He had been captured early in the war so he hadn't been promoted and was placed in middle-ranking jobs until the end of his career. Soon after he retired in the early 1950s, he and Waveney moved down to Exmouth with Robin and Margaret. The other children were old enough to follow their own paths. The family looked upon this move to Exmouth as a new start, but in fact Waveney's quality of life deteriorated with their relocation. She had a lively personality and found it difficult to be with Maurice, who became rather solemn, especially after he retired.

This solitude and lack of activity did not suit Waveney. Her daughter Margaret is sure that the CCC was a lifeline for her mother, as she revelled in the stories and adventures of her fellow members. She did try to keep herself busy through her involvement with the parish church councils, regular household duties and corresponding with her many friends and relatives. She was actively involved with helping out in the local church, running a bookstall and raising money for the parish.

In 1965, just before his sixty-sixth birthday, Maurice had a heart attack and died quite suddenly. Waveney had adjusted to life in Exmouth and remained there, though she spent most of her time visiting family members, including her fourteen grandchildren.

She was one of the members of the CCC who outlived the magazine. She died in 1999 at the age of eighty-nine.

Rosa

Born in Burton-on-Trent on September 13, 1896, Rosa initially joined the CCC as Rosa Dartle, basing her name on the character in Charles Dickens' David Copperfield who 'needed to know everything'.

Rosa and her elder sister Ella lost their mother at a very early age when she died giving birth to a son, who also died. Following her death, their father, who was a builder, sent both Rosa and Ella away to boarding school, where they spent most of their childhood and teenage years.

Once she left boarding school Rosa moved to London and attended a course at a school for cookery. She spent her time during the Great War working at Coutts Bank. She eventually made her way back to Burton, where she met and married her husband, whom she refers to in the CCC as KV, even though it has no obvious connection to his real name, Harold. They married in 1920, at which point Rosa left her job.

KV had served in the Royal Artillery during the Great War, first as a private, and ended the war as a captain. Then he returned to his old job at Bass brewers. Bass was based in Burton, but KV and Rosa moved to London, where KV worked for the London arm. He was a 'commercial traveller', which meant that he acted as a representative of the firm, visiting pubs and checking their methods of storing the beer, their equipment and procedures.

Rosa had their first child, John, in 1923, then Katharine Margery in 1925, and finally Elizabeth in 1928. The family moved to St Albans in 1929 and KV commuted to London for his work with Bass.

When the Second World War started KV continued

to work for Bass in London and served in the Home Guard on evenings and weekends, though he later re-enlisted with the army.

Rosa sent the following article to Ad Astra about the day-to-day activities of her family at the beginning of the war.

1940

. . . Do you not find it a terrible waste of time going to the shelter during the day? I just carry on with my work here as I simply couldn't get through the duties and meals if I didn't!

I don't go unless I hear gun fire (there's a warning on now, but I'm at the dining table) and then I do mending, silver, letters etc. which I save up for such times. (Ad Astra)

I wonder if the enemy intend deliberately to bomb our hospitals, and if this is a sort of preparation for chemical warfare? It is a ghastly thought, yet I do not feel that our resistance could be weakened by any dastardly action that could happen. I joined the Labour Party recently feeling that here are some definite ideas of progress, especially in Education. I hope that by the time the girls are old enough to need me very little I shall have become a little experienced and able to be useful in some humble capacity.

I have always felt that until more and more women take part in organisations and local government and so on, we shall not get on, or see the reforms we all desire. I was asked to be on the Food Committee and of course consented. But isn't it funny how *I can't get away from food*! This committee has not done anything useful so far, but is to watch prices and report on overcharging and make suggestions for the good of the populace. I'm hopelessly ignorant about committee procedure, but no doubt I shall learn.

The great thing in all this strange life we are living, is to be able to feel some hope for the future out of all the present chaos, it's only by trying to gain experience of all kinds, that I feel I can have any excuse for continuing to be – when so many are suffering who are so undeserving of the horrors that have come to them. I'd like to thank you for your Editorial labours, in these difficult days. Good luck to you all the time, a long life to CCC.

Rosa Dartle.

Throughout the war Rosa and her family hosted several evacuees at their house in St Albans. They first assisted some of Rosa's friends, who arrived with a week's worth of rations and stayed for eighteen months. After this family relocated, the billeting officer asked if Rosa would be willing to take in two teachers. She saw this as a fantastic opportunity for her children to have education on hand, and was delighted to do so. The teachers always came home for lunch, and the headmaster of the school eventually asked Rosa if he could join them too, so Rosa was often busy in the kitchen during wartime days. This role was not as trying for her as it could have been, as she was one of the few CCC members who was naturally a domestic person, happy in the home and very fond of cooking.

The next excerpt was written in either 1940 or 1941. Rosa's son John had already left school and was working at the local motor body works.

My Dear Ad Astra,
This week I received and sent on Number 47, it was very much appreciated. Like you, we have very frequent air-raid warnings, and of course all and every night. We had our entrance hall made strong for a refuge, with beams, 9 upright and 3 across the ceiling, the idea being to hold up a roof over our heads. John has made 3-tier bunk beds and secured them to the pillars, and the children sleep here every night. We

had a wall built round the porch, outside the front door, to minimise blast. The adults in the house sleep in their beds at present, but this weekend I must move them all downstairs. I think we have had some fires, and several casualties in the town from our own dud AA shells going through roofs! But the worst features of the attacks that have come to pass so far are the . . . . but folk were safe in shelters and away from windows. Also we have an assortment of delayed action bombs which sometimes go off during the day! Isn't it astonishing, the way we can get used to so many and great dangers? I was tickled to death thinking of you three in your bed, and you in the middle!

KV has tedious journeys to London and back each day and his office buildings have suffered. They sometimes work in the cellars when the d.a. bombs have not exploded or been removed. Last week I had some refugees from E. Ham, who came to get a few nights' rest. Now the children sleep on the bunks I had their rooms vacant and the refugees thought it was heaven to sleep in a bed after 3 weeks in Anderson shelters. Their home was gone but they returned to their work quite cheerily after their week's respite. They said our noise here was nothing compared with London and E. End. It seems heavy to us, but it is relative, like everything else no doubt. For my part, I go on from day to day, cooking, washing, shopping in between the sirens, canteen on Mondays, first aid on Thursdays, Recorder practice on Fridays, my only relaxation. We are all very well and very cheery, Margery has lots of homework, and works until 9.30 p.m., when we all retire to bed to rest if not to sleep.

You asked about my sister, at Pinner? Well, she spent the summer in the W. Country leaving her husband and two friends, a teacher and office worker, to fend for themselves, and she has not yet returned. I have had one post card from her in two months and to tell the truth I am so disgusted at her lack of sense of duty that I can't bring myself to write and enquire. How *anyone* could be away, just staying places, for weeks on end with no job worth doing, beats my understanding. I really feel ashamed.

John is busy at the Motor Body Works fitting up Ambulance bodies and Mobile canteens, also they had an order for large numbers of bunks.[*] They do work that comes their way, he has to spend one night in three at the Works, standing by in readiness, as it is also an ambulance station.

*These are being made by John's men too, and we hope next wk to be able to have bunk beds in our own shelter. Meanwhile we're still in the communal bed! (Ad Astra)

He gets some sleep on these nights, but not very much. KV now does regular duties every 4 or 5 nights with the Home Guard. Lately I have taken to bottling in jars with those clamped on lids, using the Campden preserving tablets. We have done plums galore, also pears, apples and carrots in dice. I am now paying 8d per lb for onions, for I have a few 'everlasting onions' in the garden. Do you know them? They grow in clusters, you take what you want from the group and it goes on growing. I am having the lawn dug up for potatoes next year. We have 50 feet width so can spare half of them quite easily. I feel this is a very hum drum account of us all, but I think you will see how fully the days are occupied. The three teachers are still here and likely to remain, so all I can do for homeless people is to offer temporary shelter for a week or so at a time and this I do.[*] Our city is full to overflowing. I think because the LMS railway is still functioning normally and we are far enough out of London (20 miles) to seem compara-

*I've had a poor lass from next door to John's factory. She was dazed from lack of sleep and so grateful. (Ad Astra)

tively safe so men can travel up and down and settle their families here.

After confirming with Bass that he would be re-employed upon his return, KV joined the army and worked as an Area Petrol Officer. He was responsible for controlling and managing the supply of fuel to the east of England for the army.

Near the end of the war Rosa added to her duties by working part-time on the production line in an arms factory in St Albans. Afterwards she returned to her domestic life in the home and KV went back to his job at Bass until he retired around 1956.

Rosa and family remained in St Albans until the mid-1950s, when they moved to Highgate in London. There she established much stronger connections with the CCC women who lived close by, such as Elektra and Cornelia.

KV died from heart failure in 1964 at the age of seventy-two. Rosa moved to Cambridge, where Elizabeth, her youngest daughter, had settled. She lived first in a flat and then in sheltered accommodation, and spent the majority of her time with her children and five grandchildren. Rosa died from cancer in 1977 at the age of eighty-one.

3

A Day in the Life

BLOOD BATH Yonire

(RED LIGHTS : NOT FOR THE SQUEAMISH .)

(NOTE : I'M WRITING THIS BECAUSE IT REALLY WAS FUNNY —
SO DON'T, PLEASE, BOTHER TO SYMPATHISE — WE'RE ALL
GRAND & FULL OF BEANS.)
"never forgotten"

More & more, as I grow older, do I wonder
if there really is anything in astrology: I am a Sagittarian,
(born midnight, Nov. 25th 1907) & every horoscope stresses
my prone-ness to accidents, but also my good-luck & general
optimism —

WELL — you all know about most of the others.
Here is the latest:

Last night E. & I were watering the garden &
spraying the roses (with a stirrup-pump & Clensel) —
E. was pottering around with his pipe when I went
indoors (about 10-p.m. or so) carrying a few roses which
I had not been able to resist cutting —

There is a white bowl of roses (French — rare
vitreous china - very lovely) on the mantlepiece —

Written by Yonire, c.1955.

One of the most appealing aspects of the magazine was the opportunity it provided to read about 'how the other half lives'. Given the diversity of the women, the CCC was brimming with unique stories and experiences. Their mutual desire to expand horizons and to see the world through someone else's eyes meant that the women were always questioning each other and sharing anecdotes about their everyday lives. Often they reminisced about the past; as the women were born at the end of the Victorian era and lived through both world wars, they had witnessed incredible changes in the world and society.

Yonire, Cotton Goods and Amelia were some of the members who wrote detailed and entertaining accounts of their lives and their adventures, much to everyone's delight.

Yonire

Born in Edinburgh in 1907, Yonire was raised mainly by her aunt, with little support from her absentee father. A lawyer by training, it was suspected that he suffered a nervous breakdown after fighting in the First World War. Yonire's mother died when she was nine, and so her aunt took her and her younger brother in. Her aunt was married to a baronet who was the Chairman and Chief Executive of Benline Shipping, and they lived in the historic Luffness House near Aberlady. They were quite wealthy, so Yonire and her brother were well cared for and grew up in Edinburgh high society. She attended West Heath public school and then enrolled at the University of Edinburgh. Yonire claimed that she was 'expelled' from the university for selling the Daily Worker *in the quad. This may have contributed to her expulsion, but it is more likely that she failed her first-year exams. She was renowned in both her family and the CCC for her tendency to exaggerate. Following her time at university she did a diploma in dietetics at the School of Domestic Science in Edinburgh. Before she married she also spent her time organising a Girl Guide Rangers troop in the fishing village of Fisherrow.*

After several failed engagements, Yonire met her future husband Elliot and instantly fell in love. Elliot was a tenant farmer and a distant cousin of another wealthy shipping family, who used to invite him for weekends. It was during one of these visits that he and Yonire met. Elliot had little to offer her financially, as he was struggling and on the verge of bankruptcy, but she happily left high society for him. The pair married in 1934 and Yonire moved to Elliot's sheep farm in the

Scottish borders. Although moving from a house with a staff of over thirty to an isolated farm was a major adjustment, Yonire quickly adapted to country life and became an avid hunter, riding as often as she could. She also spent a great deal of time reading philosophy, which resulted in her conversion to Catholicism soon after they had married.

Yonire and Elliot had their first son, Bill, in 1936. It wasn't long afterwards that she joined the CCC as one of its original members. Three years later, in 1939, they moved to 'Dodridge', a farm twenty miles south-east of Edinburgh. They had been struggling as sheep farmers and decided to switch to arable farming. The family remained there until 1960 and had four more boys: Jock in 1940, Sandy in 1944, Adam in 1945 and Mike in 1947. Elliot spent the war years on the farm, as his was a reserved occupation and he was a captain of the Home Guard as well. They contributed to the war effort by taking in numerous evacuees throughout its duration.

Yonire's submissions to the CCC were always typed on yellow, green or blue paper, but they were even more colourful in terms of her descriptions of events. She submitted this article about a 'day in her life' to the CCC in 1948.

1948

Murder in the Organ Loft or What Would You Have Done Chum?

And don't say you wouldn't ever have been such a b.f. as to get yourself into such a mess because YOU DON'T KNOW, or do you?

I have wanted to get this off my chest and on to paper for months but never dared for various reasons. However, this time I'm going to (at least) write it down.

I first met Sebastian when he was rehearsing for the Edinburgh Festival at which he was performing as a soloist, well, actually, I first met him in Paris when he was at the Conservatoire and I was staying with some people, but that was ages ago and we met again, as for the first time, last August. He liked Edinburgh, and after the Festival was over, stayed on, getting himself various jobs. He is extremely popular with the Moray McLaren, James Bridie, Eric Linklater types and a very nice chap, if a bit excitable AND inclined to drink far too much. We liked him and he liked us and he used to come for odd weekends and go for extremely energetic bicycle runs with the boys and play our battered piano far into the morning watch and drink himself into a coma which he slept off with no apparent ill-effects (my aunt said she had never seen Sebastian fully dressed, until the other day when she met him in Edinburgh. He was always recovering from a heavy night when she came to Dodridge!).

He is extremely vague and composes all over the place, and, believe it or not, I got a long-distance call from a conductor the other day to ask if I could possibly find the slow movement of his concerto which might be knocking about the Dodridge dining-room! (I don't think it was, anyway I couldn't find it. But I *did* remember that Seb. had been working on the Slow movement when he was staying with Borealis so I've passed the buck to her.)

I only once had any emotional bother with Seb. and that was after a party here when we went out into the garden on a wonderful night in September to cool down before bed. I got the impression that he was making love to the night, rather than me, and it didn't seem important, anyway, I just disentangled myself and went indoors.

I have never thought, and neither has Elliot, that he

was interested in me as a lover. He likes me and we have similar musical passions and tastes and he can talk to me for hours without boring me. *And* I like the way he plays the piano. He is *very* fond of Elliot and Dodridge and the boys and turns up often and unexpectedly but always fits in very well. Even my aunt, who has always regarded my boy-friends with suspicion, looks upon Seb as peculiar, but nice and *safe*!

Well, that was how I thought about him too. I used to go around with him quite a lot to concerts and opera and whatnot and I sometimes acted as his secretary at rehearsals.

I wanted to hear Cortot when he was in Edinburgh but had not booked a seat soon enough. Seb. said casually, 'I can get you into the Press quite easily.' I still thought I had a chance of a returned seat but I hadn't, and finally I found myself having a drink with Seb. and a couple of critics before the concert. Seb. left me with them to go and rehearse and returned before the end to collect me. We all went and had something to eat at a pub. Then the critics left us to write their copy and Seb and I wandered over to the bar (which has a Late Licence). *Now* I think it is probable that Seb. had been drinking pretty heavily all evening but at the time I assumed he had had no more than I, which wasn't much.

Suddenly Seb. stretched himself, beat his chest like a gorilla and said, 'I want to play *Bach*.' It seemed a good idea and I wanted Bach too. The question was *where*? Seb. lives in digs and has a studio but the studio is closed at 10 p.m. (it's in a block of music rooms, etc.) and he can't get in because the outer door is locked. We could have gone back to Dodridge, in fact, he wanted to, but I didn't think my sister-in-law would appreciate Bach at 11.30 p.m. till Lord knew when, just under her room, so I refused to let him come home with me. We discussed all the Edinburgh pianos we knew but none of them seemed right. Either their owners were away or they hadn't met Sebastian and I felt it was hardly the right moment. In fact, if I arrived with a strange man, when they were in bed, saying he wanted to play Bach, and they saw Seb. looking a bit primitive and woolly, I doubted if they'd react well at all.

While we were on the point of reluctantly giving up Bach and going home to bed (me at any rate) Seb said, 'Got it! We'll play Bach on the organ of St John's Church' (St John's is a very fashionable West End Church bang on the corner of Princes Street).

I said: 'How will we get in?'

He said: 'I've got a key.'

I said: 'Seb! Where did you get it?'

He said: 'I played the organ there one Sunday.'

I said, 'Come on then,' and we went. (In case it may seem strange that I thought so little of gatecrashing into St John's, I'd better explain that I was used to playing Church organs at queer times. If you remember, I began my singing career under Dr Greenhouse Alt who was, among other things, the organist of St Giles in the High Street and he would quite often take me up there to sing at any time. The Hall where I had my usual lesson was bad from an acoustic point of view and if we had a concert coming off (me singing, I mean) he'd often say, 'This is *hell*, come to St Giles,' and we'd sing up there (quite often with a bunch of bewildered American tourists being shown all round us!). So the idea of St John's didn't perturb me in the least.)

We went along, Sebastian worked out some Fugues and I wandered down among the pews. It was quite lovely, the moving lights from the Princes St., Lothian Road traffic shone through the stained-glass windows. The Church was dark (except for the organ-loft light) and peaceful and I sat in a pew and listened. He played a fugue or two – then 'Jesu, Joy of Man's Desiring' – then 'Sheep May Safely Graze' then more fugue, then he started improvising. Seb. *is* a genius, if he doesn't kill it with drink, and it was utter bliss to be sitting there listening, until the music changed, very subtly, it got nastier and nastier, more and more horrible and macabre and Black mass and mocking and sinister and beastly.

I got up and went to the front of the loft and said, 'Seb! *Stop* it! Seb, STOP!' but he didn't take any notice. I ran round to the back and switched the organ power off and then pitched into him and blew him up and said he'd got to play something decent and calm to leave the Church as we'd found it. That it was infernally bad manners, if nothing worse, to treat other people's places of worship like that.

He looked at me and said, 'You look wonderful when you're angry. It suits your type, you're too heavy and big for normal emotions, but *anger*, you ought to get angry more often. Then I'd fall in love with you and then I could *really* write. That's what's wrong with my concerto. There's no real *passion* about it. *Please*, Betty, go on being angry.'

Well, I laughed (later I wonder if the whole of the rest might not have been an attempt to annoy me and get me angry for the sake of the Concerto! Unfortunately, he succeeded rather too well!) and I said I must get home, and *please* play something nice and calm to leave a pleasant atmosphere behind us.

He played one of the stock voluntaries on the verge of parody the whole time but it did. I said, 'I'm sorry you've mucked up a wonderful evening, but it can't spoil the first bit, which was perfect. And now, come *on*, Elliot will think I've had a smash. I'll drop you at Mrs D's on my way.'

The organ-loft light switched on and off at the *top*. I went down the stairs first and Seb. waited to switch off, when he did and we were in pitch darkness, I couldn't find the door-handle (it turned out to be a Yale, high up in the door). I was grumbling for it when S. came down saying, 'Where IS this ruddy door-handle?' and he bumped up against me in the dark. I was wearing a short dress, a loose coat, French knickers, I mean flimsy open v. short ones and a lace bra, and a suspender belt, nylons and high-heeled openwork shoes. He began fondling me and kissing the back of my neck and ears. At first I was just mildly irritated and concentrating on the door-handle. Then I got annoyed and swung round and slapped his face. That did it! He got me jammed against the door and I very soon realised he meant business.

I tried everything, argument, scorn, anger, pleading, force (even my old standby, 'Release method No. 3' as taught by the RHS failed because I couldn't get a leverage because of the b— door), I even prayed! And it may have been an answer to prayer that I discovered I could get my shoe off *and* use it. He had me in a sort of cross-grip, with my right arm below his, too low to jab my fingers into his eye, and I couldn't bite, because he had his arm round my neck and mouth (I never thought of screaming till long afterwards). Well, I slipped my shoe off and socked him as hard as I could on the head. His grip loosened at once so I socked him again and then as I got my arm really free, *again*. He just slumped on to the floor and lay there.

I climbed over him and up the organ-loft stairs and found a light. I switched it on and saw him lying in a pool of blood with the top of his head battered in, unconscious, and, for all I knew, dead. I was quite certain he was dead.

Well, what would you have done?

I thought over my chances of escaping the gallows if I went over to the policeman still on duty outside the Caledonian Hotel and said, 'I've just killed a man. We were playing Bach in St John's. It was self-defence,' and decided they were poor. I then wondered if I could conceal my traces and slip out. It was unlikely that the body would be discovered till next Sunday and Seb. quite often disappeared without bothering to tell his landlady. Could they fix the time of death? Against this, I'd been wandering all round the Church and leaving fingerprints everywhere. I had been with Seb. quite openly and obviously. The Barman had probably heard us planning to go to St John's. Anyway, I'd be certain to be questioned and I'm a rotten liar. Concealment was out of the question. The next point was, whom to tell? I lit a cigarette. I was sitting on the top step of the organ loft with the body most horribly beneath me and proceeded to think it all out very carefully. I thought Superintendent Merilees would be best. He has a weekend cottage near us and he knows us very well and he's nice and he'd break it to Elliot and get my brother (and lawyer) and everything.

He might even help me to conceal the crime! I was just finishing my cigarette (no point in rushing to my doom!) when the corpse suddenly shuddered, groaned and sat up. (I *still* can't get him to believe I was upset. He just says, 'Sitting there, smoking a cigarette, and *gloating* over me!') My relief was so terrific my knees gave out and I couldn't stand. So I just continued to sit and look at him. He was frightfully dazed and had a splitting headache but he was quite conscious. We got the bleeding stopped and the mess washed up and my goodness! I don't know HOW real murderers even clean up. It was awful. There was blood *everywhere*. I found water and pails and cleaning things downstairs below the church but it took hours. Then I had to help Seb. to the car (parked about $\frac{1}{4}$ mile away). This wasn't so bad as at that time of night it just looked as if he were a bit drunk. We got him to bed and rang up a VERY safe Dr friend who promised to see if his skull was fractured and to ask no questions. Actually, he did, he couldn't think what he'd been hit with, the slipper had very narrow $3\frac{1}{2}$" heels, it had made *holes* in his head.

I then drove home and got back about 2 a.m. to find E a bit worried, we sat and talked till 4.30 a.m. or so and E went in next day to see if Seb. were really going to live. We had a very anxious time for a week or so until it was obvious that he was.

But it has put years on to my life.

Yonire was known as quite a character in the CCC, with her amusing submissions of somewhat embellished escapades. She also contributed many stories about her numerous activities, such as photography and dog breeding. She processed and developed her own film in a darkroom in the family home and belonged to a photography correspondence magazine.

Her interest in breeding dogs led her to both show and judge them at the West of England Ladies Kennel Society and the prestigious dog show Crufts. Elliot would often assist Yonire with these events by showing the dogs for her, since she suffered from physical limitations. Years before she had fallen when riding, and when her horse rolled over her, it broke some of her ribs and injured her back. As a result she suffered from osteoarthritis in her back and hip, along with various other ailments. Due to her compromised health, Yonire expended little energy on housework and spent the mornings in bed with her typewriter. This was her favourite activity, as she was able to write, read, smoke and listen to music. She wrote prolifically for CCC, contributed regularly to the kennel-club journals Our Dogs *and* Dog World, *and submitted articles to various magazines such as* Farmer's Weekly. *It was through this periodical that Yonire was commissioned to write a book about Jack Russell terriers. In 1962, she published* The Jack Russell or Working Terrier *(reprinted in 1990).*

While travelling to dog shows throughout England, Yonire often passed through Herefordshire and liked the area so much that she convinced Elliot to move there in 1961. They intended to buy a farm but opened a pub in the village of Kinnersley instead, called the Kinnersley Arms. The family remained in Herefordshire after they retired from the pub in 1970.

Despite chronic health problems, Yonire was full of life, so it was a shock to everyone when she died suddenly in 1979, at the age of seventy-two. She had been admitted to hospital with a broken ankle but caught pneumonia and developed complications. The women in the CCC *were devastated by her sudden absence and many struggled to continue to write after her death.*

Cotton Goods

Cotton Goods was known as the one working-class member of the CCC, a status of which she was very proud. Though she was better educated than the majority of her peers, and her father had been middle class, she married a working-class man and lived in a working-class community. Cotton Goods felt particularly aligned with this group politically as she was a socialist and ardent early Labour supporter. Her contributions to the magazine often represented working-class views.

Born in 1893, she grew up in Oldham in Lancashire, where her father was a manager in a cotton mill. She was the eldest of three children and her mother died when she was nine years old. Five years later, her father remarried and had three more children, whom she helped to raise. Once she finished school, Cotton Goods qualified as a teacher and taught for several years, first in Oldham and then in a small village called Bickerstaffe in west Lancashire.

After one failed engagement, Cotton Goods, by then in her late twenties, married Albert. She had met him through a penfriends scheme during the war. Albert was a working-class man, an overseer in a cotton mill in Lancashire. The pair settled in Accrington, where they had Betty in 1923 and Jim in 1925. They then moved to Spring Hill, a district on the outskirts of Accrington, and had Irene in 1930 and Nancy in 1935.

One of the topics that Cotton Goods liked to discuss in the magazine was her Lancashire background. She was extremely proud of her roots, which is why she chose her pen name for the magazine. The following extracts are some of the articles that Cotton Goods

*wrote about her father and her experiences of growing
up in a family of cotton workers in Lancashire.*

1950

Woodstock

Recently I referred casually to the Woodstock Spinning Mill where my father worked for 50 years. I said
I might write about it sometime and someone (Sirod, I
think) said, 'Please do.' No doubt I have mentioned
incidents connected with this mill before – it was such
a big part of my life.

Woodstock! I think I always knew it was a lovely
word. To me as a child it represented security,
romance, adventure. Our food and all necessities
depended on t'Woodstock – as did those of most of
the people I knew, from the Managing Director, my
father's greatest friend, to the littler half-timers who
attended school with me.

The manager, Hamlet Cocker, was the most out-
standing figure of my childhood – I always thought he
was the origin of 'According to Cocker'. He was so
handsome, and had the loveliest voice I'd ever heard. I
think my father loved him, for Hamlet Cocker's photo
was the one thing he saved from the wreck when he
lost his home. Socially, he and his family lived on a
higher plane than we did, but we often visited them
when my mother was alive. My father's second wife
was a mill-girl with few social graces. On one occasion she accompanied my father to a party at Cocker's
and horrified the company by asking for 'one o' them
slavver-chop pears', 'slavver-chops' being the local
name for big juicy jargonelles.

The clerks in the office were our friends, especially
the ever-changing office-boys, and all the foremen
were familiar figures to us children, but the workman
I liked best was the lame roller-coverer. Cripples often

had this job, as they could sit down while at work. This particular man was nicknamed Billy Toffee, though his real name was Taylor. I used to wonder why people laughed when I addressed him as Mr Toffee. Later, he committed suicide.

The spinning-rooms were infernos. All the 'hands', especially the men, were almost naked. There were grades among workers – first fully-blown spinners called 'minders', then piecers, little piecers and tenters. Before anyone became fully qualified he 'joined at minding' or 'joined at piecing'. These men and boys (from the age of 11) wore nothing but white corduroy trousers and clogs. The tenters were girls who wore striped cotton skirts, white overalls called bishops (they were rather like a bishop's surplice), clogs and – out-of-doors – shawls. At that time I did not mix with the factory hands, but I thought they had supreme courage – not because of their arduous work but because they addressed my father as GRANVILLE. I was in awe of my father, and for anyone to be so familiar as to use his Christian name! Of course, as I grew older I realised that Christian names – from 'bosses' to the lowliest workers – are always used in Lancashire factories. At least, they *were*. Nowadays, when the new 'bosses' have been sent by their parents to public schools and have lost touch with the work-people, they are more formal. I like the homely attitude but I must confess that present-day owners are far less brutal, and many are more truly democratic than the old mill-owners. The workpeople, too, are better educated and can meet the owners on their own level industrially.

Speaking of 'joining at minding', did I ever tell you of the proposal my friend Mary once had? She was 17 or 18 and must have fascinated a rather pitiful factory-hand. He met her one evening and offered his hand

and heart in this manner – 'Mary, Ah've bin wonderin' if yo' could tek a fancy to me. Ah don't drink an' Ah don't smoke. Ah'm joinin' at mindin'. Ah play second cornet in Royton Brass Band an' Ah wouldn't ax yo' for IT till yo' were turned 21.' Poor Jimmy! In spite of all these qualifications, Mary turned him down. T'Woodstock (as it was always called) was a 7-storey building – or actually 2 buildings – situated in a valley with wide, rolling moors behind it and a branch railway running through the mill yard. It was in a lonely spot, our house being the nearest building, and we were about a mile away. My father always fetched the wages from the bank. He generally had a cab, but on those occasions when he walked, he always had a bodyguard of a few hefty men. I can well remember my father's loaded stick that he always carried to and from work. On winter evenings when the hundreds of windows of the factory were lighted up, it looked like a huge fairy palace in the heart of the hills. What romantic tales one could build then! Our house was 'at t'top o' th' Woodstock', meaning at the top of the lane leading to the mill. It was a strange old stone house and had once been an inn in the old coaching days. It had many windows, all with deep window seats, also huge cellars and a well in one of them. We children used to sit in those window seats and watch life go to and from t'Woodstock. Once when the office staff were having an outing the mill caught fire. Oh, these factory-fires were exciting and terrible. This day as we sat watching from window seats, and feeling as if the end of the world had come, a carriage driven by Mr Cocker and containing my father and others swung by our corner and away it went, like a Roman chariot, to t'Woodstock to save the offices. My father and the others seemed like gods to me and t'Woodstock like their paradise.

I've told elsewhere how we children used to accompany my father on Sunday mornings to the mill; how we rode on the 'bogies' and how one dreadful morning my father found Mr Cocker drowned in the mill-lodge: he'd fallen from the topmost storey while examining some repairs.

I've told how my father was dismissed by the directors, who all belonged to a certain chapel and put one of their congregation in his place. This was done while the new managing-director (after Mr Cocker's death) was in hospital. It nearly broke my father's heart because he loved t'Woodstock. He never told anyone but went out as if to work every day and wandered about till 5.30. My family only found out at the end of 3 months when their dividend sheet was not signed, as was usual, by my father. A great fuss was made and my father was re-installed, but as inside-manager, but he never got over it. Then came the 1914–1918 war, then the boom, then the slump, then bankruptcy and t'Woodstock became derelict. It's working again now, but I see it as something like 'Mandelay' in *Rebecca* as it lay in ruins, and with it my father a ruined old man.

I enjoyed this so much. (Janna)
Thank you CG. This is v. interesting. (Sirod)
Enjoyed. (Isis)

1955

I have mentioned my father in recent articles and, through dwelling on one side of his character, I have done him an injustice. May I give a little character sketch of him?

He was the eldest son of a big family, four sons and one daughter. He was well brought up in the Victorian tradition, educated at a good private school, attended church, went to work in the office of a big spinning mill and by the time he was 21 had an assured position as secretary and salesman. Those were the days of cotton supremacy – plenty of orders, good dividends but, alas, also slavery for the mill-hands. All his family had good positions in cotton, the men, that is, in his generation. The woman's place was at home unless she belonged to the 'lower orders'.

The first seeds of Socialism were sown in me when I was forbidden to associate with the factory-hands (whom I found more to my taste than many of the more genteel children). If ever I took a new friend home, the first question was: 'What does her father do?' The girl herself did not come into the picture. Of course, my father's family were staunch Conservatives and Churchillites, Winston first entered Parliament as MP for Oldham. Not so my mother. In fact, her family was a different cup o' tea altogether; they weren't so conventional and were great fun, always either prosperous in a gay way or absolutely on the rocks. I adored them.

Life promised to be a fair voyage for my father – good job, good health, good looks, and a good and loving wife and a couple of healthy children (Granville and me). I remember nothing but happiness for the first few years of my life.

Then when my father was about 30, his bad luck began with my mother's illness, which started while she was carrying her third child. He was wonderfully good to her all the three years she was an invalid, every thing was done that could be done to ease her and make life pleasanter. She loved him dearly. It has always been strange for me that, when she was dying, she asked me to take care of him, strange when you remember that I had younger sisters and a brother who would need care.

Her death did something to him. I cannot remember any stint of whatever we wanted before that, but now he began to be abnormally careful about money, although he still had a good position.

He did not take much interest in us children but I think it was due to a sort of shyness. We had a good house-keeper who looked after our material needs and my Auntie (his sister) was goodness itself to us. He seemed very remote, spending most of his leisure in reading or roaming over the moors. He was almost a complete stranger to me.

Then, five years after my mother's death, he married Georgie. Lord knows why. He had always held aloof from mill-girls, though he might easily have found one who would have been a good companion to him and a good mother to us, but he chose one who was ignorant and inexperienced. She came from a respectable family and was young and strong but hopeless as a housekeeper. Within five years, she had three children of her own to look after as well as us children of the first marriage. It was too much for her – in fact, it would have been hard for a far more intelligent woman. After a few years, she was in debt all over the town, though my father had not been as close-fisted with housekeeping money as he was over our clothes. She let the house go to rack and ruin till it was really filthy. She neglected her children and had low companions who led her to drink and so forth. It must have been hell for my father to whom respectability meant so much. I did all I could to preserve cleanliness in the house and to care for the little ones whom I loved dearly. They were born when my maternal instincts were awaking. It was a losing battle all the time and my father grew more and more unhappy. It was only then that we children began to love him. My half-sister, Vera, who had never known him in his pride, thought the world of him. He began to be generous and kindly and took greater interest in us. He asked me to be patient with Georgie when the dirt and debts got on top of me; I was astounded at his tolerance, he who had always been so arrogant at one time. I think he had to suffer in order to learn these lessons, but it seemed to me that his suffering was in excess of his deserts.

For years Georgie was a thorn in his flesh and, no doubt, his work at the mill suffered – he was often up half the night searching for her in her low haunts. He was dismissed. This was the bitterest blow he had ever sustained. He could not bear to tell anyone, so for three months he set out as if to work every morning and roamed the moors till it was time to come home. At that time he had enough money to produce his salary as though he were working. When the next dividend sheets came out, they were not signed, as usual, by him, so my relations, who had shares in his firm, began to question and the whole story came out. There had been some jiggery-pokery and a special board-meeting was held and my father re-engaged, but his spirit was broken.

Then came the slump, a terrible period in Lancashire's history. My father lost every penny; he mortgaged his home and lost that and at sixty-odd years of age was a complete pauper, without even dole. He was dependent, as was Georgie, on his family for even a crust. A bitter pill for a proud man. One good thing at this time was that Georgie began to behave herself. I must here say that she was always kind enough to me, it was the filth that upset me most and her neglect of her children. I think a time of peace might have set in for my father after this, for we children banded together and got him and Georgie a comfortable flat (strange to say, it was part of the school that he attended as a boy that had been converted into flats), but another blow was in store for him. He went blind. He was seventy by this time and too old and broke to learn Braille, so he was cut off from books and from his walks over the moors. His only recreation was talking. He had always been a quiet man, seldom speaking unless he had something important to say, but now he seemed to want to make up for all those years of reticence, he would talk interminably. I was sorry for Georgie. Another funny thing was this. He had been rather particular about his speech in the past but, in his poverty and blindness, he talked the dialect. For one short period when he was in hospital and suffering a lot, he used terrible language, swearing at the matron and so forth, although he was very, very averse to swearing as a rule. I never heard him say more than a mild 'Damn' in all my life.

To give Georgie a break, I invited him here for a holiday during 1942. He developed a bad carbuncle on his head and was very ill, so our Dr sent him to hospital. He had been in hospital in Oldham previously but was unhappy. This Oldham hospital had once been the Workhouse, so my father thought he was 'one of the old Bastille inmates'. He did not understand the changes that had come about. In Accrington hospital he felt independent as he knew we were paying for him. He never came out of Moorlands, some of you may remember my articles at that time. He lost all interest in life, became a mere shadow of himself, both physically and mentally. He was not senile but indifferent to everything and everybody. He lingered for about two years and died in 1944. It was while Micky (of Phoenix) was staying with us during the 'doodle-bug' period . . .

Most of the pictures of my father that are on my mind are sad ones but I try to keep clear one or two belonging to the happy days of my very early childhood. On Sunday mornings my father would always take us older ones to the mill where he went to collect the post. There was a Sunday post those days. While he was busy we were allowed to play in the cellars of the spinning rooms. Here there were the 'bogies', long low trucks on which we had rides to the detriment of our Sunday frocks. Then he would take us up the 'hoist', a primitive sort of lift, to the top of the factory (7 storeys high) where we could see the country for miles around – mostly lovely moorland, so different from the begrimed town beneath us.

After dinner we would go for our Sunday stroll, perhaps to my Grandma's to tea, my father in his frock-coat and silk-hat and my mother in her grey silk dress with her short fawn cape and pork-pie hat. We were dressed up to the nines and felt very important in spite of the discomfort of our Victorian clothes. I'm glad he had those few years of happiness.

The same year that Cotton Goods submitted that article to the CCC, she and her husband Albert separated. They had not had a happy marriage and, though they had lived in the same house, they were essentially estranged and led completely separate lives, barely speaking. Therefore, in 1955, Albert moved in with his elderly mother so that he could take care of her, and Cotton Goods moved to Derby to live with their unmarried son Jim. Nancy, the youngest of the children, also lived with them for a few years.

Cotton Goods spent much of her time writing, as it was her main passion. She wrote letters to family and friends, diligently submitted articles to the magazine and frequently corresponded with many of the women separately.

Amelia

Amelia was known amongst the women of the CCC as a 'true lady'. Born in Quetta, in what is now Pakistan, in 1904, she was the eldest and only girl in a family of four children. Her father was a major general in charge of the English forces in Quetta, where Amelia and her three brothers spent their childhood. Eventually the family relocated to England, and Amelia went to various schools in Bexhill, Ringwood, Alverstoke and Bath. When she was seventeen, she moved to Lucerne, Switzerland, for a year to attend finishing school.

Amelia's mother died when she was fourteen and, in 1923, when Amelia was eighteen, she became her father's escort, travelling with him and accompanying him to major functions. It was in this capacity that Amelia met her future husband, Charles, who was also in the army. They married around 1928 and had four boys: Richard in 1929, Tony in 1933, and twins John and Peter in 1935. Their family was constantly on the move due to Charles's career and they spent time in Canada, Malta and various locations in England.

During the war, Charles was stationed on the Isle of Man, and Amelia and the boys lived first near Winchester and then close to Bristol. Once the war ended, the family moved to Aldershot, where Charles was the commanding officer of the Royal Army Pay Corps Depot.

In 1947, Charles retired and they bought a home in Glazeley, near Bridgnorth, in Shropshire. Only a few years later, in 1950, Charles and Amelia separated. Amelia moved to London and lived in a flat by herself, while Charles and his sons stayed in the family home. After life as an army lady, this was a drastic change for Amelia. She had to learn to survive on her own.

London was the most reasonable option for Amelia as her father was there in a nursing home, and her brothers Peter and Bruce, with his wife Audrey, plus their cousin Jim had settled in the capital as well. Peter and Jim owned a company called Clean Walls that removed the smog and soot from the walls of buildings. They hired Amelia as their secretary, an opportunity that proved to be a challenge for her as she had much to learn about the practical skills required for office work. Though Peter and Jim didn't really need her in the office, she worked exceptionally hard and succeeded in establishing a new life for herself.

Amelia was an incredibly strong and resilient woman, and this was evident in the adventures that she shared with the CCC. She did not tend to write about her personal concerns, as some of the others did, but she was eager to share her London experiences. In the following article, written in December of 1952, Amelia described the days when London became enveloped in the Great Smog.

1952

What Did You Do in the Great Fog?

Well. What an experience! Never have I seen such felted darkness or had the strange weight that pressed impalpably upon my eyelids. It was all very queer and unpleasant and, of course I know it cost the country untold wealth, but I wouldn't have missed it for a good deal.

On the Saturday morning I left my Putney lodgings in good time, $\frac{1}{2}$ hr before my usual time because I am still very conscious of being purely an 'over-head' on the books of 'Clean Walls'. None of the Representatives come in on that day and my cousin the other Director is also away so my brother, Peter, and I are alone in the Office and do all sorts of tidying-up jobs in those awful

BOOKS. Crossing the Common I could see only two yards ahead and it was strange to move in so shrunken a world, only faint and muffled sounds penetrated the fog and my foot-steps rang loud upon the frosty ground. In the allotments each bean-stake and cabbage leaf was rimmed with silver and all colour was drained out of every thing . . .

At last I reached the bus terminus on Putney Common and found to my relief that the buses were running. If you can use such a word to describe their progress. Slowly we lurched along and the six or eight passengers began to feel a 'We're all together now' feeling. When we got to the Fulham Road we found nine buses all in a row whose drivers had given up the struggle and we could scarce forbear to cheer when our valiant man swooned slowly past them and they fell in meekly behind us. We all grinned at each other with the exception of the two inevitable 'ghouls' who always seem to appear at any time of crisis. They sat cosily together and recounted horrifying tales of the many disasters due to fog and other Acts of God with which their lives had been richly peppered. When we reached Hyde Park Corner, after a ride lasting over an hour, several of us went to the front of the bus and thanked the driver.

There were very few buses coming in and those which did arrive came in big convoys all of one number, so I decided to walk the rest of the way and set off up Park Lane making good progress. Buses which started level with me were quite a distance behind me when I got to Marble Arch! Every one I saw seemed to feel as if they were having quite an adventure except of course the older people, who were finding the smoky smell very trying to their throats.

After lunch with my brother in a restaurant filled with fog I changed my books at Marylebone Library. I took the Tube (or Underground, I have not yet learned to discriminate between them) and of course it was crowded with everybody who had had the same idea. We surged into the trains as you can imagine. I still find these crowds exhilarating so enjoyed it all. I had to change at Edgware Road and while I waited for my next train a man, inspired no doubt by my kind face, leaned close beside me and poured into my willy-nilly ear the story of his business life and plans for the future. His utterance was as blurred as the visible world about us and as the vapour eddied round us the whole encounter seemed like a dream. I had no wish that it should become too real so I got into the next train that came in tho' I knew I'd have to change again. Everything was disorganised but eventually I got to Putney and did some shopping in the High Street then visited my father to his great joy as he was not expecting anyone. The buses had stopped running by now (4 p.m.) so I walked to Roehampton which isn't far but I was glad to get there. Poor Audrey had lost her voice but we had a cheerful supper never the less and the fog seemed to lift a bit at 9 p.m. At least one could see that there were houses on the other side of the road. At 10 I thought I'd better get home and Bruce got the car out but when we were ½ way he had to give up. It was like a blanket and his lights were of no help at all, rather the reverse. So out I got into the murk in a part of the Upper Richmond Road, which I didn't know at all, but I didn't tell Bruce this or he would have abandoned the car to escort me and would never have found it again. I seemed to walk for ages and the light from the street lamps just penetrated so I got along all right.

When I'd been in for a little time I rang Audrey up to say I was OK as she was a nervous type and would have visions of my coshed corpse being stumbled upon in the dawn. Unfortunately this was not a good thing as Bruce had not yet shown up! It turned out that he had great difficulty in finding his way across the garden which is only about $\frac{1}{2}$ a tennis court but beset with a swing, sandpit, drying-line supports and other snares.

Everything one touched was filmed with grime and I had an impressive Hitler moustache from breathing in all the choky stuff. At about 4 next afternoon I set out again to visit Father, it was fairly clear and I got a bus all right and again he was very glad to see me and grateful too (so often now one gets the feeling that he forgets that it's quite an effort to get to the Nursing Home, not nearly so convenient for any of us as the Hospital). I was with him for about an hour and then started home. The fog had closed in again thicker than ever. It seemed to press upon one and was quite difficult to breathe. Street lamps threw only a feeble glimmer in their own immediate neighbourhood and between them there was quite a stretch of inky darkness, I had to keep one hand on the wall or I would have lost my way and to cross a gateway was quite an adventure. 'I do not ask to see the distant scene; One step enough for me,' as the hymn has it. At the big crossing on Putney Hill there were lots of lights but they only seemed to make the fog more impenetrable. It looked solid! and I could only see one Zebra stripe and the island in the middle of the road was quite invisible. There were a few people about there and several of us plunged together into the unforeseeable future and crossed the road in safety. On a news stand behind us the placard shrieked 'Woman stabbed in fog' and a voice pursued us, 'Yes, it's a perfect night for crime.' I parted from the convoy with some reluctance. 'The night is dark and I am far from home,' I thought sadly. Actually it isn't very far from the Putney crossing to the Bishops' house and I know the road having walked along it often. There were very few people about of course and it took me quite a long time but I got in eventually to find Mrs Bish tearing her hair because I'd been gone so long and also because Rose hadn't come to cook the supper. I told her there were no buses running and that it would be silly for Rose to try to walk because of the time it took. She calmed down after a bit but continued to be rather 'upset' all the evening and golly what a bad cook she is, *and* what a muddler. I pleaded fatigue after my 'long walk' and retired to my own room as soon as supper was over and there I wrapped Christmas presents and wrote some cards and so to bed.

Monday wasn't so bad, buses ran normally but the feeling of comradeship had gone and everyone seemed rather peevish. I got to the office early so as to give everything a good clean-up. We don't run to a 'char' yet so I do the dusting and Hoovering every morning as another sop to my conscience. Even though I'd cleaned all outside surfaces my fingers were black by lunchtime and so were everyone else's. The grime got into every drawer and cupboard.

But I will always remember the beauty of the frost filaments on every leaf, the visible world was suddenly so small that one could not help noticing tiny details that would otherwise make no impression. If my typewriter hadn't let me down at the beginning of this article I was going to say that I felt as if I was inside a pearl. This sounds rather silly and exaggerated but it did give me a strange feeling to be so enclosed by white vaporous walls, in such a silent little world, a world in which all colours were muted to dim greys except for the white frosted edges of leaves and branches.

Enjoyed this fascinating description of the fog. (A Priori)

June 7, 1953

I'm There

This is an article by your Special Correspondent which Cornelia and Cotton Goods had better skip, also any others who are sick of the Coronation.

As far back as January when I first started taking my early morning walks through the park, I thought that the Achilles Statue at the Hyde Park Corner end of the Carriage Drive was a good place to see the Coronation Procession. So I got Peter to send down a sleeping bag from Glazeley and I stocked a bag with Aspirin, marmite sandwiches, choc biscs, Primula cheese, Ryvita, large, easy fitting shoes, and extra pr of stockings. When I left the office at 5 p.m. last night it was pouring, but *pouring*, so I thought it would be silly to sleep out and sadly prepared to make my middle-aged way homewards. My brother, Peter, knew that I was disappointed so suggested a visit to the New Theatre (if any room) and supper at Lyons Salad Bowl. We left the sleeping bag in the office and had luck at the cinema and supper, then we walked down the Carriage Drive at about 8.45 p.m. and at the Achilles Statue there was still room, and it wasn't raining and everyone looked so cheerful that my years slipped from me and, confirming Peter's long-held opinion that I am crazy, I decided to stay the night and be blowed to the weather and a rheumatic future. He nobly struggled back to Baker Street and brought me the sleeping bag and an inflatable pillow of his own.

So here I am, at 9 a.m. on Coronation Day after a night filled with alarms, other people's excursions, and lots of rain. My bag is clammy. I've been broad awake (interrupted by rain) since 5 a.m. and it is just 10.30. The Queen has just left the Palace and of course those who are interested will be hearing the very same words as we are hearing so there is no need for me to comment further on that.

This has already proved a most excellent vantage point because all the troops from Knightsbridge Barracks and the big military camps set up in Kensington Gardens have come swinging past on my right and turning through the arches and away down Piccadilly or Constitution Hill. At squeak of dawn coaches with liveried drivers and footmen came fast, going north. They returned later with their distinguished but undistinguishable occupants, the men in peers' robes and their wives in full evening dress with tiaras (rather gruesome at 5.30 a.m.). Of course we also cheered wildly:

1. Municipal Dustcarts

2. Small speckled dog of unknown breed

3. Runner in singlet and pale blue shorts escorted by police on motor bikes. Who and what can he have been?

(At this moment a string of Army Lorries, jeeps etc. is going through the archway, I wonder why.)

Little files of soldiers move about, I suppose they are all different and are engaged in relieving those who have been long on duty but they all look alike in their smart No. 1 dress, have a busy but purposeless appearance. Certainly the weather is not being too kind and it is chilly and rather damp. Mercifully the exceedingly noisy young people who made the night hideous have now calmed down a bit so we can hear the wireless.

The lorries are now explained, they contain the mid-day meal for the men lining the route.

At 5 a.m. this morning the news of the conquest of

Everest came through by 'grape-vine' or jungle drums. I'm finding it most exhilarating to be in this great crowd, ignoring the rain, remembering and singing songs of the 14–18 War, strange how 'Tipperary' and the 'Long Long Trail' and 'Pack Up Your Troubles' still survive while the more recent ones are already forgotten.

As the loud speaker broadcast the happenings in the Abbey we grow quiet. All through that long Service the crowd kept silence.

It has been most impressive. The rain came down relentlessly and under umbrellas and improvised shelters we crouched following the words in our Programmes and newspapers. As one we rose to shout 'God Save Queen Elizabeth!', as one we sank again into the wet and chilly ground. At the end of the Service the roar of the National Anthem shook the air. And then we took out our squashy sandwiches and with joking and laughter shared them with our neighbours. Near me were 4 Dutch girls, a Swedish couple, a Pakistanian and several Americans, hard-up ones. Curious how one always feels that all Americans are rich, just as all Europe thought, after the Napoleonic Wars and earlier, that all the English were wealthy 'Milords' and for the same reason.

Soon, however, the head of the Procession came along. It halted when the leader was at the Marble Arch and of course stretched all the way back along Piccadilly and Trafalgar Square, down Whitehall to the Abbey where the Queen's coach waited. 'Our own' BBC Announcer was halfway between us and Marble Arch and told us about the different bodies of troops as they came by. The marching was superb, every column split into 3 to come through the Apsley Gates and joined in one again absolutely faultlessly. We roared and roared the Mounties, the Highlanders, the

Ghurkhas, the Women's Services from overseas got special cheers. Our own Air Force too and then the Army, file upon file marching as one heart lifting and glorious. When the Colours of every Regiment went by I put my face in my hands and cried remembering the times I had seen one of the Colours of the Duke of Wellington's Regiment carried by Charles while he was yet a subaltern and that recently Tony had carried the same Colour to be laid up in Halifax Parish Church when the Battalion went to Korea.

The Navy too went by in great style and got its usual extra cheer. How wonderful the Marines are. I've not mentioned the open carriages. Full marks to the rulers of tropical countries who endured the cold rain which saturated their lovely uniforms, Queen Salote of Tonga was the high spot here. Waving one hand graciously she repeatedly mopped her smiling face with a large handkerchief held in the other. She was *loving* the whole show. I was sorry for the little Sultan of Kelantan, who shared her carriage. I remember him from my days in Malaya, Bill the Lizard we called him, he was so thin and frightened looking. The Sultan of Johore, big and burly (and with a *very* roving eye) would have been a better boy friend for her.

Then the Guards came, resplendent in bearskins and scarlet, the colourful Bargemen and Yeomen and then at last at last the glitter and flash of the Household Cavalry with behind them, gleaming like everyone's childhood dream of fairy land, came that great golden coach. The din of the cheering was so great that it could not be heard! My voice cracked and I could cheer no more.

The Queen looked more lovely than one could have believed possible. Her youth and prettiness were trans-figured into exquisite beauty by the glow of dedication and happiness which radiated from her. That heavy crown, the purple, and the gold, all the pomp and splendour – the beauty of her spirit triumphed over them and made them subordinate to that spirit and the vows she had made. Never, never shall I forget the sight.

As soon as the Procession had passed the crowd started to break up and I was swept along in a thrilling stampede, carrying my sopping wet sleeping-bag which now weighed about a ton and my bag of needments. As I was alone I was not afraid of losing my party so rushed along willy-nilly with the rest enjoying the irresponsible sensation of being chaff before the wind.

Miraculously soon I was on a bus bound for Roehampton. I am not yet so old established a Londoner as to be put out at finding a 30 bus turning out of a road where it didn't oughter be, so was luck-ily spared the annoyance this caused to some people. I reached Bruce's house in time to see the Royal Family on the balcony for the Fly past (on TV) and was so very glad I had seen even so small a glimpse of the Queen in the flesh on her Great Day.

Soon Audrey, Peter and I went up to London again to meet Bruce and his son Jonathan who had had seats in Whitehall. We met them and made our way up to the Mall (oh the decorations there are a dream of loveliness!) towards the Palace. We got into one of the stands on the right near Constitution Hill where we had a view of the Balcony and also, to our left, of the first triumphal arch on the Mall and the pearly towers of the Abbey beyond the trees of St James's Park. There was a big crowd in front of the Palace which grew and grew until it filled all the space and looked from where we sat like a huge rag rug. No rain now but hurrying clouds and some wind. Bruce,

Jonathan, Audrey and Peter got 4 seats in the back row, and I sat just in front of them sharing Audrey's umbrella with a large comfortable woman who was nice and warm to sit next to. She soon told me the story of her life and I told her ditto (Bowdlerized!).

Dark it grew and darker and then the Balcony was illuminated while the Queen made her broadcast. Then she came out with the Duke. So tiny she looked like a little fairy and how we yelled again and waved. They stayed quite a long time waving to us. Then she pressed the button which turned on the Lights of London and all the buildings glowed with unsuspected beauty and the Mall looked quite out of this world. Then the Duke went in and she was alone with us for a little time.

God bless her.

I had hoped to stay put and watch the fireworks come up behind the Abbey but other plans prevailed and we left our nice seats and set out for some unspecified vantage point. Unfortunately the fatigue and excitement of the day now proved too much for Jonathan and he burst into tears. So we went home.

My face felt like cardboard and I was madly thirsty and it was a struggle to get to the office next day. But I'd do it again next week if I had to.

Unforgettable and unique (for me) experience.

I did enjoy this description, so vivid and amusing. Thank you for taking the trouble to do it for us! (A Priori)
I did envy this. (Barnie)
So vivid. We must keep this. (Ad Astra)

Amelia stayed in London for the rest of her life but withdrew from the CCC around 1970. She remained close friends with Elektra, who lived near by.

She always had a strong bond with her four boys and it was a terrible tragedy when she lost two sons in 1985, Richard from a heart attack and Tony in a car accident.

Once again she was forced to draw upon her great inner strength.

In her later years, Amelia enjoyed gardening, sewing, embroidering and spending time with her six grandchildren. Eventually she moved into a nursing home, where, a fortnight later, she died unexpectedly from a heart attack at the age of eighty-four.

4

For Better, for Worse

a priori

At the cost of raising issues on which in CCC we have for some years agreed to differ, I felt I should make some comment on Yonie's theory that she has never been able to indulge in sexual intercourse unless there was the possibility of conception. Does this mean, Y, that since the menopause you have lived a totally chaste life (and one subject to arthrosis of the hips, remember!). Dear me, what a lot you have missed! For at this time, it seems to me, married life takes on a new pattern, and the act of love is in itself creative (or any act of love I agree), totally apart from any chance of conception. It is creative because it helps to build up a warm and loving emotional relationship at a time when many marriages may be going through a bad patch, owing to the changes in life-style which couples may have to face at that time. Adolescent children, and those who have left home for University or jobs are in my experience, far more sensitive to the kind of atmosphere in their parents' home than many older people realise. They like to come home to a loving and peaceful atmosphere as a refuge from the stress they often face in their own lives, no matter how successful or happy. It seems to me a natural thing that two people who live

Written by A Priori in 1974.

There appears to have been an unspoken understanding amongst the CCC that husbands were rarely to be discussed. The women could easily have chosen to do so, but it seems that they did not because it would have been seen as a betrayal of the sanctity of their marriage. As a result, husbands or marriages were probably the topics least discussed in the magazine. If they were, each woman wrote about her marriage in a very different way. A few shared confidences, but the majority barely mentioned marital matters at all.

A handful of the women in the CCC had extramarital affairs, but they seldom disclosed them in the magazine. Instead they confided in selected members within the club with whom they had closer personal connections. Even though the CCC was an open group that encouraged frank discussion, many members still did not see it as a vehicle to 'tell all'.

There also seemed to be an understanding that boasting about one's marriage was unacceptable. When husbands were mentioned, it was generally when a member had marital problems and needed emotional support. As a result, the articles about marriage or husbands generally had a negative slant, despite the fact that the majority of marriages in the CCC were evidently happy and fulfilling ones.

In the following articles, Isis, Accidia and Roberta share the problems that they faced during difficult times in their marriages.

Isis

Isis was one of the lesser-known personalities in the CCC. Born in 1906, she grew up in a household of five children, where the two eldest were her significantly older step-siblings. Her father was a clergyman in the Church of England. In 1920, she lost both of her parents in the influenza epidemic that devastated Europe and she was sent to live with distant relatives until she went to read history at St Hugh's College, Oxford. There she met her future husband Alistair, who was studying history at Exeter College. He was the brother of one of her good friends at the university. Isis's time at Oxford was significant for her as she had an academic family background and considered herself an intellectual. She chose her CCC name 'Isis' after the River Isis, the name given to the River Thames at Oxford.

Upon completing her degree, Isis taught in South Africa for a few years. She then returned to England, gave up teaching permanently and married Alistair in 1936. They moved to just outside London, where Alistair became a schoolmaster teaching history. Here Isis gave birth to Thomas, the first of four sons, in 1937. With the advent of the Second World War, Alistair was commissioned with the Territorial Army, moving all over the country but spending the majority of his time on the Isle of Man. In the meantime, Isis moved to Wiltshire to live with Alistair's parents and was able to see him occasionally when he was on leave. She gave birth to Peter in 1940 and David in 1942. After the war, the family moved back to the outskirts of London, where Alistair resumed his pre-war job. Here Isis gave birth to their fourth son, Matthew, in 1946.

The following pieces were submitted in 1952 over the span of twelve consecutive CCC magazines. In them Isis writes about the events that took place in her life between 1946 and 1949. Even though she was a member of the CCC during those years, Isis only shared these accounts with the other women well after they had happened.

Revelations or Coming Clean

I think the time has come when I can tell you the whole story of what was happening here from 1946 (April) when Matthew was started – to 1949 (Sept.) when I entered the Catholic Church. It's all one story, really: story of a crisis. I only hope it won't be terribly boring.

You may remember that, in 1945, when we all returned here and started our family life again, I wanted a fourth baby. But after we had discussed it very fully, Alistair told me to put the idea right out of my head, as it would upset all the educational plans he had for the other boys, and also cause overcrowding in this house, which he already considered much too small. I succeeded in persuading myself that he was probably right and that it would be better to concentrate on our three, and enjoy them, and not hanker after another baby. So I set about it very thoroughly, even to the extent of getting rid of practically all my baby clothes and equipment, at a time when these things were difficult to replace. By the spring of 1946 I had renounced all thoughts of ever having another child, and was quite content with life as it was.

Alistair and I mostly made use of the safe period, it *was* safe for me, because my cycle was 28 days exactly, like clockwork. But if we did have intercourse at a fertile time we always used a Rendall's Pessary and no other method. We had done this ever since Tom's birth. Peter and David were 'timed' for when we wanted them, except that I 'dawdled' about two months before getting started.

One night at the end of March 1946, A suddenly took me unawares and unwilling (not feeling in the mood), disregarding all protests – when I asked, 'What about precautions?' he answered, 'Oh, to hell with precautions. They spoil everything. Besides, it's quite unnecessary at our age. We aren't as fertile as we were.' I said, 'Are you *quite* sure you want a baby exactly at Christmas time, because you'll certainly have one.' 'Rubbish,' said Alistair; and I resigned myself. Next morning I worked out exactly when the baby would arrive, December 24th. The worst possible time. Poor Granny would be called upon to have the boys for Christmas or else to come up here to look after them (which Alistair would most likely not agree to). In any case we should all be separated. I could have wept. And yet I was *thrilled*!

We were at the seaside in the Easter holidays when I missed my first period. 'Nonsense. Rubbish,' said Alistair. 'It will come. You'll see. You've miscalculated it.' But when the fact was established he was *furious*. How dared I do such a thing? How *could* he have known that *one* risk would be one too many? I was equally furious with him. 'I warned you, didn't I?' And so we reproached each other. I tried to resign myself to the more trying aspects of the situation, but felt profound resentment about it all – yet mixed with joy and excitement. All most irrational.

Alistair at this time was only just out of the Army, and none too pleased at being back in his civvy job. Another thing which contributed a great deal to the bad state of things between us was that, following a sort of nervous breakdown while on an instructing job at Wimbledon, A was having psycho-analytical treatment, almost every day, up in London. He used to go up after school each afternoon, and return home about 7. The effect of this treatment was to make him completely and absolutely wrapped up in himself and totally indifferent to everything and everybody else. It also made him morose, and exceedingly irritable. Moreover, he was absolutely terrified of anybody knowing that he was being analysed, and I was ordered to keep the secret, no matter what lies had to be told, to everybody who might enquire where he was. In fact I was constantly telling his friends and relations that he had gone to the London Library, or to the dentist, or just shopping; until I was sick of it. He seemed to regard it as the most dreadful kind of disgrace, and said that of course if it were known he would lose his job. This wretched business was going on throughout 1945, 1946, and the greater part of 1947. It made him well enough to do his work, and it released a great deal of the extreme resentment he felt against his mother. He became able to laugh at her instead of helplessly raging. But as for improving his relations with me, it certainly did not help and on the whole the total result was negative. They broke him down, but did nothing to build him up. His philosophy of life remained cynical and sardonic and empirical, though rather less bitter and angry. He still had faith in absolutely nothing, except just a little faith in Freud, perhaps.

This being the old old story of the eternal triangle, I'd better come now to the third party; but first I must make it clear that this business did not begin until Matthew was 6 months old. It sort of stole upon me unawares, so that although the 'third party' was quite a lot in the picture from June 1946 onwards, it wasn't until June 1947 that I was in love with him. And I don't *think* it would have happened but for Alistair's preoccupation with himself and his analysis, and the general estrangement and lack of sympathy between us all this time . . .

In 1946, X was about 50, and everybody liked him and called him 'a nice little chap'. Actually he isn't all that small – about 5 ft 7, tho' he is certainly no Adonis, he is quite pleasant to look at. Rather like a smaller and more refined edition of Ernest Bevin. He has a well-shaped head, high wide brow, greyish brown hair brushed back and not very thick; horn glasses, blue eyes, nice features, expressing great firmness of character beneath a very agreeable and friendly manner. He obviously has a first-rate brain. Not only is he an extremely good doctor (you hear tributes on all sides to all sorts of aspects of this) but he is also a classical scholar, and reads Thucydides in his spare time and is well read in general. He was always interesting to talk to, when he had time. And he has a remarkable gift of sympathetic understanding and a nice sense of humour. He was almost always cheerful, with a sort of boyish gaiety in the way he would tear up and down steps like a ten-year-old, and turn round to wave before leaping into his little grey car. We had always liked him. At the time of Tom's birth, when he and the Sister were with me for the whole of the last hour and a half, I remember being rather exasperated by their heartless jesting and badinage across my writhing form. Still, it was more reassuring than too much solemn bedside manner, and I joined in during my lucid intervals, and quite enjoyed it. But never never had it occurred to me, before May 1947, to regard Dr X as a potentially romantic figure.

I went to him for all the routine pre-natal visits, and he saw Matthew into the world most efficiently as I have before related. While I was in the nursing home we had two rather serious conversations in private, first about M's chances of survival, and secondly when he broke the news to me about Matthew's cataract. On these occasions there was no joking in his manner, but just the quiet and serious sympathy you would expect. Of course *he* knew then about Matthew's abnormal condition, though apparently he couldn't be absolutely certain until the end of M's first year. It was just a very strong suspicion. At least, that's what I gather from combining what he said about it with what the nurse and matron at the maternity home told me later.

In the Christmas holidays immediately after M's birth, the boys all had chicken-pox, and the doctor came then, as well as routine visits to Matthew and me. Then he caught flu and was pretty bad and we had visits from two new young partners. Before the January term began, it was necessary to get a certificate to say that they were all clear of ch. pox – and I wrote a note about it to one of the partners, very apologetically asking if one of them would look in when passing by one day. Much to my surprise, latish one Saturday evening, a foully cold day – Dr X himself turned up. The family was gathered round the fire, and he came in and inspected the boys' torsos and wrote the certificate, and talked and joked with them. Alistair went on reading the paper, more or less, and took very little notice. Then Dr X turned to me and asked abruptly, 'How are you?' I said, 'Oh, all right thanks' (actually feeling fairly foul), and he then said, 'I want to see the baby, and can we talk upstairs?' M was already in his cot. I took the Dr up and at the top of the stairs he asked, 'How is your period?' so I said I'd been going on merrily ever since M was born. He started talking about fibroids then, and seemed in quite a flap. We sat on my bed, with Matthew on my knee, and he looked him well over, especially his navel and tummy, and the circumcision scar. Then he went on and on about fibroids, and said I must come and see him in about a month's time if the flow had stopped. Then he asked when the oculist was going to see M – which was fixed for March, and asked me to remind him to arrange the consultation. We went downstairs chatting, about *his* influenza and how he was still feeling pretty awful but there was so much work to do that he had to keep on etc. He reminded me again to come see him, and went off. Alistair asked, 'Whatever did he want to talk about?' and 'Fibroids? Rubbish. You haven't got any,' and went on reading his book. True to the principles of all his family, A does not believe in anything you can't *see*. He considered all this a great fuss about nothing. *Please* believe that I am writing all this without rancour. A is entitled to his own opinions even if they irritate me! Besides it's all past and done with.

X by the way is not one of those doctors who are delightfully vague about babies, and leave mothers to muddle along as best they can. He always had good advice to give, on the most trivial points, such as the best way to help M's very snuffly nose (for weeks after his birth, he continued to exude the most awful stuff from his poor little nose – and it sounded very distressing). This doctor took the keenest interest in every detail of M's progress and always treated him as if he were the sole heir to some ancient dynasty – a really precious infant. This alone was enough to make me love him! . . .

Our next meeting was in the hospital, unexpectedly, 2 months later. Alistair and I had taken Matthew in before his first eye operation for the pathologist's examination. We waited about for ages in the little private patients' waiting-room. I was filled with the most irrational panic and depression, feeling quite certain that M would never survive an operation on his eyes. (Too idiotic – a little thing that doesn't take 10 minutes.) Matthew was by now a really lovely babe – $4\frac{1}{2}$ months, normal weight, pink and blooming, very contented, and really (I truly think) very pretty. He slept in my arms and my tears rolled down upon him. Alistair stood by the window looking as miserable as I felt. Suddenly, in walked the Sister and our doctor. The Sister went to speak with Alistair; the doc. bent over Matthew and me. He exclaimed loudly: 'But is this the same baby? Why he's *beautiful*! What have you done to him? Did you feed him yourself?' I smiled at him, feeling a glow of gratitude. 'Sister,' he called out, 'Mrs R has 4 sons. Isn't she lucky?' (I remember seeing a notice in the *Daily Telegraph* about 4 years before. 'To Dr and Mrs X – etc. A son, who only survived a few hours.' I had forgotten it until that moment. They have two girls.) I looked at Matthew, and felt ashamed of my moping fear, and suddenly much comforted.

After M had the operation, I forgot that he'd be visited on his return from hospital, so it was a surprise when, on a brilliant April evening, I was carrying hot water up to the bathroom for the boys to wash at bedtime, and through the hall window I saw the familiar little grey car outside, and the door bell rang. The doc. had a look at Matthew in his cot and then was able to clear up some confusion in my mind about the various eye drops and lotions which I had been given at the hospital . . . That was about the 22nd of April. Some three weeks later, when I had forgotten all about eye-drop difficulties and doctors, but was in a far from good nervy condition myself, with fibroids getting worse and worse each time, there was a really comic surprise visit at a most unwelcome time. I had no domestic help then, and David was still at home – the school couldn't take him until September. Alistair was coming home for midday dinner. Matthew needed quite a lot of attention. And this particular Monday morning, I was cooking corned-beef hash, and vacuum-cleaning all downstairs, and in a far from sweet temper. So when Dr X appeared, all tanned and merry from his holiday, he got a very sour welcome. I glared at him. 'I just wanted to see how Matthew was,' he said cheerfully. 'And you remember you had difficulty about the eye drops. Was it all right?' He nearly tripped over the vacuum cleaner. I led him through the sitting-room to the pram in the garden, cursing inwardly. David was playing outside. The doc. had a look at Matthew, chatted a bit, about the eye operation and so on. We didn't yet know whether it had been a success. M was to see the oculist in another 10 days. Then we went indoors, and the doc. said, 'And how are *you*?' I said, very sourly, 'Oh, I'm going crackers I think.' 'How are the periods?' 'Bloody,' I said. 'Well, I must look at the fibroids,' he said, very firmly. 'Not now, you can't,' I protested. 'Not inside, I only meant to feel your tummy.' 'Oh bother,' I said. 'I'm busy.' 'So am I.' So I began to lie down on the sofa, very reluctantly. 'No, that's no good,' said the doc., 'because you can't lie flat. You'll have to go upstairs, I'm afraid. It won't take long. Call me when you've got your belt off.' I mumbled something about being sure that the fibroids had gone, and went upstairs, wondering how soon the corned-beef hash would burn.

David meanwhile came in to see what all the argument was about, and wanted to come up with me, but Dr X propelled him out through the window, and shut it firmly! When I got upstairs I found that only one bed was made, as I'd been interrupted, so I pulled my bed clothes up just to look respectable, and lay down on Alistair's bed when ready. The doctor came in and pummelled my tummy and pressed and massaged it very nicely, all the time chatting briskly and cheerfully, to put me in a good humour. When he had finished, he pulled my dress down and gave me a final fatherly or brotherly pat on the tum. Said, 'It's all right. Those fibroids aren't giving much trouble. They may die down, or they may become tiresome later on, in which case we'll have to do something about them. I'll send you some tablets for the bad periods. Try to rest the first day, and don't *worry*.' I had sprung up from the bed and was going to see him to the door, but of course my stocking began to descend, and I felt a fool and annoyed with him. He grinned sweetly at me and said he'd show himself out. He departed leaving me still muttering curses and wondering how to get the carpets done before dinner.

When Alistair came in I told him the doctor had been to see Matthew. I didn't mention the rest, because he'd only think (as I did) what a fuss. But when he went upstairs for something, he noticed my bed, which I'd still forgotten to make properly and asked me about it. I then told him the rest, partly because David had made some remark too and he looked so scandalised and suspicious that I burst out laughing. 'Darling,' I said, 'it was all *most* professional. Dash it all – you can't really entertain dark suspicions of dear old X *can* you?' and Alistair laughed too. But said he thought it was rather a nerve to flow in like that and conduct an uncalled-for examination. However, I certainly attached no importance to it at all, any more than X did.

To be continued.
This is going to be rather long, I fear. I am so sorry;

also that it is so medically detailed, but that is hardly avoidable. I'll try to get more of it done in fewer words next time, when the tricky part begins. I do hope I'm not being wildly indiscreet. But (a) I'm sure you *will* keep it under your hats? Won't you? (b) X comes out of it without a stain on his reputation, so I don't think it can matter and the more detailed, the more accurate, I think.

Revelations – Part 2

Up to the middle of May 1947, the point I'd reached in the first instalment, Dr X was no more to me than just an old friend and a very well-liked doctor. The mischief was done some time during the next six weeks.

Alistair and I had to take Matthew to see Mr Adams, who had done the needling operation, to know whether it had been successful. We learned that it had not, but that it could be repeated, and often had to be done half a dozen times before it succeeded . . . But at this consultation we met Mr A's partner whom we both instantly disliked. He was a very peculiar young man, apparently suffering from enormous vanity and conceit. He interviewed us before Mr A saw Matthew. He suddenly fired at us the question: 'Do you consider that your baby is mentally deficient?' This idea had never even occurred to either of us. We most emphatically assured this doctor that M did not seem in the least m.d., only rather backward in his development which we thought his bad sight accounted for entirely.

When we got home, Alistair expressed his opinion of Dr P in no uncertain terms, although we did talk over the possibility of his being correct. However, our own quite honest and definite opinion was that

Matthew's backwardness was purely temporary. One thing which weighed with me was that he had learnt to feed from the breast so successfully, after a very difficult start. And he always seemed so responsive to us. However, I went on brooding over this horrible possibility, and felt that I would like a reliable opinion on it as soon as possible. So I found myself writing to X telling him that we were perturbed at the mention of definite mental backwardness, and asking if he could possibly give me an opinion about it. Alistair meanwhile began a prolonged period of leaving me severely alone. For the next 2 or 3 months he scarcely spoke to me, never talked, and never touched me, except for about 2 very miserable mockeries of intercourse, neither of which could be described as better than nothing. (Actually this was the state of affairs almost all of the 8 months after M's birth.) No conversation. No love making.

On one of the last afternoons in May, having done my housework, and had lunch with David, and fed Matthew, I had a bath and changed into a summer dress, and was just sitting down to write something for CCC when Dr X appeared – in answer to my note mentioned above. He was wearing a natty summer suit, and appeared to be in no hurry at all. When I asked, 'Shall I fetch Matthew in?' he said, 'Not yet. Come and talk to me first.' We sat down – I on the sofa and he in a chair close by, and I told him all about the interview with Mr A and the partner – at the mention of whom Dr X grinned inscrutably to himself. He then told me that at this stage it was really not possible to say definitely whether there was anything seriously wrong with M. He said that the two conditions, congenital cataract and mental abnormality, were frequently found together; but that Matthew did have, from the first, a tendency to a

lolling head, which was possibly a bad sign. On the
other hand, he was emphatic that the infant might not
be irremediably backward – might possibly develop
slowly and in a normal manner; he agreed with me
that M did not, in general, look like a really m.d.
baby, if you made allowance for his almost complete
lack of sight. He bid another look over M – especially
his head, neck, back and tummy, and gave me bits of
advice. I put M back in his pram and sat down again,
thinking that the doc. would now be pushing off. But
I had said in my note that there were some other
things I would like to ask him about. I had thought
that it would be very disastrous to have another pregnancy, and that I had better get sound advice upon the
best methods of birth control, in case our usual ones
were not adequate. Dr X said, 'I think there was
something else you wanted to ask me about' – and
came and sat beside me on the sofa, very much to my
surprise. Still more to my astonishment I found myself
overcome with sudden embarrassment, as if the subject of b.c. was not one which I could possibly discuss
with him. It really was a bit difficult, with him sitting
so very close beside me – much more like an old
friend than a professional adviser. However, I took the
plunge, and asked him about the relative safety of
sheaths, caps and pessaries. What was still more surprising was that he also suddenly appeared to be
embarrassed – about half way through his discourse,
after firmly telling me that only sheaths were 95%
safe. And believe it or not this business-like discourse
tailed off into silence, which prolonged itself for several minutes! It is all as clear to me now as though it
were yesterday and not just over 3 years ago. (The
details of this whole affair are still clear to me, dates
and all, partly from having cryptically recorded them
as they happened, and from much reflection upon

The NURSERY WORLD

VOL. 30. No. 501. WEDNESDAY, JULY 31st, 1935

3d

Contents

Letters about Baby
By Sister Morrison
S.R.N., C.M.B., H.T.S.

•

Bottling the Summer
Fruits
By Doris B. Sheridan
M.C.A., H.S.C. Diploma

•

"My Charge"
By Ursula Wise

•

Knitting and Fashion
Pages

•

Children's Supplement

•

Readers' Letters about :
Bronchitis & Nasal Catarrh
The Mother's Diet
Dancing for Children
Constipation, etc.

Insist on Cow & Gate Rusks!
"The Book without the Risk."

All of the members of the Cooperative Correspondence Club wrote using pen names. They first started writing to each other after one woman, calling herself UBIQUE, wrote a cry for help in 1935 to the other mothers reading this edition of *The Nursery World*

The CCC magazine circulated twice a month. For each edition, the women in the club wrote articles and mailed them to the editor, AD ASTRA, who would compile them in often beautifully embroidered linen covers

The members of the CCC were incredibly varied in terms of geographical location, social status and personality. COTTON GOODS, seen here with her children Betty and Jim in Lancashire around 1927, was known as the one 'working-class' member of the magazine, something of which she was very proud

The war years. WAVENEY is seen here with her husband Maurice and their four sons in 1939. Maurice had just received the news that he would be going away to war. Two years later WAVENEY would learn that he had been taken captive and was a POW

Originally the magazine was intended to be an outlet for intellectual debate, so the women were often involved in heated exchanges. One of the most argumentative of the group was A PRIORI, pictured here, holding a copy of the CCC, in Scotland with her three daughters Sally, Vicky and Jane in 1941

With the advent of war, women's roles changed and many of the CCC were able to take up work. SIROD was one who had several jobs throughout her life. She is seen here with her sons Bill and John in 1947, working on the once derelict farm in Dorset that she and her husband purchased during the war

As the women went through various changes in their lives, they often relied upon the magazine to provide a support network. ROBERTA, seen here skiing in Switzerland in the mid-1950s, particularly valued the magazine as a source of friendship while she was going through her divorce from her Swiss husband in the early 1950s

ACCIDIA, a mother of seven with an inattentive husband, found solace in the magazine as it provided her with the communication and adult companionship that was lacking in her life. She is seen here with five of her children at Harewood Estate in Yorkshire in the early 1950s

YONIRE was one of the liveliest personalities in the group. Seen here in around 1950, she was by no means a 'typical' housewife and was often likely to be found on her bed, smoking a cigarette, with her typewriter on her lap, typing letters to friends or articles to the CCC

Ten years after the magazine began, the CCC recruited four younger members. ANGHARAD was one and she proved a welcome addition to the group, soon embarking on a long professional writing career and sharing exciting stories with the group. She is seen here at her desk in Mountain Ash, Wales, in the early 1960s

After the war, the women started meeting officially as a group once a year, although certain members also met up more frequently. These parties were typically held at ELEKTRA's house in London or at AD ASTRA's large home in Essex, where WAVENEY and ELEKTRA are seen above in around 1965

Another gathering of the group in 1969 at ELEKTRA's house in London. Not all of the women were able to attend every year. Seen here in the bottom row: (from l to r) AMELIA, CORNELIA, A PRIORI, anonymous, ELEKTRA, BARNIE. Standing: GLEN HEATHER, SIROD, JANNA, AD ASTRA, anonymous

Just as the women had shared stories about their children when they were young mothers, as they aged they frequently wrote about their grandchildren. ROSA is seen here in Ilford, Essex, with two of her grandchildren, Peter and Robina, in 1960

AMELIA was known as the 'lady' of the CCC, and she is seen here on the day of her grandchild's wedding in 1986 in Worcestershire

In general, the husbands of the CCC were not involved in the magazine. A PRIORI's husband Lough, however, seemed to be an exception and was well known and well liked among the women. He is seen here at a CCC gathering in London in 1977 with AD ASTRA, A PRIORI, ELEKTRA, ROSA and ACCIDIA

It was largely through ELEKTRA's (seated, on right) dedication to the CCC that the remaining articles still exist today. She was determined to see them shared with the world and has lived to see that moment, having reached the milestone of her 100th birthday, celebrated here in London in March 2006 with ANGHARAD, ACCIDIA (standing) and Jenna

them; and from having written them up in story form later on, only a year or so ago. After I have finished this account of them, I don't propose to think about them any more; but in any case, they have now lost any emotional power, although the emotional flavour of them remains very clear, in memory.)

So long did X remain sitting there, looking half embarrassed and half rapt in thought, that I began to wonder whether no sick people were awaiting his attentions anywhere, but no doubt it was not a very busy time, in such beautiful summer weather. (This was a Tuesday, which later on I learned was his free afternoon, when he could take it.) I fear that the thought was now born in my mind 'How nice it would be to think that I attracted him a little, even at 41 years old, and he such a nice and capable and successful person.' It was a cosy, warming thought, soothing to my vanity, and just a little comforting to the unpleasant reality of the possibility of our poor little Matthew not being normal.

After a while, he got up to go, but still lingered a little, looking at my books, and chatting about various things. I went on for a long time thinking about that visit. When he said good-bye he asked me to let him know when M's next operation was to be, so that he could visit him in hospital. Quite unnecessary as he would be told at the hospital. I certainly wasn't in love with him yet, for I was only feeling flattered, and looking at it from a purely self-centred point of view. But I certainly felt a good deal uplifted and elated by that afternoon's conversation, and amused that he had suddenly lost his usual brisk professional confidence and became all bashful and personal. Alistair noticed my elation, but it didn't interest him particularly.

Matthew had his second operation early in June . . .
I had occasion to telephone him about 8 or 9 days

later, to tell him Mr A's verdict, which was that the op. had had a certain degree of success, and that one more should do the trick and open up the clouded retina and let in light. M was to go into hospital once more, as soon as a bed was available. It was this conversation on the telephone, I do believe, which sunk me. X's voice, coming over the wires, was so sympathetic, and gentle and kind, that it just made my innards and heart go all jellified, and from that minute I *never stopped* thinking of him every moment of the day, whatever I was doing and wondering where he was and what he was doing and so on. Yes, I was done for. I'd fallen, hopelessly. I had not thought that way about anybody for sixteen years, or more.

I began to go off my grub and to sleep badly, and worst of all, to wake up very early in the morning crying, tears just streaming. So I suppose it was not surprising that, before long, the brilliant idea occurred to me that I might trot along to X and get a tonic or perhaps a sedative, or something like that . . .

I laid my plan very carefully, because Alistair was to know nothing about it. I must get to the surgery as soon after 9 a.m. as possible, only waiting for our new daily girl (she only lasted 3 months) to arrive and take charge of Matthew. It was a long way to go, nearly 20 mins in the bus. And Matthew would have to be given his breakfast when we had ours, instead of at 9 as he usually had it. Also, I intended to look my best and be very carefully groomed and turned out!

It all worked out beautifully, one Monday morning and I set off, so nervous that my hands and feet were stone cold, on a warm summer morning. There were a lot of people waiting to see X and I couldn't sit still, but smoked cigarettes and prowled about, and finally found a quite naughty French novel in a corner bookcase, which I sat down to devour. I thought it would help me to feel thoroughly wicked! (It had his wife's maiden name in it, and a date, 1933 or 34. I was pleased for even these scraps of indirect information about him.) But I couldn't take in much of what I read. As my turn came nearer, I wished more and more that I hadn't come. Whatever was I going to say to him! There was nothing the matter with me, except ___. By the time it *was* my turn, I assure you that my knees were wobbling and my teeth chattering and I felt really sick.

Inside his room, I began to stammer something about 'Perhaps I ought not to have come. You know how your tooth stops aching when you get to the dentist's waiting-room? Well, I don't think there's anything wrong really, but I'm all jittery, and I wake up crying, and have horrible dreams or don't sleep . . .' While I spoke I first walked up and down, and then perched on the side of the examination couch. X stood looking at me thoughtfully for a minute. I got the distinct feeling that he knew *exactly* what was the matter with me. Then he sat in his swivel chair before the desk, and drew the patient's chair up close to it, touching. 'Come and sit here,' he said, fiercely. I went. With his right hand he took my right hand in an ordinary shake-hands grip and with his left he felt my pulse. Still holding on with the right hand, he wrote down a note with his left. Then, still holding my hand, he began talking. He talked for about 10 minutes, about the strain of present-day living; about the enviability of sheep and cows and dogs; the need of relaxation; the effects of childbearing and nursing upon mothers of mature age; and a whole lot more. While he talked, I studied his face, as though I wanted to sketch it afterwards. Having been on the verge of tears, I was soon smiling at him most calmly. Then he wrote some more things, still with his left hand, and as he still held on firmly to my right, I yielded to an over-powering impulse and squeezed his hand hard. He made not the slightest response, and put on a most wooden expression, a 'poker-face'; but he didn't withdraw his hand either. So I squeezed again, hard. Still no response, either way. He went on holding it. Then he said: 'I'm giving you some mild sleeping tablets. I want you to take one every night for a week. Take a second if the first doesn't work, but not too late on in the night. When you've had seven good nights, stop them; and come and see me in a fortnight.' Then he let go my hand after giving it a little shake. I thanked him and took the prescription. He saw me out.

I was in a complete daze, felt as if I was walking on air, and that nothing – *nothing* in the world mattered any more . . . O fatal day! I remained in that same state of captivity for another 15 months at least, and was not really free again for nearly two years.

Well, those sleeping tablets (Soneryl) were such a comfort to me – being quite unaccustomed to such things, that I forgot my instructions and went on taking them for a fortnight. Given by him, I suppose I regarded them as almost sacred; anyway I took 14 of them, and had mostly very good sleeps. I went about all day in a daze, very happy and unperturbed by anything that might happen; but not very efficient in my duties I imagine. It made me so much better-tempered with the family, and altogether I thought it was a good thing. I loved only in the present and did not consider how a thing like this was likely to end. Whatever way is almost sure to be disastrous. Unfortunately one does not realise it in time.

I lived for my next visit, and once again everything fitted in beautifully . . . This time I had also a request to make – could he possibly speed up Matthew's admission to hospital? They had promised to let me know in a few days, and I'd heard nothing . . . My turn soon came, and I was with him once more. I told him that the sleeping pills were marvellous, and asked if I could please have some *more*. When he heard that I'd taken them for two weeks instead of one, he looked rather horrified and I thought he was going to be angry. But I smiled sweetly at him, and he got no further than the first two words of scolding. I then told him how the hospital negotiations were hanging fire and asked, 'Would it be in order for you to find out about it?' He at once rang up the hospital and enquired. They said they would let me know by tomorrow.

I got up to go. 'Um. Come and see me again next week, will you?' asked X, in not at all a professional sort of way. 'I'll try,' I said, 'but this time is really the baby's breakfast-time, so it's not always easy.' . . . X laughed, and he looked at me exactly as though he felt the same about me as I did about him. This may of course have been pure self-deception. But, I did, still do, think otherwise. I think that for about 4 or 5 months from the hand-holding episode, X was quite prepared for a flirtation of moderate seriousness, provided that it could be done discreetly. However, I must leave you to judge that . . .

Matthew's third operation was lucky. It did the trick. And this is how I heard. David and I went to visit M the day after the operation; it was a Friday. That was X's regular hospital day, though I didn't know it. David and I were in the waiting-room, D was behind the door, which was open. I was near the window, facing the door. Suddenly X appeared outside the door, and came in, and towards me, his face beaming with joy. 'I wanted to give you the news – the eye operation has been successful this time. Mr A was able to tell right away.' I was stunned by the good news – and couldn't speak for a minute. X went back to the door and was about to shut it when he saw David. The look he gave him was far from benevolent. It was on the tip of my tongue to tell D to go and look at the lift outside, but I thought he might fall down the shaft, and then I'd never forgive myself. X turned back to me, and we just sort of looked at each other for a minute or two. Then he said in quite a cross voice, 'I'm going away at the end of the month for three weeks.' I said, 'I hope you'll have a lovely holiday,' and meant it, but the words came out rather faintly and flatly, and X grinned to himself. Then he went off, without another word . . .

I'd had to start thinking about b.c. again because Alistair had suddenly begun to notice my presence about the place again, and seemed suddenly keen to resume normal cohabitation. This was not surprising, I suppose, since love has a remarkably beautifying effect, and A certainly sensed a change in me. And I didn't mind his making love to me at all. It was quite a relief to my nerves. My feelings for X were on the whole not very sexual. They were more a sort of adoration than actual passion. So I was able to respond to A and to enjoy coitus. Nor did I think of X at all when A and I were having intercourse. In fact the idea of doing so seemed almost sacrilegious, in a strange way . . .

I now began to hatch a most elaborate plot for meeting X as soon as possible after his return from his holiday. My idea was to get Alistair and the boys away for the last week in August, without Matthew and me; and to get X to come here to do Matthew's diphtheria immunisation (which I intended to have done anyway. All the others were done.) . . . I manoeuvred him to the required date, and it looked as though my plan should work out nicely. All that

remained was to telephone X as soon as possible after
their departure – that would have to be at his
Saturday evening surgery time; and to be prepared for
the phone being answered by somebody else, in which
case I would sound like a daft person who's got the
wrong number. Then I would ask him to look in and
do the immunisation within the next few days. After
that, warning him in advance that M and I would be
alone. I thought that would give him a chance to get
out of it if he didn't like it. The plan worked out quite
marvellously in every detail, and resulted in a most
momentous visit one lovely hot August afternoon.

(In next instalment you will hear about that, and
the following phase – up to the time, I think, X 'saw
the red light' and turned all cautious, and I also made
a feeble attempt to break free from this obsession.)

Am enthralled with all this! (Janna)

1952

Revelations: Part 3 – Aug.–Nov. 1947

Let's see. I'd got to where my deep-laid scheme was
about to come off . . .

He came just after 5 o'clock on Thursday afternoon. I had spent a restless few hours, unable to settle
to anything, and nearly faint with joyful anticipation.
After opening the door to him, I said – not very audi-
bly – 'It's nice to see you again,' at which he smiled
and got a bit pink. We talked first about his holiday,
in the Isle of Wight; and the respective 'polio' scares
we had had in our families; and something about the
political and economic situation and other general
topics. Then I fetched Matthew in and sat with him in
the middle of the sofa and took his dress off.

There is room on our sofa for three people to sit
without touching each other; so I was surprised, albeit
agreeably, that X should sit so close to me that his
coat sleeve scraped my bare arm quite hard, and he

really was *leaning* against me. I expected that he would move up a little, but rather he leaned even harder. This, my instinct told me, was the crucial moment. If I had turned my head round and said, 'Are you close enough?' which was what I very much wanted to do – I think that would have been the start of an affair. In fact, I am sure of it. I don't know what stopped me, except that it was *not* any high moral sense. I did not think of my duty to Alistair, nor of morality in general. In those few seconds I did have an apparently irrelevant thought about X's car standing in the road – its number and appearance probably known to a number of our neighbours, who also knew that A and the boys were away. It seemed therefore desirable, for the sake of X's reputation, that the car should not be standing there too long. That much I do remember thinking, as I sat there with a wildly beating heart, feeling that it would be so easy now to 'hook' him into kissing me, and then goodness knows what. Instead, I carefully did not turn round to look at him, but began talking very fast about Matthew's tummy and navel which were so much more bulgy than they ought to be – and he felt them, still leaning against me, and as I talked I leaned against him – but that was all. I was terribly red and blushing by now, and breathing very rapidly, and I thought how much he would notice it. Then the dangerous moment passed. He pulled the little table over, with his bag on it, and began to concentrate his whole attention upon the immunisation stuff and the syringe, and began talking again as he did so. I held Matthew on my lap, with his head on my knees, and the doctor injected the stuff into his left arm. Instantly, young Matthew set up a most tremendous yelling – an absolute howl of indignant pain – and at once I snatched him up against my bosom and hugged him, and stroked his back, meantime glaring indignantly at X as though he was a murderer! I didn't realise that I was doing so, until he began laughing and told me! But anyway, Matthew had effectually broken the spell. X got up and went back to the separate safety of the arm-chair, while I rocked and soothed my poor sobbing baby. As soon as we could make ourselves heard, we continued to talk, and X stayed on for quite a long time – he was here nearly an hour altogether . . . He seemed to be in no hurry to go; so we went on talking. It was all very happy and pleasant. When he had gone, and his parting words were, 'I'll come and give the second injection in a month's time; meantime – keep in touch,' I felt terribly flat, and began to regret most bitterly having let slip such an opportunity. I didn't really know what I wanted; it was all very conflicting and disturbing. I suppose I just wanted to be sure of whether he felt the same as I did. One thing at any rate I *was* sure of . . . was that I must see him again as soon and as often as possible. He represented kindness and friendship and sympathy. (Also, I wanted him to have a good opinion of me, even if he wasn't in the least in love with me.) . . .

The next thing that happened was really rather funny. I had got so beastly run-down by this time, and was so unhappy, restless and dissatisfied etc. with all this indefinite state of affairs, that when I caught a heavy cold, it just wouldn't go and a very noisy and alarming sounding cough developed, which so annoyed (and worried) poor Alistair, that at last, in desperation, he said, 'For heaven's sake go and see X and get your lungs seen to, and get rid of the cough.' I knew perfectly well there was nothing wrong with my lungs, and I'd often told A that if he'd kindly rub my chest hard with Vicks, once or twice at bed time, or even bring up a nice hot lemon drink after I was in bed, it would soon go, but he couldn't be bothered with such fiddling things – so he sent me to the doctor. I had mixed feelings about going – and did not want to relish the idea of X examining my chest. But it was, at any rate, a chance to see him and talk to him, and not to be missed, especially as I could go openly and without guilty feelings of deceit. So accordingly I got myself up with excessive ease and set off Saturday evening. A, seeing me apply the lipstick, asked, 'You're not putting that on for old X, are you?' laughing, and I said, 'I don't want to look *too* ill.' It so happened that there was only one other person there, so I got a marvellous innings that evening – well over $\frac{1}{2}$ an hour! I told him that my husband didn't like my cough, but that I'd had *my* lungs etc. gone over most carefully at another hospital only $2\frac{1}{2}$ years before, with all the tests – so I wasn't worrying . . .

Then he said suddenly, 'Well, I suppose we must look at the chest. Get this off,' and he pulled at my jersey. He turned away while I was pulling it off, and then told me to go over by the fire and came and did all the back, with stethoscope etc. Then he asked me to turn round, which I did, but kept my arms folded over my bosom, and did I feel an absolute fool, because I have *never* before minded how many doctors looked at my chest, but I COULD NOT not mind this time. I took one quick look at him and he was carefully not looking at me, and then I looked all round the room until he had finished; and then put my jersey on, and I don't know which of us was the pinker or redder by the end of it. It was terribly funny. He then gave me a linctus, and more tonic (which was not the slightest good) and I departed, still feeling slightly embarrassed.

A week later, A was still fed up with me; I think he was afraid I was going to pass out on him. I told him

I only wanted a rest. Could I take Matthew away somewhere for 3 or 4 days? A said, 'You'd better go back to the nursing home and lie up there for a bit. I'll fix it. How long do you want?' I protested violently against this *extravagance*, when we could have gone to his parents at much less expense for 2 weeks; but finally gave in, and said 4 days would be enough. Actually I was there for 5. And I think I wrote about it at the time, so will only now deal with two aspects.

(1) X's visit, (2) something I read there which made me think . . .

On the second evening as I came from my bath, Sister H, who is a most attractive and terribly competent young woman, said kindly to me, on the stairs, 'Shall I tell Dr X you are here, if he comes?' . . . 'No, don't bother him if he comes.' But I felt sure she would . . . On Saturday morning I felt sure he was coming, so I got all glamoured up, and put on an old black silk dressing gown with flowers on it which still looked quite nice, over a pretty nightie, and sure enough, about 12 o'clock, Sister H showed him in. My heart did a most colossal somersault, and he came in, looking thoroughly confused, come up and *shook hands* – as though we were at a garden party or something – and said, 'How nice to see you' (What an inept remark, I thought), and I simultaneously said, 'What a surprise.' He sat down on the bed, and Sister H looked a little surprised at the greetings we exchanged and we all made conversation very cheerfully. He asked a lot of questions – I explained how A had pushed me in here for a rest, and he said he thoroughly approved, and would like me to stay another week. However, I put my foot down and said I must go home on Monday. In the end, after much argument, *he* ordered Sister H to 'keep me till Tuesday'. He said he'd send tonic (ha-ha!) and sleeping tablets.

After this, the matron and Sister both came and cross-questioned me about whether I was worrying about anything about Matthew, etc. etc. To all of which I just said, 'Oh, no, just tired, that's all thank you.' They were *very* sweet and kind. I felt enormously better after the 5 days.

The Christmas before, a friend sent me a book, Bruce Marshall's novel *All Glorious Within* . . . I began to read it, and several times thought, 'Oh, I don't like this – can't go on with it,' and chucked it to the foot of the bed. But curiosity made me go on, because it told me all sorts of things I never knew before, about the Catholic Church, and Catholics, and priests and nuns and what it was all about. I wanted to know more . . . But it gave no more than information. It gave me a darned uncomfortable feeling inside me, that there was an awful lot wrong with me; that I needed to be taken to bits and made up differently; that if I ever wanted to be well and happy again I would have to start by seriously trying to begin at the beginning by keeping the First Commandment . . .

My conscience told me that I was all upside-down because I was loving X *and* myself, instead of God; as well as more than my husband and family. I had lately been pondering on the possibility of getting free, by a divorce for 'cruelty' – for which I rather thought I could make out quite a good case. After that, I'd get a job, where I could have Matthew with me, and wait for the possibility of X's wife either pre-deceasing him (very unlikely) or running away with somebody else. But the Bruce Marshall book reminded me that I had taken solemn vows in marriage, and that it was meant to be a life-long arrangement, and couldn't just be undone as easily as all that. All very uncomfortable and conscience suggested also – is there no fault on your side which makes your marriage unhappy?

Couldn't *you* do something about putting it right?

Next instalment should cover 6 months, the one after 10 months, then a final wind-up, six months of 1949 – chiefly about talks with the Friar, and Dr Strauss.

Revelations – Part 4

It is becoming harder now to write this and I think that writing it has helped a lot towards getting it out of my system, so that it has no longer nearly so much importance for me. Still, the end of the story is altogether a different matter from the beginning and as we progress from romance to reality, so to speak, it should become more interesting both to write and (I hope) to read. (By 'Romance' I don't mean that these things did not happen; but that they were at the time clothed in a false subjective light, which makes them of no value and significance in comparison with the events which followed after them.)

I didn't see X for nine weeks after returning home from the nursing home, after that brief rest, full of new strength and good resolutions. During that time, there was the episode of The Note. This was a major tactical error on my part, and I think it was the turning-point in our relations. Either it suddenly put him on his guard; or possibly his wife may have seen it. Up to now, anything I had written to him was such that the whole town might have read it, and no harm done to anybody. But this note, in a reckless moment, I signed, 'Yours, with love!' I wrote it without thinking, and then, out of sheer bravado, let it stay, and after posting it, thought, 'Maybe he'll not notice, or dismiss it as a slip of the pen.' But it gave me a sleepless night. I wished I hadn't.

Gosh! I send everyone notes like that! Even Jockie's Headmaster!
(Yonire)

How it came to be written was this: I had to get, every three months, a fresh supply of the pills for bad periods. Needing these, early in December, I rang up to ask for them to be posted (from their dispensary). I think there was a patient with him, as I was in a bit of a flutter, and after ringing off, imagined that I had sounded rather off-hand. So I foolishly wrote this quite unnecessary note to say that I hadn't meant to be rude. And signed it as I have described. And there-after wished very heartily that I had left well alone and not been so idiotic.

After Christmas, we were occupied with the matter of having Matthew examined by a Specialist . . . I told Alistair that I would get the introductory letter from X. I think Alistair thought that I would ring up about it; but after having sent that silly note, I felt shy of ringing up, and preferred to face him in person. I rather hoped that X might have forgotten about the note.

It was January 15th when I went to see him about it – a cold morning, and I was the first patient to arrive. Mrs X opened the door and showed me into the waiting-room. The gas fire was not lighted, and I asked her not to bother to light it yet if she'd rather wait until the others arrived. I talked a little to her, rather constrainedly and I fancied that she looked at me rather curiously. She is a small, pretty, very dark and vivid woman, with a manner which I thought (I'd only spoken to her two or three times before) was friendly only on the surface, with a very guarded and reserved 'underneath'. Mentally I had always labelled her 'hard', and though I never doubted that *he* was probably devoted to *her*, I had always wondered whether she was equally fond of him. She soon left me, and I had not long to wait before he summoned me in. At once I was aware of a complete change in his manner. It was neither the open cheerful friendliness of the time before all this began; nor the manner of the previous summer and autumn, with that undercurrent of some kind of feeling which definitely seemed stronger than – or distinct from – just sympathy and kindness. This was a manner of unusual gravity, of guardedness and caution, and something approaching severity. I felt chilled, miserable, and uncomfortable. I took refuge in extreme business-likeness, and without any conversation, simply asked him if he would kindly write the letter for Dr L.

I sat by his desk while he wrote it, and he took a long time about it. He asked an enormous number of questions, and went back over the history of the pregnancy and birth in minutest detail. His manner relaxed a little as he went on, but he remained very serious and did not once smile. Neither did I. I felt not the remotest inclination to smile. Altogether the composition of the letter, written by hand, took something like half an hour. When he had finished and I stood up to go, he handed it to me, and said: 'Come and see me as soon as you can after your interview with Dr L.' This surprised me a little, as he was emphatic about it – but I didn't bat an eyelid, only murmured, 'Right.' Thanked him, and was shown out by him, somewhat solemnly. 'Gosh,' I thought, 'Mrs X *must* have seen "Yours, with Love".'

I never described to you Alistair's very ghastly interview with Dr L and I won't do so now. I hope that neither you nor I may ever live through a day like that again. Dr L told Alistair his diagnosis in private. Outside his house, A called a taxi for us, and I asked him what Dr L had said. A said, 'I won't tell you now,' and my heart sank like a lump of lead. But even then I had not the remotest inkling of the verdict. Late that evening when I was at work in the kitchen, A came in and told me, and he was crying. I don't think I ever saw him cry before – and only twice since – also about the same thing. I could only stare at him and say, 'But he may be mistaken! He surely *is* mistaken, Matthew doesn't *look* like a Mongol.' Alistair said, 'I'm afraid it is absolutely definite. He said there was no possibility of doubt.' . . . But after Alistair said that – I did not any longer doubt the fact. Obviously no doctor would state it so emphatically if there was a shadow of doubt. I asked, 'There's nothing to be done about it?' 'Nothing at all,' A told me. I then tried to comfort A and to make him feel that we could help each other to bear it. But whether through my fault or not, I don't know – it wasn't very successful. That evening, perhaps, we were truly united in our misery; but after that first shock, I had the feeling that A was, unconsciously, feeling that I ought to be 'punished' for Matthew's condition. I felt that he positively hated me for being the mother of a defective child. At any rate, there was a complete barrier between us, and nothing I could say or do or think seemed to get over it. It was a complete nightmare.

X had told me to come and see him as soon as pos-sible. Every vestige of desire for a love-affair or flirta-tion or anything of that sort was completely banished from my mind by the weight of this frightful grief – naturally. But if I could have had his real love – that would have been another thing. *That* would have been an anchor in the storm. At any rate, it was not possi-ble to be anything but completely natural and human, in the circumstances. I went to him the morning after next, with a mind blank except for what I had come to tell him. He already had a letter from Dr L, but he asked me, very gently, to tell him what Dr L had said. 'He said –' I couldn't get any further. I just cried and cried – for the first time since our visit to London.

Luckily I had an enormous handkerchief in my pocket (I always borrow Alistair's when all mine have vanished) so I was able to cover my face and my tears, and X sat perfectly still, looking at his feet, until I had finished, and my voice came back. 'Anyway, there is nothing we can do about it,' and I got up. But X said, 'Wait a minute,' and I thought, 'You're damn well not going to hold my hand again,' so I gripped the arms of the chair. And he talked for quite a long time, *very* gently and kindly – and it was extremely helpful and comforting, though impersonal. He was explaining that Matthew would in no way suffer from his disability; that he would be happy; that he would probably make a certain amount of progress, in time – and so on, stressing the more hopeful aspects of the matter. This gave me time to recover and to draw deep breaths, and regain calm. Finally, when I thought it was time to go, as we got up, he said, 'If there is ever anything at all I can do to help, I will be very glad to do it' – again looking at the floor and not at me, as he said it. And so, thanking him and having powdered my face at the mirror over the mantelpiece, I went out into the cold, cold world.

We had just a few more meetings before the end.

During this month I went to see X once, having a small bit of things to ask him; and we had a pleasant talk, but it was still not quite as before . . . He also talked about the coming National Health Service, about which he had great misgivings, and doubts about whether to work in it . . . I came away rather depressed at the thought that, if he stayed outside the NHS, he probably wouldn't be our doctor any longer . . .

A week or so after this, I visited an old friend of mine in the country (Surrey) and spent the day there. She is about 8 years older than me, and long ago she gave me a lot of good worldly advice upon various matters connected with my boy-friends, and love-affairs and what not. I suddenly decided, after we'd been talking about life in general, and comparing notes, to ask her advice about this X business. I gave her a brief outline and told her that I could no longer endure this uncertain negative state of affairs, and that I had a wild idea that perhaps if he was no longer our doctor it might be easier to start an affair with him, or at any rate to establish a more satisfactory kind of relationship, exactly what I didn't really know! Rather to my surprise, her advice was to go ahead and grab him. *How* I was going to do this, I had not the faintest idea, but it so chimed in with my own wishes in the matter, that I thought it excellent advice and determined to put it into practice as soon as a chance occurred.

As it now was time to fill up the new registration forms for signing on with one's doctor, I accordingly made that the pretext for my next – and last – visit to X. May 22, 1948. A Saturday morning. First I asked him for some more 'period' pills, and sleeping tablets. Then I asked him for the forms to fill up for registration. He said that he *still* was not absolutely certain about the NHS but that I could fill up the forms and return them to him, and he would pass them on to his partner if he was not going to keep us on. He asked which partner we preferred and I told him. Then I said, 'There was something I was going to tell you – but perhaps you know it already.' Long pause – and not receiving any encouragement, I said, 'It would be best, I think, if I didn't see you any more. If you know what I mean.' There was an awful silence for a minute. Then he said, very coldly indeed, 'Yes, I agree. It would be better.' Another pause. Then, 'When your duty and your inclination don't go together, you must make them.' I tried to

What a SAP! Honestly Isis – He is. (Yonire)

recover a little self-respect by laughing at this and say-ing, 'So easy, isn't it?' Then I got up, and said, 'OK. We go on to Dr B's list then. And I must thank you for the ointment for Matthew, which has quite cleared up his trouble. Good-bye.' And I literally 'swep' out', after forcing a light smile at him. He had stood look-ing rather astonished during this speech, perhaps expecting tears or reproaches. Luckily he did not have to show me out, as his wife was just opening the door to some new arrivals. He said not a word when I left the consulting-room – and as I went out at the front door I said goodbye to Mrs.

The shock was so great, I suppose, that I felt absolutely nothing at first. It was like being a third party looking on, with detached interest, at something concerning two other people. I did my shopping and went home; and later in the day, filled up the medical forms, and wrote a letter to go with them. It was a long letter, but entirely unemotional. I wrote as though about something which had happened a long time ago to me and somebody else, and scarcely used the word 'you' at all. Said that I was sorry it had hap-pened. Explained why I thought it had – and inciden-tally for the first time mentioned that things were bad between Alistair and me, just casually. Said he wasn't to think it was a sort of Hollywood romantic notion, because I'd really wanted something better than that, and didn't visualise breaking up any homes etc. Said I could see I had been mistaken. Also that he could be sure that it was entirely finished now, in so far that I should not try to meet or speak to him; nor would I play any tricks with the sleeping tablets (he'd just pre-scribed me about 100 of these!) as this would not be fair; and I thanked him very much for all that he had done for us, and wished him all good luck . . .

Meanwhile poor X I suppose must have been in a

bit of a panic, remembering that 'Hell hath no fury like a woman scorned' and he did then the only thing that I blame him for. He wrote (before he got my letter. He would not have told A if he had known the state of affairs between A and me) to A at the school, got him to come and see him, and told him about that last interview. Alistair had now for several months thought that I was certainly in love with somebody; but he imagined that I was secretly meeting some old boy-friend of the remote past . . . I don't know what passed between X and A – it was not until long after that I knew of their interview. Perhaps someday I shall ask A. But it had the effect of making A treat me exactly like Mr Barrett of Wimpole St. and a very naughty little daughter. It was *unbearable*, especially as neither of us told the other anything.

Isis – I wish I were married to
Alistair! I'd teach him! (Yonire)

1952

Revelations Part 5: May–October 1948

Dr X answered my explanatory letter, briefly, but very kindly. He said that it made things much clearer. He hoped I would soon feel much better and happier; and if at any time I thought that psychological treatment would help (because I had referred to that possibility in my letter to him) he would be glad to write, if I wanted him to, to whoever did it.

The next ten months were mainly a sort of living death – with one brief interval of something better – that was the two months following the electric-shock treatment. In July I was writing to Dr X to say that if he had no objection I would write to him about 3 or 4 times more, just to relieve the sense of utter desolation; but that, naturally, I would not be expecting any answer. I did write again – in November and December, and in April of 1949; and each time I wrote, the next day or day after, he would come along this road in his car, driving slowly, on his way to some other road. It was his way of answering! It always cheered me up a little . . . From May till September, 4 months, I don't really know much about what was going on, partly as a result of the electric shocks. They made me forget everything that happened in those 4 months, but nothing whatever of what happened before, which was the main object of the treatment! . . .

All I can remember was that I cried every day, sometimes for hours on end, that is, if I was alone. All the time I was alone, in fact . . . With Alistair it was mostly stony silence and he would sit and stare at me for what seemed like hours on end. He seemed to be suspicious of everything I did, every letter that came for me, every letter I wrote. If I went out anywhere, when he was at home, he always asked where I was going, and how long I would be and whether I was going by bus etc. etc. . . .

The person who perhaps helped me most to get through this time was Dorothy K . . . Well, DK helped me a lot, by her warm human sympathy, and for that I shall always be grateful . . . She recommended a psychiatrist who had a nursing home where shock therapy, ECT, was given. After the summer holiday, Alistair and I went up to see him . . . To begin with, this Dr first had Alistair in to talk to him, for half an hour. Then my turn came . . . Dr RR stared at me as if I was something quite beyond the pale. He spoke to me in the tone of an indignant father whose child has been behaving very tiresomely. He asked, 'What is this I hear about this doctor?' To that I answered nothing. What answer did he expect?

Next question: 'Are you in love with him?' I said, 'Yes.'

'Is he in love with you?' I said, 'NO.'

At this, Dr RR stared. It obviously wasn't the answer he had expected. It wasn't the right neurotic answer. He looked rather shaken. Next he said, 'I've heard about this unfortunate child of yours' – in a tone that suggested he was referring to some disgraceful incident. To this I said nothing. What was there to say? After which he asked if I would be willing to come and have treatment at his place. I said, 'All right. I don't mind.' And that was that.

I spent 3 weeks at Dr RR's place . . . It wasn't a bad place on the whole; the staff was very good and the patients seemed extraordinarily normal; the treatment was unpleasant but not actually frightening – though I wouldn't have it again for any money, I'd rather be shot . . . But it produced no fundamental change; one came out with just the same difficulties and problems and weaknesses, and things lacking, as one had before. The root of the matter remained untouched. What that was had still to be discovered.

1952

Nearly the End of the 'Revelations'

. . . Then, one day in 1948, C [CCC member Campo Allegre] sent me a name and address, of a Franciscan Friar, in East London. She did not know him personally, but only through a mutual friend; and she said that he was particularly gifted in helping people with nervous and neurotic troubles, and helping to reconcile people whose marriage was going to bits, and so on . . . My response was to think: 'Oh, dear, it is *very* kind of Campo, but really it is quite an impossible idea. I *couldn't* go and discuss my soul with a priest, and especially a strange alien R. C. Even with a C. of E. person it would be a revolting business; but with one of these weird unknown people, it would be terrifying.' . . .

After the work and fun of Christmas were over, I began to have a feeling that I would soon be a nervous and mental wreck again, and that there was nothing to look forward to. The only remedy I could think of for the moment, since I felt unable to make any effort at all to get interested in outside things, was to begin reading the Bible – a chapter a day; and I began this on Jan 1st . . .

A friend (very Protestant) lent me, at the same time, *The Robe*, which is, of course, a Protestant book. But it helped a great deal. It gave me another push in the direction of finding my way. I never thought I'd finish it, it is very long-drawn-out; but became too interested to stop. But pious reading, though it may help to dispose the mind to accept further inspiration, is not much good by itself, unsupported by any efforts or exercises of the will. The effect was to produce a state of conflict (by emphasising the contrast between ideal and actuality), which expressed itself in outbursts of rage against Alistair and the boys, quarrels, arguments; a feeling of desperation, an urge to *weep*, to commit suicide – anything to get away from the unbearable prison of the here-and-now. Hence my running away for a day; and various efforts to stage a suicide, by taking a huge quantity of aspirins and by trying to cut my throat, and by fixing up a hanging apparatus in the garage! This state of conflict and efforts to 'escape' went right on until April 1949, and culminated in the quarrel with Alistair when I struck him in the face.

It was about a month before this, however, that things were so bad that I finally decided that it could do no harm, and *might* conceivably do some good, to write to this Friar, whom Campo had mentioned, for advice. I wouldn't need to meet him, I thought; if he could read and write, he would perhaps be willing to give advice by post . . .

. . . wrote an interesting letter back, saying that he had an idea that part of my trouble was an over-active imagination, which created conflicting images, and that thoughts and images fed each other, and chased round in a sort of circle, like a snake eating its tail. Also that, in Dr X, I had fallen in love, not with an individual, but with a type. He said he would have to meet me once or twice in order to help further.

I was much struck with the shrewdness of his analysis, and it was obvious that here was somebody who was more than ordinarily understanding, and clever, and apparently quite human and kindly as well. I began to think it might be interesting to meet him – curiosity was aroused. He should be easy to talk to, and not embarrassing, and he hadn't mentioned religion or Catholicism . . .

So when he suggested a time for an interview, it had to be Saturday morning, because he taught in a school. I agreed to come, having first asked Alistair if I might. He said, 'Do what you like.' Fr. K gave me minute directions about how to get to the Friary. . .

On arrival at the Friary, my knees knocked together and I longed to turn and flee . . . In the doorway a young man, not more than 30, of much more than average height, and big build, in the brown robe and sandals of the Order, stood and smiled at me for a moment before entering. He had the most beautiful face I had ever seen . . . I think I must have let out an almost audible gasp, and Fr. K, who has more intuition than the average man, smiled more broadly as we shook hands. I got a distinct impression, which was encouraging, that he also quite liked the look of me, as well as being aware, without a trace of vanity, that I liked him . . .

The interview itself will have to be described next

time. I will only say this, in addition: that not only did I feel convinced at once, before he even spoke, that I had found a friend, but I also realised that here was an exceptional person: and more than that – there was something about his presence which made me exceedingly and uncomfortably aware of my shortcomings and general rottenness.

1952

The Friar and the Psychiatrist

Being the continuation of the Long Story, now nearly Concluded! . . .

He [Fr. K] showed me how the X business had arisen out of the trouble over Matthew, and that it was an 'unreality', independently of whether or not it had meant anything to X himself. I had told him that my feeling for X had very little sex in it, and that Alistair and I had a satisfactory relationship on this plane – in general – though not on other levels, and from this he deduced that in X I was seeing a type or ideal which I failed to find in Alistair – rather than actually 'falling in love' with X himself as an individual. And he referred to the futility of this search for the ideal types in individual people . . .

He then said that I needed sympathetic friendship, at which he himself was not much use, but he could put me in touch with somebody who was and would do so . . .

Next he said, 'My advice to you for the moment is, in order to correct this emotional unbalance, please practise being a complete vegetable. It isn't very romantic, but it is very necessary. Try not to react to any stimulus whatever, whether pleasant or otherwise. Make up your mind that you *will not feel* things: great elation, deep grief, anger, excitement. Refuse to be upset, in any way. Be a turnip. Or get under an umbrella of indifference, and shelter there from all disturbances.' I said I would try. 'Take, as your motto, for the next few weeks: "I couldn't care less." It will do you a power of good. And by that time Dr Strauss will be able to help you.' . . .

The three weeks following this interview was by no means an easy or happy time. Fr. K's personality had the same effect as the pious reading, only much more so. By emphasising the contrast between the ideal mode of human life, and the actual which prevailed in my case – it caused most intense conflict and in-bred bitterness. He was a living reproach to me, showing me what I could have been (as all of us could) if I had had the right end in view, instead of lesser ends such as: getting my own way, getting married, having a family, finding an ideal lover, and so on. Some of them excellent ends in themselves, but always lesser ones . . .

Just before Easter came the climax of trouble and bad feelings. I spent one night walking about in the garden to get peace and fresh air, while A remonstrated with me, trying to persuade me to come in and go to bed like a reasonable person. I lay on the grass for some time, and longed to be under it. After that we quarrelled and I hit him. Then I took the aspirins – around 50[*] of them and passed out, more or less for a day, feeling unutterably frightful. Either just before that or just after, I wrote a desperate note to Fr. K saying that I *could* not and *would* not live with A another day, and hoped I would soon be dead. I got a note back by return telling me that I was a 'very bad turnip' and that decisions could never be taken when one was emotionally upset; and ordering me to get a sleeping draught from the doctor and to sleep for 12 hours and not be an utter fool.

[*] *Not quite sure if it was as many as that! (Isis)*

On Good Friday, two days after the aspirin business, I rose from my bed and took the boys to church for part of the Three Hours in the hopes that it might induce a better state of mind, even if only for a day or two. It did. But in any case, after hitting Alistair I had felt a lot better and not exactly guilty, but completely shocked out of my hatred of him *She ought to hit him* – permanently, as it turned out . . . *oftener! (Yonire)*

I also went to church on Easter Day and on all the subsequent Sundays up to Whitsun, and also Ascension Day. This was something I'd not done for 18 years. I thought it rather peculiar myself, but felt that 'desperate ills need desperate remedies' and possibly after a time some benefit might be apparent, though I could not imagine what it would be or how it could come about.

Meanwhile the appointment with Dr S was fixed up . . .

May was the fateful month which brought the turning point. It was on the last day of May 1949 that I made the final decision in my own mind. (My 43rd birthday!)

But first there is a bit more to be said about April. In the first week, I was alone here with Tom, the others being down at A's parents. I took T to see *Monsieur Vincent*, which we loved, and I think it further helped me on my way, though not consciously. And at this time I wrote my last letter to Dr X – a very miserable little note, blobbed all over with tears – just to tell him that I was going to get treatment from Strauss – in case he wanted to tell S anything. I ended by saying that I should not be writing to him any more. At this time, and for another month or more, I still felt very keenly and deeply the loss of X and the wound left by my leave taking of him. It did not seem to have been healed by time, as yet.

Isis met Dr Strauss on two occasions . . .

Then on May 3, I saw Strauss again, this time a shorter interview; rather indecisive, and he was quite 'nasty' to me. He told me that I was in no way neurotic, nor did I need any shock treatment. He suggested that the cure lay in my own hands; also that I was abominably self-pitying, and never seemed to realise what my poor husband had been through. All this was said in a most gentle and kindly way, 'more in sorrow than in anger', so to speak. I left him, feeling bewildered and disappointed, and also rather appalled at the thought that, since there was nothing the matter with me he could cure, I would have to do something about it myself; nor was there any excuse to take shelter behind . . .

Just after this, I met Caryll Houselander, the friend whom Fr. K said he would introduce me to. She is somewhere about my age and lives alone in Chelsea. She is a writer, painter and wood-carver and a very striking and remarkable personality. She was born a Catholic, like Fr. K. She has done a great deal of work for and with mentally defective children. She helped me a great deal, in the long talk we had, although rather indirectly. I told her a lot of my troubles, to which she listened sympathetically, but the most valuable thing was all she said about Matthew, and about all such children, in general. I can't relate it all here. We also talked about religious matters in a general way. I found, to my surprise, that our ideas were very much in agreement. It helped me to discover that most of the Catholic faith was already inside me, and it would not be some strange thing quite outside which would have to be assumed. Even then, however, I still had no mind to change . . .

Next, I went up to Forest Gate again on a Saturday morning for a talk with Fr. K. All rather different this time . . . He told me some (hard) truths, which were very painful to hear, and generally tore me to shreds and cut me to the quick. It was all highly unpleasant, and as I was already over-tired and on edge when I got there, it wasn't long before I dissolved into tears. I hoped he wouldn't notice as he was not looking at me while he talked but was doing scribbles on a piece of paper. However, he did look up suddenly and I was caught. I had been feeling extremely angry with him being so unkind; I felt like throwing something at him and had quite made up my mind never to see him again. Seeing my tears, which I was trying hard to conceal, he asked in a most kindly-elder-brotherly-way: 'My dear, have I said anything to hurt you?' I thought – what a question! But the kind words and tone surprised the tears away and made me able to find my voice. Until then I had not been given a chance to speak. I explained, or tried to, some of my rather muddled feelings on the matter and how far I agreed with what he had said. Nobody had ever before told me what I'd always known but never admitted to myself – that I had married Alistair for all the wrong reasons. It would be more comforting to my vanity if he thought I had married because of some overwhelming physical attraction, rather than because I was afraid of being left on the shelf! In any case, I felt angry with him for digging this out of its dark hiding-place, and exposing it to the light of day. He went on to advise me to have a really revealing heart-to-heart talk with Alistair about our relation-ship, some time soon . . . When we parted, he had agreed to come to our home as soon as possible, to meet Alistair and the boys.

Before that day, which was 6 days later, I had already arrived, through further great inner upheaval and many tears, at the inescapable conclusion that I would never attain sanity and happiness unless I made a further effort to take a further step. I realised that going on Sundays etc. to parish church was not going to provide any solution to the problem. It merely produced a feeling of vague pious satisfaction, a sense of duty performed, but this was not what I was looking for and needing. I wanted to share in that something which Fr. K, and Dr Strauss, and Caryll Houselander all shared, and which I began to realise was a life on another plane. A supernatural life – and a living faith. I had known 2 or 3 people who had this too and who were not Catholics; but they were people who were so good by nature that they'd have had it even without being Christians . . . It began to be borne in upon me that if one had not this supernatural life by nature, then one must seek it by grace, and if that quest for grace led you to the door of a new and unfamiliar Church, you must nevertheless follow it until you found what you sought.

Isis remained married to Alistair and embraced Catholicism. She frequently attended pilgrimages during the first few years of her conversion. While Catholicism continued to be an important focus in her life, she still suffered from bouts of depression.

Matthew was cared for in various homes throughout his life, visited by both Alistair and Isis. Though Isis spoke of him, his other brothers never really knew him. Matthew died in 1974.

Alistair and Isis lived in the outskirts of London until he retired from his teaching position in the early 1970s. They then moved to Oxfordshire, where they spent their time reading, gardening and socialising with neighbours. Isis died in 1989.

Accidia

Accidia's husband John was an honest and hard-working man, but he had an old-fashioned view of marriage and, as previously mentioned, was not an attentive husband. She wrote the following in late 1952 after he was promoted from tutor in Adult Education to Deputy Director of the department at Leeds University. This was just one of the many times when she struggled during the course of their marriage. She explained, 'I was always the number-two wife. Number-one wife was John's work, always, always, always. That's why I was so lonely I think.'

November 4, 1952

Elevation

John has just been appointed Deputy Director of the Dept of Adult Education at Leeds. This was hardly the bolt from the blue that it sounds since he had more or less been doing the work for the past year, though without the title and without the emoluments. Naturally he is pleased; who could be otherwise? Considering that the outbreak of war in 1939 cut right across his career and that 1945 found him transformed from the prosperous bachelor of pre-war days into a £350 p.a. man with wife and two children and no hidden assets, meteoric rise is perhaps the correct term here. A not inconsiderable asset of the new job is an increased salary and we can at least feel that there is not the crushing need to examine every coin twice before spending it, or better still, not spend it at all. Heaven knows, there is plenty to spend any spare money on!

We started married life in 1942 with a piano and a frying-pan, a moderate wardrobe each, and far too many books (or so our various landladies thought) and slowly and painfully we have acquired furnishing, adequate if not aesthetic, and five offspring. John and I are both extremely short of clothes and could disburse £50 each straight off on a very modest refurbishing of our wardrobes. The house lacks all kind of civilising touches and could swallow £500 without a belch. In fact, it will probably be years before the improved standard of living makes itself felt, especially now that the children are coming to the expensive stage. At the moment I make all their clothes, but can hardly be expected to tackle boys' suits or school uniforms. Also, I feel that we could be a little more ambitious in the educational field than we have hitherto allowed ourselves to be. But the expenditure most likely to take the gilt off the gingerbread will be on a house since sooner or later we shall have to leave this University property which we tenant and go to live in that horror of cities, Leeds. This will mean buying a house and, although the value of house property has depreciated considerably these last 6 months and is likely to depreciate still further, the sort of house we seek (large garden, adequate bedrooms, not impossible to run single-handed, in fact, the Georgian-style residence of desirable aspect and demeanour that exists in 'every imagination' and never in fact) will hardly be bought for an old song.

However, to turn from the Yorkshire preoccupation with finance, what of the job? Naturally, it's predominantly administrative (a pity, as John prefers teaching) and from my point of view it's the nearest thing to reasonable grounds for divorce that I have yet come across. We live, move and have our being in an atmosphere of University policy and politics until at times I feel I could *scream* if I have to listen once again to what Professor X said about the desirability of setting up a committee to consider the possibility etc. etc.

This week John was away all Saturday, physically at home but mentally at the University all Sunday, out from 8.30 a.m. until 11.00 p.m. Monday, out from 8.30 a.m. until 10.45 p.m. on Tuesday, out from 8.30 a.m. till 5.00 and 5.30 until 11.00 (a dinner this time, lucky man!) on Wed and so it goes on . . . AA wrote a good article on 'frustration' and I think that one of the hardest things for the educated woman to do is to accept the almost purely domestic role that marriage, childbearing and the modern lack of domestic help forces her into, whilst her husband goes from strength to strength and inevitably has less time to be at home and to be a companion to her. At the moment I feel I am slap in an emotional muddle and am having a hard time to build up the courage to face a future so different from what I had hoped (when we came here it was for John to be the warden of the residential college and the assumption was that I should take a fairly active part myself since I should be on the spot and always available in the evenings). Frankly I am lost in a sadness for the past. (Sorry if this sounds ludicrous to the older and maturer beings who regard 34 as pretty green!) When John got the job in Cornwall as WEA tutor organiser we had almost no money, we lived in a small house in a typical Cornish street and we had a 1933 Morris 8 which did incredible things on Cornish hills and we had time to enjoy each other and the then two children. Hell! And now we've got (on paper) what seems like a good salary, a somewhat improved house and a 14 h.p. car in reasonable condition and we haven't a moment to sit back and listen to a concert or to chat without the shadow of damnable Dept of Adult Ed. Learning in the background. Promotion is a lonesome thing, God, not for he who is promoted, but it's a heartache to the wife who finds her time at the sink and stove no less and her loneliness considerably more. What increases the melancholia of this wife is the knowledge that the Director of Adult Ed. at Leeds is a complete monomaniac for the work, and the effect of this on his wife and four children is not such as to encourage me to heights of cheerfulness. The snag is, of course, that the man himself cannot see that he is becoming more and more absorbed until around his entire sleeping and waking life winds the strand of THE WORK. Mercifully John, and I myself usually, have a sense of humour (which Director and wife regrettably lack) so perhaps, this, if no other virtue, will prevent our calling upon Elektra's expert services to salvage our marriage!

AA, I feel you may have wise words to utter on this problem of lonely wife keeping home fires burning and rearing children while husband deals with the affairs of the world and has less and less time even to notice whether fires are burning at all or children reared (unless they make too much noise). My impression is that you are naturally self-contained and have cultivated this so as to lead to an inner self-contentment that is not *fundamentally* impaired by the behaviour of external beings or objects. If this is a correct deduction I should welcome any helpful advice. Just now I vacillate between the picture of myself entirely domesticated, providing that secure and pleasant home background for husband and children to enjoy and relax in (the lazy devils!), sweetly listening to the joys and miseries of their day etc. etc., and that of myself as living a life of my own (inner, not outer at the moment) and not really identifying myself with anyone else – Neither of these extremes

seem ideal, but I can't seem to hit the middle way –
Personality defect, I expect.

I think you will in time. (Sirod)
Yes. I think so too. (Rosa)

*Accidia wrote the following article when she was
expecting for the sixth time. As mentioned in a previous
chapter, at the end of her entry 'Longing for Lucilla',
Accidia miscarried shortly afterwards.*

September 11, 1954

Perhaps it would be well to end with a thought for the
day about John and his part (not biological, of course)
in this affair. John has the great disadvantage and the
great advantage of naturally taking many things for
granted. This means that he never fusses over me,
never gives me presents, never remembers my birthday, assumes that I am happy, contented and well
unless I positively *scream* at him that the contrary is
true. (His excuse about not bringing the odd gift home
is that, when in commerce, he found that it was the
unfaithful husbands who were for ever loading their
wives with gifts – Ergo, no gifts means fidelity and if I
ever receive an unexpected pair of nylons or a length
of terylene I may know the worst.) He becomes enormously preoccupied with his work and pays no act of
attention to anything else for days at a time. (If *I*
wanted to be unfaithful nothing would be easier to
conceal.)   *How often have I said just this! (Ad Astra)*

He would drive the very feminine type of woman
round the bend in no time because he would forget to
talk to her, would never notice what she was wearing
and would be not in the least concerned with what
she did with herself during the day. Now, all these
traits can at times be both irritating and depressing for
a wife but their golden side shews clearly on occasion.

Take the matter of children. John thought four enough but if I wanted five and was prepared for all the work involved, well he wouldn't fuss and he more or less forgot about the matter for nine months and has remembered it from time to time since for a brief moment. His attitude to six seems to be similar; five is enough but if six it must be . . .

He is out and away a great deal so that he forgets about the children for hours at a time; when he remembers, he gets a certain kudos from confessing that he is the father of five (and he enjoys the varied expressions on the faces of his listeners). But what about earning the money to feed etc. the children? Well, John would always work twice as hard as the next man whatever the number of his dependents; he has a genius for getting jobs that have previously been done by two people; if work is not there he makes it; he has all the northern puritan ingrained attitude to work so he doesn't work any harder because there are five mouths to feed than if there were only two. He is not a connoisseur of food so he doesn't miss his caviar and wines (anyone who can empty the coffee pot with apparent relish three hours after it has been put aside after a meal, or fry up together cold potato, an odd piece of fruit cake and some cold rice pudding or a piece of meat pie at 11.00 p.m. cannot, I feel, have much of a palate!).

Both he and I have moments of great gloom about the house (I particularly after a visit to Elektra's), but this dissipates and we neither of us notice for long periods at a time. If we go out to dinner, or visit some exquisite ménage, presided over by a *soignée* hostess, we sigh momentarily, but John is mentally off and away on some mettlesome steed of adult education even before I recovered my sense of values. All things considered he is the ideal husband for me, even if I don't always see it and, considering his mental and physical health, it would appear that I approach in some degree the ideal wife for him.

Following John's promotion, he became so absorbed in his work that he could 'think and talk about nothing else', and this eventually led to a nervous breakdown in October 1956. For financial reasons he needed to return to work, but it was clear to John and Accidia that a change was in order. John had met Roby Kidd, a high-profile Canadian in the field of adult education, at a conference and had been offered a job with what was then known as the Indian Eskimo Association (IEA) of Canada. He accepted and moved the entire family to Toronto, Ontario, Canada. For Accidia, this was one of the happiest times in her life as they lived in a nice neighbourhood with plenty of playmates for the children. Also, she met several contemporaries with whom she developed lifelong friendships. In Toronto Accidia gave birth to her seventh child, Benedict, in 1961.

John missed academic life and did not see eye to eye with the Chairman of the IEA, so he found a new job in adult education at McMaster University in Hamilton, Ontario, in 1965. Both Accidia and the children were opposed to moving there with him, so he tried commuting to Toronto (forty-three miles) just on weekends. After a year, Accidia joined him with Benedict, Lucilla, Humfrey and Julian. The rest of the children, now in their late teens and early twenties, left to pursue their own careers and academic paths.

In Hamilton, Accidia and John's marriage nearly failed. John only focused on his work and Accidia felt isolated, with few companions aside from her children. Looking back, she felt that they had married too young and just grown apart. Essentially they lived separate lives. They did, however, stay together primarily for the sake of the children.

In 1969, John decided he would like to retire, so they returned to England and settled in Tunbridge Wells. Quickly he realised that retirement at sixty was a mistake and he took up a job with the Open University, where he worked until 1988. He had to travel quite a bit as he gave lectures in political science all over the Sussex area and also had to go twice a week to Milton Keynes, where the Open University was based. With the children leaving home, Accidia had a great deal of free time. In 1972, she applied to work for Marriage Guidance (MG) and was accepted. Within three years she was promoted to tutor and, in 1976, she joined the training team at Rugby, where she worked once a month training counsellors.

In 1988, John retired and they moved to Dorset. Accidia had hoped that, with his retirement, she and John might travel. However, John basically withdrew from life, and for his last eight years he generally remained in the house and preferred to be alone, reading in his study. Accidia spent this time working for the Dorchester chapter of MG (which changed its name to RELATE) and attained a senior position. After John's death her life did not change significantly, as she felt that he had essentially left her years before.

Though she was officially retired at the age of sixty-five, Accidia continued to work for RELATE until the age of eighty-two. She particularly enjoyed this as she always took pleasure in learning from and about people and was interested in the different theories of counselling.

Accidia wrote for the CCC from the time she initially joined in 1951 until the last edition of the magazine in 1990. When she lived in Canada, the magazine was posted to her last so that she could still be included while living abroad. She entertained the other CCC women with various articles about life in Canada and certain experiences unique to North America. The CCC had a strong influence on Accidia's life, and when asked to reflect in 2004 as to why she liked the magazine, she explained:

I think it was a chance to forget about being a mother, forget about being a wife, forget about a very restricted lifestyle, and get the stimulus. It was friendship really, because I was incredibly lonely . . . and I lacked adult friendship, so it was friendship by proxy. It was a marvellous antidote to loneliness.

Accidia still lives in their beautiful cottage in a small village in Dorset. She suffers from bouts of loneliness as four of her children and nine of her eleven grandchildren live permanently abroad. However, she visits her three children who remained in England and travels with her youngest son, Benedict. She is exploring a Buddhist way of life that emphasises focusing on the present rather than reflecting on the past or worrying about the future. This means that she no longer looks at old photographs because they cause her too much sadness.

Despite her frequent melancholy, Accidia is a very active person, both physically and mentally. She is remarkably well read and intelligent, with a sharp wit and a wonderful sense of humour. She walks four to five miles a day and is always pleased to have visitors and activity around the house.

Roberta

*After Roberta had moved from Kent to Davos with
her four children, she continued to write extensively
for the CCC. The magazine was a lifeline, as she was
devastated when Walter told her that she and the children should not join him in Johannesburg because he
had met another woman and wanted a divorce.
Roberta decided to remain in Switzerland, and she and
Walter agreed that all four children, Nick, seventeen,
Christopher, fifteen, Guy, nine, and Suzanne, seven,
would live with her.*

*The following extracts were written by Roberta when
Walter was travelling back and forth between Johannesburg and Davos to complete the divorce.*

*In these passages she specifically mentions Amelia, as
she was going through her divorce around the same
time.*

1953

. . . Well thank you for your loving thoughts and mes-
sages. I did appreciate them all more than I can tell
you.

I do want to meet *Amelia* too, as she says we are in
the same boat, and I should like to know if she has
also experienced the same emotions and 'change' as I
have done.

It is like an answer to my prayers, it is like waking
up from a bad dream and knowing one can go on and
all is well, that what has been can't come back, but
gladness and thankfulness are truly within my heart. I
DO thank God for the luck which has been mine and
shall always be grateful, but now there is no sadness

about it, no longing, no dreadful heart ache to be back in England and 'safe' and at home and cared for and 'under the wing'.

I don't know when or why or how I thus emerged. I only pray it is *lasting*, but one day I found myself at peace, calm, not wishing to 'go back' or return or wishing and longing for what had been . . . I just was able to accept it for what it was worth and realise it is over and in the past. I am able to accept Davos, and enjoy it with its lovely scenery and warm autumn days, accept with pleasure the life which is now mine, accept living and being alone, and accept the task of having the children on my own.

I can truthfully say that such peace within me I have not known for years. I have been torn, twisted all inside me, mentally at sea, never at rest, seeking what I did not know, but I was terribly restless mentally, and I know at one point I would have cracked up and was terrified. I did not sleep properly and woke thinking of Walter and the future and writing imaginary letters to him, one day all loving and one day all hatred and bitter; one day begging him to come back to me and the children, to beg him to remember, to think, and another time hating him and thinking all the most fearful things I could, full of self-pity and martyrdom stuff, but now I have floated free, free, free, bliss. If the clouds do come again to close me in, I don't think it will ever be the same, I hope not.

I suppose it is the natural reaction to having been tossed and torn and buffeted right and left, and I sought love from everyone, all of you, and my friends at home, my mother. I needed reassurance that I was not the cast-off person and not worth loving as I deeply felt. I grasped at every tender word and kind act or thought for me. I was, I suppose, *full* of self-pity.

I looked at my lawyer with eyes full of tears and

made his heart be sorry for me! I melted my father-in-law's heart, so that he wrote to me how sad he was for me and, though he always felt divorce was a matter of *two* people being wrong, in my case he felt I was in no way to blame. Now I did NOT do any of this with a motive, nor from artificial feelings. They were only too real, my heart was bleeding and I showed it. I was afraid and I showed it, people were sad and sorry for me.

It was as if I was burning in a lonely fire and starved of any love and had lost forever any self-esteem I had, but somehow I am out of it, my head rises above it. I could not at this moment ask for anyone's pity, I don't send out weak waving tentacles seeking bits of love to suck and gain strength from.

I only know I am at peace and those who have been fond of me still are, and those who matter in my life do, and those whom I feel are my real friends always will be. Your thoughts for me, shown by your joint letter, made me cosy and happy inside but not weep and long to throw myself into the first pair of arms open to me! So you see perhaps after all you have a stronger Roberta among you and a bit better one than a few weeks ago. I hope so. I am so much happier as I am, than as I WAS.

I read somewhere recently that to dwell and brood on one's shortcomings, sins and faults is a SELFISH person, and I suppose that is what I have been. Too wrapped up in myself, my drama and sorrow, though truthfully I have always had time and feelings for others too, but I do see what the writer meant and hope I shall now STAY above it, keep as I am and not worry you any longer with my long wails!

Thank you, all of you, for all you have done to help me, for your loving and encouraging words. I am grateful.

I hope you will but I hope you will write your wails too and may they be small ones. (Sirod)

PS I have just roared with laughter, for this entry is about as Selfish as anything can be, nothing BUT self!

Again, I read recently that one can weep from the depth of the soul *not* because one is unhappy or miserable, but for what has been and is lost and cannot return. How true this is. Roberta

March 27, 1953

. . . Walter is supposed to be back at the end of April to see the bank, if he comes I don't know, and when he does it will be rather odd. However, he writes and cables and sent snaps to the children and writes to them very lovingly, and it is so odd how he writes to me, can't understand it, however, there it is.

Some time there will be another lawyers' conference to face but perhaps I shall be away and it must be postponed till May. Next week I am taking Guy and Suzanne to see their grandfather for two days (in Zurich). He wrote to me so lovingly and said whatever happens I am part of his life forever and his home is my home and not to forget it, so we shall make the effort and go down and see him. He will be delighted at the progress G and S have made all round, so hope it is a happy time, though sad too it will be, if you know how I mean! I DO feel it is my home and always shall, so let's hope the new bride won't ever visit it!

Now that I know Davos is to be my home for as long as I can foresee, I realised it is now or never to get together a home of my own. As I have said before now, I have just the dining room, bedroom and Suzanne's furniture here of my own, the rest belongs to the flat. Quite by chance I saw the new flats being built three minutes from here, they are utterly charming.

The rent is not much more than I pay here[*] and I would have the top floor. Marvellous views, two balconies, two bathrooms, all very, very modern of course and new, and to me, charming, lift, cellar for skis and bikes and so forth.

But unfurnished, of course. (Roberta)

I have to let the owners of this flat know at the end of the month if I want to leave or then stay for six more months. The new flats won't be ready until July at the earliest, so now it depends whether Walter can afford for me to have an unfurnished flat. I have written and wait a reply.

Of course one can weep to think I left all my Aga saucepans and lights and most curtains, and piano, and three divan beds behind! All would have been so useful here now, also brooms and hundreds of odd things, *all* kitchen stuff and cabinets, oh well, who could foresee? And the horrid thing is that had I brought ALL the things it would have cost no more than the sealed van which came anyhow!

The heart struck a sad note yesterday. I heard that all the cine films, which had been stored with a friend in England, waiting to see where we settled, have been shipped to South Africa. All those precious and lovely films, which Walter took with such care and affection of the children, our gardens (in colour), skiing holidays, the houses where we lived and the boys camping. He had filmed all the children since Chris was 40 hours old. Now no longer, indeed, NEVER shall I see them ever again. He had written stories for the children to act in and filmed them so beautifully, he had taken exquisite colour films, indeed all his films were artistic and NOT just bits and pieces of boring show off by the kids. Now I begin to wonder if all the photographs too have gone, but I think not, as my mother had them, so shall somehow bring them back here, though if W wants some of them he can, as after all, they belong to him.

Anyhow I feel happy about the new flat if it becomes mine, and when I saw it again today it had my feeling about it, and in a moment I could see how I would arrange it and how it would look when ready and finished. Just as I had that awful feeling of disaster around Saltwood, the *first* time that I went inside, so do I feel sunshine and rightness about the flat. However, we shall see, and after all I may have to go on living here and make the best of it.

Walter, I know, will not deny it to me *if* he can afford it, it depends . . .

Amelia, I am of course interested in you. We both stand on the same plane! Though your life seems active and busy and worldly compared to mine, but do you have any plans for getting a home together for yourself? I think you having to leave your own precious home the most awful part of all. To think of the things which you loved and cared for still standing there as you left them. This pain has been spared me of course, but I don't think I could rest or settle if I knew Saltwood stood as I had left it with Walter living there! Indeed I know I could not, and every time I went to bed I would think of my own room left behind at 'home'. I DID do this for two long years and HATED my furnished white hospital-like room. Hated it and kick and kick against the grain. For you it is worse, and after all you ARE living in furnished rooms and not with a stick of your own. I have the bliss to be surrounded by my own bedroom stuff which I adore and sleep in my own dear bed and am covered with my sheets and blankets. I do know how you must surely feel and deeply sympathise.

But in any case your own 'lot' seems so utterly unfair and UNJUST to me. I admire you deeply for picking up and going FORWARD and not being bitter, and oh the agony of not having the boys with you for Christmas as I read in the last magazine. This I could NOT bear, you are wonderful I think and again you have a more bitter past than I have, namely the fact that your children can go and see their father and home. Mine cannot. There will be no pull, no coming to see me after seeing father and HIS home and way of living. I think there is much to be thankful for what I am saved. I deeply know how lucky I am over this. It makes life 1,000 times easier not only for me but for them too. Only of course your boys are older and able to adjust themselves and understand. My two young ones could not. It would be Hell for me, anyhow, to live with them running to and fro in holidays . . .

Walter's pain lies within himself and it WILL be punishment and agony to see his children such short times in life. Only I know how much it means to him, but he has chosen it after all! So on we go, don't look back, take today and think of tomorrow! As another door shuts etc. etc.

Much love to all of you and longing for news of you ALL. Do ALL write, please! (Not to ME but for the mag. A fat mag is such bliss and joy to me, so take up the pens and WRITE!)

November 2, 1953

Finale à la Noel Coward

I must try and clarify my thoughts and not give any false impressions, hard to do but will try my best.

On October 25th I had a telephone call from Walter, who had arrived in Zurich! It was as natural as breathing to speak to him. I was neither nervous nor upset. We talked for some time and then arranged for me to go down on the Wednesday (this was

Sunday) and we would meet at the lawyers' for a conference.

This we did. Both Walter and I were nervous at first and shy with each other, but after a time all was easy and smooth going. We could talk naturally and normally. He looked at me and I at him, then I said, 'Why don't we call it off? You know as well as I do that we could make a go of it given the chance.' He hesitated and said, 'Yes, I think so too but where and how? Johannesburg is out of the question, the children could not be educated down there and now I have to go forward. I can't work over here nor go back to London. No, it won't work.' So on we went. It was hard going, for of course it all took place in German. Finally, feeling rather exhausted, we left the office at 5.30 p.m. and W and I went off to have tea together, quite normal and natural and we talked a lot. The odd thing is he does not appear to be very happy, but one can expect that after all! He looked awfully well and as charming as ever, those big brown eyes looking at me not coldly but with warmth and heart and feeling, all very odd. After that he drove me to the friends where I was staying. Before I got out of the car he put his arms round me and kissed me and said one or two things, ending, 'And please don't cry, I feel it as much as you do.'

The next day I collected Guy, who has spent a few days in Zurich with Vater and seeing Walter, and came back to Davos. W was entranced to find Guy so well and speaking such perfect Swiss-German. Guy was calm and quite undisturbed by seeing his father again. He enjoyed it but came back happily to return to school and asked no questions as to when he would see him again, or why and when did he have to go back to Jo'burg etc. etc. All normal and casual and happy . . .

I went down again on Sunday afternoon and W had got me a hotel. In the evening he had wanted to take me out to dinner, but had finally to dine with the head of the bank etc., so Nicki came along to see me later in the evening and we had a good laugh and chat about his German holiday . . . The next morning I was up early and ready to face the fray. For once I looked my *very* best! This DOES help one's morale.

The Conference began and went on and on. I lunched with my lawyer and W with his. Then we met again and it went on until nearly 7 p.m. I was done for at the end of it, worn out like a wet rag and so was Walter. I felt like a chair up for auction, and oh, discussing money is always grim. Finally we all came to terms and the contract was drawn up in rough. Meantime, Nicki took Sue back to Davos by train. It was too late for me to get the afternoon train and I could not face the last train home after all that, so Walter said go back to the hotel and we will dine together. We did, and both were rather weary, and instead of W being on top of the world having got what he wants, he was down and depressed. However, we had a lovely dinner and he took me back to the hotel and kissed me goodbye and thanked me.

Now the finale came this weekend. W phoned me and asked me if he could come up. I said, yes, why not? It will be the first and last time you see the flat or stay under my roof. He came at 5 p.m. on Saturday and of course I did my best to have the flat looking charming, which it did! I bought flowers and had a lovely chicken pie for supper which I had made etc., and table looking its best. Pride, pride, knowing SHE does nothing in the house, neither cooks, does flowers or anything. Yes, she makes curtains and her own clothes, but that's all, otherwise does not lift a finger except in the office! So we went to meet him at the station, and it was a perfect day, blue sky and snow everywhere. We have just had our first real fall, everywhere looked charming and I thought to myself, keep your SA, here is beauty and peace and reality.

I made up the bed for him and he took a bath and all was normal and atmosphere not strained or queer. On Sunday he fiddled with my radio and went for a walk with Sue. (I took him tea to bed where he was snuggled with Suzanne, just as they used to be.) Then he took us all out for lunch. Again, we were blessed with a perfect day, and I told him to look at it all and drink it in and remember it when he looked on bleak brown grass and flat countryside, and not to forget his own country . . .

In the afternoon we talked and read etc., and I got tea with a very nice homemade iced cake. Before 6 p.m. Walter packed and we had our last words together. He thanked me for everything and asked me to be brave etc. etc. We made our last money arrangements for the next few months, and then he was off after putting his arm round me and kissing me and stroking my hair. Whatever he felt inside him I shall never know, nor does he know my real feelings, or maybe we both do. Anyhow off he went. The next day he phoned me and almost wept but I was calm. He said he had written to me in the evening when he got back and that was that. In the evening he and a businessman from the bank went to Germany and he flies from there on Wednesday back to Johannesburg and his new life.

Yesterday I had a convention to sign and that has been sent down and the divorce begins. It won't be over till four or five months have passed, then he can re-marry and that is that. I feel no bitterness, no jealousy, but still a terrible pity for Walter and deep aching sorrow. For whether he wants to or not deep down, he has cooked his goose and there is no return. What happiness awaits him no one can say, but real happiness cannot be his in any way, and in a few years' time? This morning I had his letter, sad indeed to read, but to be put aside and taken with a grain of salt. I can do no more and have tried to do my best. I can go forward and am just the same after all this as I was when I wrote in CCC that I am free in spirit and happy inside me.

I KNOW I have now what it takes, no tears, no sentiment. Facts are facts and, unlike Amelia, oddly there is no wound to heal over. And I feel most strongly that to feel as I do, that is to say, certain *love*, *pity* and *charity* is so MUCH better for my well being than if I felt anger, hatred, bitterness towards Walter, but I don't, and my soul is not poisoned. And it is better to feel a kind of tender love and pity without remorse, than be het up and wild inside. I can't explain but I hope it may be understood. I know well it WILL be different when he is married and wants to see me and she is over here too etc. etc., but cross my bridges I won't. We both know full well that what is between us is for life, that nothing can break the truth of it, but our lives are now separated and I am here leading my own life, and he faces a new one leading his life, all the same?

But the years which pass don't bring one closer, that I know full well, nor the separation from his children won't bring them closer when they meet from time to time, but in spirit there is NO breaking that tie, it is life long. I do not believe that Time or Circumstances break it. However that is that and one way and another Noel Coward could not have invented anything more tricky! Would it have been easier if we had met and felt nothing for each other, just indifference and even hatred? I think not, even if it makes divorce even more wicked and stupid, but I have tried to explain why I think it is better thus.

So there it is. One good thing for me is this. I do NOT have to appear in court. It is all done with lawyers and then I am told it is over. I am thankful about this in every way possible. In Switzerland the procedure is different, in Zurich one has to appear but not in the Grison, so that is fine.

The law is FAR better too for a woman in this country. Not only do I get good alimony, but a lump cash sum down on divorce (this is to protect the wife in later life should the husband die), also three insurances, so as far as money is concerned one can't complain. The English law is far easier on the man, what security does a woman have? Just her alimony and that is all.

One flaw is that when I am divorced I must pay income tax, which is very high indeed. In Switzerland it depends *where you live* on how much you pay! And unfortunately Davos is the highest in Switzerland because it is a poor Canton! But by cutting down in many ways I can manage (I hope)! I am not clever with money and if I have got it, spend it, and don't think of the morrow. W has said that if he earns more in years to come he will pay me more, but that remains to be seen, though I know he MEANS it now. Still I feel secure and will become a good housewife and model manager from now on. Although my new allowance does not begin till the divorce, then the drop arrives, however my problems are so far, far less than Amelia, bless her.

Don't weep for me, don't be sad for me, don't pity me. Remember my blessings, my luck, my good health, and the happiness I have had.

Love to you all from a cheerful Roberta!

Cornelia, I DO thank you for your most wonderful suggestion of writing a lot for my sake. You are right to feel CCC means a very, very great deal to me, but I don't want any one to feel harassed and pressed by me to write when they have no urge. I would become a terrible burden. But it was a loving and kind idea and I do thank you warmly.

Thank you so much for this, Roberta. (Barnie)
Thank you for letting us share all this with you,
Roberta, says she with a <u>large</u> lump in her
throat. (Waveney)
You dear brave high soul! (Cornelia)

Roberta continued to live in Davos as a single mother, while Walter returned once or twice a year to visit the children. He supported Roberta financially so that she didn't need to take on paid employment. They remained in contact following their divorce, with Walter often using Roberta as a confidante. Roberta did not reciprocate this openness, and this is almost certainly because he was the love of her life. She never quite got over him or the divorce. Walter, who the family concludes was a bit of a 'womaniser', eventually married four times. He was widowed by his second wife, then remarried and divorced, and finally married a fourth time to a woman he stayed with until his death in 1981.

Roberta led a very social life with friends visiting frequently. She had a passion for skiing and spent much of her free time on the slopes. In 1957, she met Tony, an English army brigadier on holiday in Davos, and a year later moved to England to marry him. For a while they lived in Nottingham, where he was based, but once he retired in the early 1960s they settled on the Kent coast.

By that point, her son Chris, aged seventeen, had moved to South Africa, and Nick, the eldest, was working in Zurich. The younger two, Guy and Sue, stayed in Switzerland to finish their schooling but both later returned to England.

Roberta's decision to marry Tony may not have been the best choice. Tony had been a bachelor all his life and didn't quite know how to deal with a wife or children. Furthermore, he had been used to mess life and had developed a dependency on alcohol. Although a very generous man, he had a possessive personality and therefore discouraged Roberta from socialising. She had been an outgoing person but in this situation eventually became quite introverted. Things did improve in the later years of their marriage, partially because Tony became a teetotaller. After thirty years together, he died of heart failure in 1988.

In 1990, Roberta contracted pneumonia and her doctor told the family that she had six months to live. They moved her out of her country home to Surrey so that she could live near her youngest daughter, Sue. The move was beneficial and Roberta not only recovered but began to regain her confidence and build up outside friendships again. She lived for another seven years in an old people's home and was able to spend that time with her family, getting to know her six grandchildren better. She died in 1996 of complications from a chest infection, which resulted in heart failure.

Roberta wrote for the CCC from its inception until the last edition. It played an integral role in her adult life, particularly throughout her marriage to Tony, when she was isolated in the country. In later years, like many other CCC women, Roberta was unable to find a kindred spirit in the old people's home, and the women from the CCC remained her closest friends.

5

'Working' Mothers

room.

I have been warned quite often that it won't work! Too much noise will ensue - or else one will wake up the other. Nicholas is longing to have Christopher with him, though.

<u>Ad astra</u> — Wife & Career. problem(?)!

I honestly don't see how you can possibly argue with Rusticana on the above problem - for the following reasons.

There is simply <u>no</u> <u>need</u> for you to do anything in the house. & you have a nurse for your children. You <u>do</u> make your own cake & preserves. But you don't <u>have</u> to do these things. Your house would probably be perfectly alright with a capable housekeeper, to run it. & as you yourself stated, you rarely see your husband. So you see you have every right to feel that you would love to carry on your career. <u>But</u> you are one in a thousand.

Written by Roberta in 1938.

Many of the women in the CCC pursued careers at various stages in their lives. Teaching was the most common profession, and several members did supply work to supplement their family's wages. When the magazine had first formed, some of the women had been restricted from working due to the marriage bar. However, this was eventually removed around the time of the war and many of the mothers returned to teaching.

Different options became available once the CCC members' children were old enough to be more independent. Several of the women took either paid or unpaid jobs for their personal interest, while a handful worked to support their families. As they embarked upon their various career paths, particularly in the 1950s and 1960s, discussions about both the benefits enjoyed and hardships faced in the working world filled the pages of the magazine.

The articles written by Sirod, Angharad and Elektra illustrate the diversity of their occupations and the high level of commitment, determination and dedication with which so many of the women approached their work.

Sirod

Sirod's pseudonym was the reverse of her real name, Doris, a name she loathed.

To some extent she was in a minority in the CCC as she came from a science background. Evidently, when she was first writing in 1938, she felt the distinction.

I am very conscious that my views always appear late and out of date but some of us must be in such a place and I know I am not one to shine at writing. Words don't come to me as they obviously do to Ubique, faster than my pen can write, at least not very often. My brain is one-sided, I am a scientist, my vocabulary is meagre and my spelling doubtful . . . I know my articles cannot compare in length or ability with most of the others.

It is probably for this reason that Sirod wrote two or three drafts of her CCC articles before she sent them out to the group.

Born in 1903, Sirod spent a happy childhood in Evesham, Worcestershire. After boarding school, she attended Bedford College, London, in the early 1920s and graduated with an honours degree in physics. She was then hired by the General Electric Company and worked in infrared spectroscopy.

In London she met her future husband, Jack, who was employed by Hoover. The pair married in 1930 and moved to Cheltenham, where Jack worked in a furniture factory. He changed jobs several times over the next ten years and then spent the beginning of the war working as a clerk in the Admiralty. During this time, Sirod gave birth to their four children: Daphne, Gili, John and Bill in 1932, 1935, 1936 and 1944, respectively. At various stages, she supplemented the family's wages by supply teaching.

In 1945, Jack left the Admiralty due to health problems. Both he and Sirod had inherited money from their parents, so they decided to buy 'Woolcombe', a derelict dairy farm in Dorset. Owning a farm had been one of Jack's lifelong dreams, yet he was not a 'hands-on' type of man and preferred the administrative details that came with the business. This meant that Sirod was left to deal with much of the day-to-day labour on the farm. This became even more necessary as Jack's health declined, rendering him physically incapable of manual labour. Faced with this challenge, Sirod tackled the farm work head-on.

She wrote the following extract shortly after she and the rest of the family had moved to 'Woolcombe'.

1945

Woolcombe

There's one thing that is quite obvious. It's no good waiting for a wet day to write for CCC. I seem to be more busy on a wet day. So many outdoor jobs have to be done just the same wet or fine and these take so much longer when you are laden down with mackintoshes and wellingtons and so many people want their clothes or shoes dried and hot drinks have to be given indoors and more mud comes in and there are more people coming and going at the farmhouse, so that a quiet wet-day write-up for CCC is absolutely impossible.

Now if you are really coming with me in our farming venture, and most of you seem to be really interested, I think we shall have to go back a bit and describe the place more. The location is 8 miles inland on the Dorset hills, which are here both limestone and chalk . . . The place is definitely suited to dairy farming and can never be expected to grow good corn crops owing to its height and situation. On

the other hand it has an excellent name in the neighbourhood for good land. I should imagine that the
farm was at the height of its prosperity about
1850–60 . . .

Since those rich 1860s Woolcombe has gradually
fallen lower and lower. A succession of owners who
let the farm off on a lease, each one spending as little
on the property as possible . . . Then this war came
and the WAEC began to give orders for ploughing up
. . . the owner who had been quietly drawing up the
rent and doing *nothing* else for years and years
decided to sell . . . several people were after it and
each thought to be canny and bide his time and get it
cheap.

Then we stepped in, just a bit quicker than the local
people. We didn't mind that the cowsheds were condemned. We intended building anyway. We didn't
mind that the house was in such a bad state of repair
that we can only use three bedrooms. We have made
our plans to have these things done in time. But I still
mind that a place can be allowed to get so bad, that
milk for human consumption is allowed to be produced in a building where absolutely no water has
been available – ever . . .

We have had the springs analysed and the water is
quite OK and is an unfailing supply. The pipe to our
one tap in the house has been condemned, so for
drinking purposes we either have to fetch from the
source or boil the water from the tap. We already
have a Lister pump pushing water through a temporary pipe up to the cowsheds, and also to my vegetable garden and the poultry troughs. Meanwhile all
alterations to the house have to take a back place to
the renovating of cowsheds, bull house, cottages etc.

End of March

On March 21st I really meant to write an article on 'Our first year at Woolcombe' but March 21st was a dreadful day. Things went wrong on all sides and in addition the weather remained as wet as it had been for the last few weeks. A year ago we waited for our furniture to come in the sunshine in the garden and Bill slept on a camp bed in the garden. This year we looked out on to a garden still hardly recovered from winter snow and a vegetable garden in which absolutely nothing had been planted. The yard which should begin to look green this time of year is just one vista of mud. I just cannot describe the mud. It's not just mud, it's MUD. To go through any gateway is a work of art, not in order to keep one's boots clean but to prevent one's boots staying behind in the MUD. The tractor with rubber wheels has had to be discarded for putting out the hay and the spade lugs are churning up the mud a little more. The cattle are a picture of still motion for they hate moving in the MUD. I spend a great deal of my time drying off coats and outer garments and trying to get socks to come clean again. If I do insist on the men and children changing their boots at the outside door, the dogs come in all muddy and the beggars do not even respect my chair covers if no one is in the room to prevent them. The cats are too lazy to go out in the wet so the rooms have to be de-catted every day or so. Bill has had a cough, not enough to make him ill, but enough to keep him in, and so, as I have no one to leave him with, I have had to stay in too. The builder's men have forsaken us, leaving piles of gravel to get in the cows' feet and half the yard electrically fenced off waiting for them to finish concreting.

But March 21st was worse than all that. On that day

two heifers, one from each farm, aborted and another was likely. In case you don't know there is a disease called 'contagious abortion' which can run through your herd and cost you hundreds of pounds. It's not exactly dangerous but if a cow aborts she does not give milk and you have to keep her and lose cash until she calves in again. There is absolutely nothing you can do about it except vaccinate all the cattle with a mild dose of it at a convenient time, such as after calving, and then they do not get it again. Then it appeared that the new dairyman who is to replace Fred and Mrs W on the machines when they go over to Brooms next week (still for us) was no good and knew very little about the job and was unusually slow at learning and cannot even drive the lorry. [We bought Brooms (72 acres) – or rather the bank did – last November because it is only a field away and has a good house and small buildings, and we can use it to house people and to run our reactors to the TT test there. There is no other farmhouse for $\frac{3}{4}$ to 1 mile away.]

Our bank manager wrote to say we were over-drawn and our builders wrote for a little more 'on account', still not giving us any of the details we have asked for. When I remind you that it was pouring with rain and I seem to have been indoors with Billy for weeks, I think you will agree it was hardly a day to consider quietly the benefits or otherwise we have received in our year here.

Now a few days later we have had three days of sunshine and already the mud is drying up. Bill and I have been out picking primroses, I've spring-cleaned the kitchen and planted my broad beans. The abortion cases are considered by the vet to be chance slips caused by the weather and the mud, and he is taking a blood test to prove it. We have dealt with the builders and told them what we think of them and have been in touch with the bank manager, who is amenable. Jack, the new dairyman, has at last learnt the cows' names and can just about work the machines, though he still cannot back the lorry with safety . . . Our TT test was a pleasant surprise, only 10% reacted . . .

A year ago we moved in. What have we done in a year? We have built up a herd of about 100 cattle and have marketed about 20,000 gallons of milk. We have installed milking machines and taken water up the hill. We have trod on so many people's corns that we have electricity to the farm but not inside the buildings yet, and telephone poles on the site. We have a state-aided water scheme under construction. We have plans out for the renovation of one cottage and the farmhouse but do not intend to carry on with these just yet. We have acquired numerous dogs, cats, fowls, ducks and geese. The two latter seem especially successful here as there is so much water available.

Ourselves? Jack is definitely better for his year here. He has lost his tummy trouble and achieved a better figure. I suppose I am better on the whole although I have had trouble with my arms and carbuncles. I have put on about $\frac{1}{2}$ a stone to my intense annoyance! But I am never lonely now . . . I suppose on the whole our assets are greater than our losses. We have certainly learnt a lot.   *You are a brave, clever girl, Sirod. (Roberta)*

As the farm work was so labour intensive and the family was isolated from other families and children, Sirod decided to send her youngest son, Bill, to a weekly boarding school just before he turned three. Jack's health continued to deteriorate and he had a heart attack in 1948. Subsequently he suffered from angina, which meant that he was even less able to help with the farm. Sirod shouldered more responsibility, receiving assistance from various farmhands and often from her daughter Gili, who had developed a keen interest in farming. Throughout this time, Sirod continued to share her many adventures with the CCC women.

March 28, 1949

How nice it will be to read this in the middle of a heat wave. I wrote about snow in Jan. and read it in sunshine when we all thought spring had really come. The cows have been picking about in the grass almost refusing their hay and today we saw the first swallows right in the midst of one of the worst blizzards we have seen here . . . This has been the culmination of a difficult week. For those who do *Yes, worst March days in Essex* not live in like circumstances it is *for 80 odd years. (Ad Astra)* difficult to explain the effect of living in a tiny community, working in an isolated place. The routine work has the effect, after a while, of dulling the wish to go out. If no one comes to the rescue, to 'boot' you out, then you almost wallow in the martyrdom . . .

It's too far at the end of the winter for our staff to relish snow; somehow about Christmas one can put one's back into it. I went up the yard to find the tractor team waiting while Syd tried to nail up sacks to stop snow drifting in on the calves. I told him I would do that job, for they had to go about $1\frac{1}{2}$ miles for hay . . . Rhona and I cleared snow off cake bags in the barn, saw to calves and fowls . . . The wind was so strong and so full of snow in places we could barely stand. Then the tractor became stuck, *Here too. I never saw* and Alf came down for spades. So we *snow really horizontal* all went up and dug out in the teeth of *before. (Ad Astra)* the wind – it was hardly bearable . . .

Later I went to the top gate to find the meat ration and the newspapers, and so found that the lorry did get through. I helped Gili to rescue some of those annoying fowls and then I took the cows out to their hay, while the others were milking. In some places the snow is a thin layer on mud, which does not make easy walking. The cows were so hungry having been taken from the kale early because of its exposed position that they plodded on ahead of me. We walked all over the field and the hay which had been put out for them had disappeared – just blown away. They followed me all the way down again so trustingly but so hungrily. I sidetracked them into another field in the hope that they would not get into a corner and start hooking each other. When I came to enquire, the only sharp hay knife was still in 'Common'. Syd was moving the electric fence, a pretty foul job in that wind I guess. So Gili and I went up to see if there was any hay left in 'Nelson' (quaint field names we have). There is an unused rick in the corner of this field; the cows seemed so ravenous we managed to climb up and take the top off and carry some out to them – although we had no knife and no picks. We pulled and tugged at that hay, which had become almost as tight as silage through weight and time. We had a huge pile inside the rails with 40 bellowing cattle waiting the other side. Then she carried it to the rails and I ran out with a load, dropping it in piles as far apart as I could. This we repeated again and again. When dealing with cows you need to try and think like a cow I always say. So to put one or two piles of hay out would be asking for trouble, or to just throw it over the rails or into a corner would be as bad. It was still snowing and blowing a blizzard but in the shelter of the rick we were quite warm . . .

Next Day.

We are still snowed in, more than ever, the drifts being really high in many places, and I don't suppose we are the only ones in CCC to be suffering. It seems so strange to see the flowers in bloom standing up through the snow, the lanes here are in full flower with primroses. I've never walked in snow before and smelt the strong scent of gorse in full bloom. We spent about two hours this morning digging the Land Rover out of a drift. It was foolish to have charged that drift but it wasn't a very large one, no bigger than the one we had just ridden over successfully. We foolishly tried to remove snow from the wheels first, which meant that the body of the car just sank further into the snow which packed like ice. If you ever get stranded in a car in snow do remember to dig under the car first before you attempt to free the wheels. The wind was still very strong but not so bad as yesterday; nevertheless, Jack had gone to bed tonight with a very bad bronchial chest. I was hoping to get near enough to civilisation to be able to get someone to post this article. We shall have to push through somehow tomorrow with three days' milk so I'll post it in the hopes it gets to AA in time for 4a.

1953

The Mild Winter Breaks

I spoke too soon, didn't I? Here we are snowed-in for ordinary traffic, with a quarter of a mile of two to three foot drifts, level right across the road. We can take the tractor across the fields all right but today we've had no papers as the milk lorry has not been up to the stand to collect our milk. There's one sure thing, it won't go sour with standing! Luckily this time the snow did not take us unawares, but it did catch us just at the end of our grocery fortnight . . .

The main roads were slippery, so J would not trust me to drive, but clear, so Jack drove himself into Dorchester to get ours and the Dorringtons' groceries. Rather foolishly we decided to return on the Roman road and had it not been for an abandoned car round which we had to manoeuvre all would have been well. When we stepped out we were into a drift over our wellingtons. So there we were, nearly dusk, about a mile from habitation, and Jack with his groggy heart. I dared not stop to think but just dug and dug. The thing to do is to get a wheel or wheels down to the road to get a grip. Luckily Jack has not seemed any the worse for his journey.

Next day the snow was much deeper, as prophesied on the radio. While I was cooking the breakfast Perce came in to say that a cow was 'down'. To have a cow down makes your heart sink in anticipation. Cows so easily lose heart and if they cannot feel their feet they give up and die. One of the dodges we have used is to lift a sick cow on a sort of sling hung from a beam and to let her stand for a while each day on her feet.

But this one had dropped right across the walk up from the exit of the milking parlour. Luckily the others could be diverted and there she lay when I got up there, propped round with bundles of straw and partially covered with sacks. She seemed to have a fit and kicked and plunged, almost pushing herself over the edge into a sort of pit of nettles and rubbish now covered with snow. She was right in the wind and her nostrils were already frozen to the ground where she lay. I managed to get a sack under her face and to put a windbreak immediately in front of her breathing. Syd brought down some old horse shafting which we rigged with chains and straw and sacks as a stretcher. Perce brought the tractor along and a strong rope. The next job was to get her on to the stretcher. She had ceased her fits and now lay panting, a nearly dead eleven hundredweight of cow. With much heaving, grunting and pulling at last we got her on to the stretcher and tied her on. Then the tractor slowly hauled. We had to take the rope off and hitch it on at a different angle more than once as she was right down a steep pathway and the pulling had to be done all from the top. In any case we could hardly stand ourselves it was so slippery and the east wind blew and blew. At last we got her to the door of the loose box. Then she had to be pushed off the stretcher which was wider than the door and pushed and pulled into the house. At last, when she was in and propped up with more straw, she was quite perky.

The afternoon was spent haying up in case it turned worse tomorrow and fixing up a temporary water supply from the stream. I walked out to break the ice again for the outlying heifers . . .

There is one really nice thing about snowy cold weather: you can appreciate the fireside in the evenings. Always assuming there are no sick animals to tend . . .

Sirod and Jack decided to sell the farm shortly after this, in 1953, as they were losing money and it was becoming too much work for Sirod. She would later tell her family that the farm years were the best of her life. The family moved to Dorchester, where Sirod worked as a supply teacher in secondary schools, giving English as a second language and art classes. She also had a passion for gardening and flower arranging, so in the late 1940s she and her friend Mary Pope started giving demonstrations. They formed a club in Dorset, which was the model for other floral clubs in the country. In 1953, Sirod and Mary toured Yorkshire, Lancashire and the surrounding area for two weeks, demonstrating floral arranging. Eventually, there were enough clubs to merit establishing the National Association of Flower Arrangement Societies (NAFAS). Mary became president and Sirod held a position on the committee, later also serving as president. Sirod would often judge floral competitions and she edited the Flower Arranger *magazine produced by the association.*

After Jack died from heart problems in 1960, Sirod moved to Weymouth because she always had a love of the sea. She became more involved with NAFAS by giving lectures, judging competitions and editing the association's journal. She also published books on flowers and used her lifelong skills as an artist to do the accompanying illustrations.

In the 1970s, she volunteered for the Samaritans, a twenty-four-hour helpline for people in need of emotional support. She did this well into her eighties. When she was not busy flower arranging, writing books and volunteering, she spent time with her eight grandchildren, who were living in various parts of England.

Angharad

Angharad is the name of a large park in the Welsh town of Pontypridd, where the CCC's Angharad was living when she became a member and chose her nom de plume. One of the last to join the magazine in the early 1950s, Angharad was invited after Ad Astra read some of her contributions to the puzzle competition in the New Statesman.

Born on November 7, 1920, Angharad grew up as an only child in a working-class family living in Hopkinstown, Wales. Hopkinstown was a coal-mining community, and her father worked in the industry. In 1939, she left Wales to read English language and literature at Lady Margaret Hall, Oxford. Following the completion of her degree in 1942, she began teaching in adult education in Norfolk for the Workers' Educational Association. She spent most of her holidays at home with her family in Wales and it was there that she met her future husband, Morien, who, by coincidence, was also moving to Norfolk. His health had deteriorated after internment in a concentration camp during the Spanish Civil War, and as a result he spent the Second World War teaching. In 1945, the pair married and moved to Burnley, in Lancashire, where Angharad gave birth to their first son, Dylan, in 1946, and their second son, Gareth, in 1949. After Gareth was born, the couple decided to move back to Wales to be closer to their family. As they had little money, they were unable to get a mortgage on a home. They therefore spent the next few years in a variety of homes in Radnorshire, with Morien commuting to his teaching job in Abertillery in Monmouthshire.

In 1953, the family moved to Aberdare in Glamorgan.

Angharad wanted to have a third child, but Morien didn't think that they could afford another one. Undeterred, she convinced her husband that if she could earn a total of £1,000 by working at home, they would then try for a third. As she had already earned some money for the family by writing stories for women's magazines, Angharad thought that she could raise the funds through other forms of writing. She decided to try her hand at play writing for television and wrote a play called Mirror Mirror, *which she was able to sell to the BBC. Angharad watched the BBC production of her play at a friend's house because it aired before she and Morien could afford their own television. After* Mirror Mirror *she wrote a second play called* The Tamer Tamed, *a supposed sequel to* The Taming of the Shrew.

During this time Angharad regularly updated the women of the CCC on her progress towards her goal to earn the £1,000, an endeavour that would be the start of a career that would last the rest of her working life.

1955

From ancestry to the hope of progeny. When I mentioned this in one issue, two of you scribbled helpful hints to me, viz. 'Ever thought of tempting him?' and 'Or cheating him?'

Neither of these is any good to me. You see, in our ménage, the control of this side of things has never been left to the distaff side. Believe it or not, to the best of belief and knowledge I have never even *beheld* a 'wife's best friend' or whatever you call it, still less learned how to manipulate one. I think this was first because he thought I would be inefficient and later because he found I was recklessly philo-progenitive and quite capable of filling his house with noisy pledges of my affection while blandly protesting every time that I didn't know the gun was loaded . . .

However, he now has ten years' expertise in keeping us both very happy and contented with no risk. (Please don't anyone scribble questions on *this* one, as I am already blushing hotly). Once he used to rely partly on dates, and then I could cheat a bit, and did, hence Gareth – so now he doesn't. I can tempt him easily enough, but he just joyfully succumbs, and a good (but alas! unproductive) time is had by all.

No need to blush here. (Waveney)

No, I must just earn that thousand, then he won't go back on his word. I'll keep you in touch with the score. Actually I have just made the first century – like this.

£25 I have saved from the TV play in the spring, £25 came very belatedly (luckily – otherwise it would have gone on holidays) from

Gosh! In CCC we don't blush – you'll come to it sister! As only one has 'been allowed' does he not like children at all? Such an impossible 'condition' as £1,000 would prohibit most 3rd children if we're a good x-section – I presume he thinks it's an impossible target. (Robina)

the WEA for a course last winter, and I've just had a contract for £56 for *The Tamer Tamed*, the play Welsh Regional is broadcasting next month. £6 to give away, £50 to put away = £100.

Angharad's first play, Mirror Mirror, *received a 'stinking review' from well-known British critic Philip Hope Wallace, who, according to Angharad, wrote that 'it was the silliest play that had ever been seen on television'. So, she explained, 'I spit on my hands and thought, it wasn't all that bad and I can do better than that'. It was in this spirit that she wrote both* The Tamer Tamed *and then* Wilde West. *Though* The Tamer Tamed *was written first,* Wilde West *was the first to be produced and was very well received. Here she wrote to the women about the success of the play and about her new part-time teaching job.*

The Eminent and I

I apologise for the unorthodox format of this – I am writing in the train and hoping I'll be able to stick it on to some CCC-size paper when I get home, otherwise I despair of getting my exciting news in, in time for 10a.

First, I've started teaching, on the 19th. It's in the Aberdare College of Further Education, a wonderful new futuristic building, and the whole organisation is near chaos. The Principal was found embezzling several hundreds of the petty cash, the PT woman is having a baby (legitimately, but inconveniently) – and has quit. They can't appoint a new Head while the old one's *sub judice*, and they have piled on to me twice the work I wanted, and I have given in partly because things are so parlous there and partly because I'm paid by the hour! I take History, Geography, Arithmetic, some English called 'Comprehension' (all new to me and needing a lot of preparation) and Social Studies. All for examination purposes (the RSA exam, a lower standard than School Cert.) and in History I have to cover a 2-year course in 1 year, in spite of having no predecessor in this subject, no text books and up to date no exercise books! It is gruelling. I went to bed one night with a paper-wrapped toffee and was asleep before I could unwrap it!

Good thing too! Frightfully bad for your teeth. (Ad Astra) Enough of that.

Last Saturday morning I received a telegram, a double-page one, saying, 'Delighted to inform you *Wilde West* has won Class A . . .' being the prize of £75 offered by the Cheltenham Festival of Contemporary Literature for a 60-minute TV play. The telegram asked me if I could attend a Press Conference in London on Tuesday, reply paid 3/-, and I said yes . . .

Monday morning I received a whopping great invitation card, requesting the pleasure of my company at 4 St James's Square, SW1 (in the Great Drawing Room, by kind permission of the Arts Council) – to meet the prize-winners and judges of the TV Play Competition, the Speakers at this year's festival and some of the Speakers at past festivals. This star-studded cast included E. Arnot Robinson, Sir Compton Mackenzie, Richard Church, L. A. G. Strong, H. E. Bates, Eric Linklater, Marghanita Laski, Nancy Spain, Rupert Hart-Davies, Robert Henriques, old Uncle Gil Harding and all.

My agent sent a telegram saying, 'Will meet you Paddington carrying Festival leaflet wire time of arrival.' I went to school Monday, asked and obtained leave of absence (no one there has any frees, but they obtained the services of a married woman teacher nearby who used to teach there but couldn't take it – but was willing to for 2 days).

I identified my agent all right – I had imagined him to be aged, and for no reason that I can conceive, Jewish. He was probably around 40, with long grey pinstriped legs and a large rangy mouth, and ex-Cambridge, married to a Welsh wife. He drove me to their Chelsea offices where the head of the firm lived in a flat above; and there in a drawing room the size of a small cinema and a view across the river of the Festival Gardens I had tea, relaxed . . . Johnson (the agent) then drove me to St James's Square and, as nobody after all was collecting the whopping great invitation cards, came in too and mingled with the great. All the VIPs of TV were there, both BBC and commercial – Norman Collins and so on. The other winners of the 2 £50 prizes were a nice lad from Cardiff (up the Welsh, 2 out of 3!) still doing Nat. Service in the RAF, and a banker from Putney. We were bandied around a lot between Press people and TV people, and had no more than a handshake with most of the writers. Robert Henriques announced the prizes, and seemed to find it very amusing and ironical that I had seen only one TV play, and that my own. The Cheltenham photographer for the local newspaper, with an eye for where the real news value lay, photographed us with Gilbert Harding. (If I can get a copy of that, as far as Aberdare is concerned I shall have arrived!) After that we talked to him. He was very friendly and downright and 'in character', very much fatter than I expected him to be, tired and sweating and drinking and eating olives and obligingly putting on his act. It must be very exhausting for him having to live up to that 'persona' all the time. I would judge he was a genuinely nice character anyway. He informed me with his customary dogmatism that I was a very clever young woman – a very nice young woman, too (with which I felt no inclination to disagree!) – and told some stories about the arbitrary treatment sometimes received by playscripts of unknown writers in the BBC.

The reporter from *The Stage* had an American accent and bet me dollars to peanuts I'd be living in London within 5 years. But I won't. I stayed the night with the Johnsons – they have 2 children and live near Hampstead Heath, and I slept not a wink from excitement. So I'll stop here, and try to sleep now.

Congratulations! Let us have all the news. (Sirod)
This is SPLENDID, Angharad. Very many congratulations! (Yonire)
Do tell us more – jolly good luck. (Robina)
Hearty congratulations. You are clever! (Janna)
Congratulations! All this sounds desperately exciting and LIFE AS IT SHOULD BE LIVED to a country clod like me. (Accidia)

Angharad continued writing television screenplays and established herself in the business. At the same time, she had reached her goal and earned the money to have her third child. After trying unsuccessfully to become pregnant, she and Morien decided to adopt. The process took quite some time and in the end it was Elektra, through her work in London hospitals, who was able to connect them with a child up for adoption. So, in 1960, Angharad and Morien adopted their long-awaited third son, Huw.

Angharad's career blossomed and the BBC offered her a contract to do four plays a year. She also became involved in writing various scripts for shows such as the very popular Dr Finlay's Casebook. Morien continued teaching and helped Angharad by typing up all of her plays.

In 1963, Angharad wrote a play for the stage, Licence to Murder. It made its debut at the Vaudeville Theatre in the West End but was not well received and only had a short run. In 1965, she decided to try her hand again and wrote a second stage play. Her inspiration came from a difficult incident that occurred the year before when her middle son, Gareth, had run away for seven weeks. She drew upon this experience to write the piece. In the following correspondence, she had just completed the play and was eagerly waiting to hear how it was received.

1965

As for the stage play, I wrote it partly with my heart's blood (it's about a mother whose teenage child decides to run away) and rewrote it desanguinised so that it would be entertaining but still, I hope, have some sort of relevance to something or other. Somebody sent Ross of *The New Yorker* a cartoon of fencers, and the one who'd sliced the other's head off was saying, 'Touché,' but Ross thought it horribly gory and wouldn't accept it until the fencers had been redrawn

by Thurber because 'Thurber's people don't bleed.' I
felt like Ross. The bloody version was releasing to
write but artistically offensive to me; the second gave
me a good deal of pleasure. Unfortunately, giving
myself pleasure won't buy baby a new bonnet, as they
say, and Morien when he read the play pronounced it
hopeless, boring, it 'never gets off the ground', the
characters are 'dull', it's dramatically far inferior to
this *Finlay* I turned out in a 3-week spurt and he
regards me as having frittered away half a year in an
infatuated haze of self-indulgent nonsense; and when I
told him I'd like Harvey Unna's opinion he typed it
out, with some reluctance, and was so convinced
Harvey would never show it to anybody, but would
ask for it to be scrapped or completely rewritten, that
he only made one copy of the thing, whereas he usually goes to the opposite extreme and makes about
six.

Harvey thinks it's good and has sent it to Michael
Codron, whose verdict we now await. It's only got
four characters and one set so it needn't be frightfully
expensive to put on. *I* think it's good too, and I
worked *very hard* on it. It doesn't aim very high but I
think it gets pretty close to what it does aim at, so
people might be kind to it if it ever sees the light.
Happy New Year everybody. Angharad.

Good Luck, Angharad!
(Ad Astra)

1966

Love from Liz, and Other Matters

Today (January 20th) I broke, with a bang, my New
Year's resolution about smoking, being now on my
13th day today; I'll try and salvage something from
the wreck by clinging on at least a bit longer to my
other resolution to shift up from the bottom of the
CCC League table . . .

Since Christmas – (appalled by the state of the

budget, I had a sleepless night on December 25th and cashed in on it by starting a new TV script at 2 a.m.!) I have written and sold one *Finlay* (about beer and funerals) and today completed the first draft of another (about school lavatories). I haven't actually received a penny on either yet, but at least I know it's on the way . . .

As for the stage play: Harvey sent it to Michael Codron, who said no. He 'liked it, but not enough'. Well written, he said, but he'd have liked more of a story. He suggested offering it to John Counsell, head of a respected theatrical family who runs the Theatre Royal, Windsor. And John Counsell said Yes! Its latest title is *Love from Liz*.

I'm not very well up in theatre background and the thing was described to me as 'Windsor Repertory.' I imagined a struggling little group willing to give the thing a tryout in a small way and when they asked me for casting suggestions (this was all by phone, I haven't *seen* anybody about it yet) I tried to think up names of struggling players who'd had one or two TV parts. I nearly went through the ceiling when Harvey said casually that John Counsell was 'trying to get Hayley Mills to play the daughter'! As it turned out, Hayley was not available, but I *remain* pretty stunned. It seems they're aiming high because it is a theatre which sometimes gets transfers straight into the West End and if they could get names with a pull, they think this might happen. On the other hand, nothing might happen at *all*. Because it is scheduled to come off, if it comes off at all, on March 4th for a fortnight. Unless they can cast it satisfactorily pretty quickly they'll drop it altogether, because John Counsell is going to Hong Kong with his wife and family to do some shows there for the British Council and he wants to get it all set up before he leaves or else call it off.

But they're seeing people tomorrow for auditions and have had copies of the play made and Harvey sounds pretty confident. So I'm keeping my fingers crossed. I'm very bucked that it was taken (provisionally) by the second person who read it . . . I can't really take in or believe that this can really be happening as simply and smoothly as it seems to be happening, and that in 5 or 6 weeks' time I may be going to a first night again. *Oh, I do hope so. Good luck. (Ad Astra)*

As it turns out, the Theatre Royal in Windsor did produce Love from Liz *that spring. Here Angharad wrote about the first night of the production. Her son Dylan, studying at Oxford by this time, went to Windsor to join her.*

I went to Windsor on Monday for the first night of *Love from Liz*. I had two other appointments to keep, with Dylan and his girl Trudi in the foyer of the theatre at 4.30 (I was looking forward immensely to this because I've never met her and, though he's quite uninhibited about how much he loves her, he's not very graphic at describing her) and with a woman called Joan Llewellyn Owen, who's writing a commissioned careers book about being a writer, and we were to meet at Paddington on Tuesday morning to save a special trip.

I had three seats booked but I never thought about where to sleep until Sunday, when I rang up in succession all the Windsor hotels given in the AA handbook, and then all the Reading hotels given in the AA handbook, and none of them could give me a room for Monday night . . . When I got to Windsor, half an hour before I was to meet Dylan, I thought if I couldn't find a place for me that night, I'd try to book a double room for Saturday (Morien's coming with me on Saturday), so I dashed into the nearest hotel, the

White Hart, and yes, they had a double room for Saturday and whoopee! they now, through a last-minute cancellation, had a single room for tonight! So I just had time to grab it, and dump my weekend case, and wash and walk to the theatre and collect the three tickets and wait. Dylan was ten minutes late and alone, because alas! Trudi had the flu and couldn't make it. Still it was lovely to see him after nearly a whole term and we went back to my (very plushy) hotel and had tea and talked, which kept the butterflies away very successfully until about half past six. And then here it comes again, that feeling, why in God's name do I do these things? Those poor players, giving their all and it's a dreary play and 'never gets off the ground', and Dylan will have to be polite and comforting and thank Heaven Trudi won't be there having to be polite too, and what a fool I was to quote Thurber in the pro-gramme note, because if the audience reads that they'll think I'm claiming to be funny, and parts of it are very serious, and I must have been *mad* to try to mix that with bits of comedy, because trying to do two things at once was *exactly* what made the last play turn out such a disaster, so why will I never learn?

Anyway, nothing would stop the hands of the clock going round, so I had to get up and go, and we got there early (because I was nervous and couldn't stay in the hotel any longer), and I thought – They won't have to worry about the audience being sticky, because nobody's going to come anyway. But they did of course. And Harvey Unna, and wife and partner and secretary came and sat next to us. Harvey hadn't been to a rehearsal because he'd been very busy with the transfer to the West End of *The Match Girls*, so he asked me how it was going to be and I said I didn't know. And the little live orchestra played 'God Save the Queen' and the curtain went up.

I couldn't believe it. Monday night or not, that *marvellous* audience! They laughed and laughed. Quite a lot of lines never got heard at all because they were still laughing at the last one, and nobody'd been rehearsing with 'pause for laugh' in their minds because nobody really thought it would happen like that. And yet they shut up like lambs for the dramatic bits. Dylan, bless him, laughed like a drain, and at the end just had time to say 'Yes – good – fine!' before dashing off to catch the train back to Oxford, and afterwards all the cast were cock-a-hoop and Harvey was galvanised into listing managers he would contact and I felt very happy. So – so far, so good!

Oh Congratulations. I thought of you on
first night. May it do very well. (Ad Astra)

Although initially well received, Love from Liz *didn't make it as far as the West End and it was the last stage play that Angharad wrote. After this she continued with various writing projects and scripts for television, such as more episodes for* Dr Finlay's Casebook. *A few years later, Angharad started writing her first book. In her spare time she had been reading books like* The Naked Ape *by Desmond Morris, published in 1967, which discussed the savanna hypothesis of human evolution. Roughly summarised, the savanna theory stated that it was in the open plains of Africa that humans evolved into bipeds and shed their body hair. Angharad found that these books and theories were 'too male centred'. She wanted to read a book that was about 'how the females evolved instead of the males' and, after she realised she couldn't find one, she decided to write it herself.*

In 1972, she published The Descent of Woman, *refuting the idea that the distinguishing features of females evolved in order to please and serve males. Angharad argued, rather, that the features of the female 'evolved*

*in her own interests and those of her child'. The book
was an international success, heralded for its feminist
perspective, and she lectured throughout the US and the
UK. However, her work was harshly received by the
anthropological community, and in the research field
she was largely dismissed as a non-scientist and pop-
ulist.*

After publishing The Descent of Woman, *Angharad
returned to screenplays, feeling that she had exhausted
the topic. She went on to receive two Writers' Guild
Awards (the precursors to the BAFTAs), one for Best
Serial in 1978 and one for Best Drama Serial in 1980.
By this time, she and Morien had moved to Mountain
Ash in Glamorgan, with Morien teaching in nearby
Pontypridd until he retired.*

*For the next ten years Angharad continued to write
for television, until an interested fan of* The Descent of
Woman *began corresponding with her about the
'aquatic-ape hypothesis', something that Angharad had
touched upon in her book. Her fan's interest spurred
her on to further research into this theory, which suggested that the ancestors of humans went through a
period of time living in a semi-aquatic setting. It proposed that this semi-aquatic phase accounted for many
human characteristics that are not observed in other
primates, such as apes. The idea originated with a man
named Alister Hardy, a well-established marine biologist and Professor of Zoology. However, he had been
hesitant to publicise it, fearing a backlash from his col-
leagues. Angharad developed his theory and went on to
publish* The Aquatic Ape *(1982),* The Scars of
Evolution *(1990),* The Descent of the Child *(1994) and*
The Aquatic Ape Hypothesis *(1997).*

*After her second book, she gave up writing television
plays and focused solely on her evolutionary research.
Her work was mostly ignored or refuted by the anthro-*

pological community until very recently. In 1995, Phillip Tobias, a well-respected South African anthropologist, admitted after gradual accumulation of evidence that the first hominids had in all likelihood lived in shaded and well-watered environments. This meant the savanna theory had been disproved and lent credence to the aquatic-ape theory.

In 2003, Angharad received a Lifetime Achievement award from BAFTA Cymru (Wales). She is now eighty-five years old and her sixth book, Pinker's List, *was published in 2005. In it, she criticises Steven Pinker's book* The Blank Slate *and his theories on human nature and politics. She writes a column every Friday for Welsh newspaper the* Western Mail. *Angharad is wonderfully bright, with a quick wit and a good sense of humour. Quiet but warm, she is a strong and determined woman who is happiest when she is writing, and she will probably continue to do so for years to come.*

Elektra

Born on March 3, 1906, Elektra grew up mainly in North London, the eldest of three children in an Orthodox Jewish family. Her father had immigrated from a poverty-stricken life in Poland and established a successful clothing business. He and Elektra had a particularly close relationship and he wanted her to join him in the family business when she grew up. Therefore, at the age of seventeen, she spent a year studying business at Regent Street Polytechnic.

In 1924, she joined her father's business and continued working with him for the next ten years. Elektra often helped her father show and model clothes to UK buyers, and would travel with him to Europe to gather ideas from the latest collections. During this time she attended St John's Wood Art School so that she could develop her skill as a sketch artist to help with designs and copies.

It was in honour of this close relationship with her father that she chose her CCC name, as she explained:

The Elektra complex – I was madly in love with my father and I didn't get on with my mother, so it was a classical story, you see . . . And because I knew how to handle my father, I became his best friend and worked with him and I was his right-hand man.

At the age of twenty-four, after one failed engagement, Elektra met and married Mark, a thirty-year-old accountant from a Jewish family. She had always been a voracious reader, and at an early age had rejected Judaism and become an ardent socialist. Mark shared Elektra's socialist principles and supported her desire to become actively involved in many of the socialist organisations that were forming in the 1930s. A lifelong mem-

ber of the Labour Party, she also joined the Workers' Educational Association, the Left Book Club and the Fabian Society. She became a member of the Progressive League, which was largely run by Bertrand and Dora Russell, Aldous and Julian Huxley, and C. E. M. Joad, to name but a few.

In 1933, she gave birth to her first son, Lawrence, and then had her second son, Michael, in 1936. Meanwhile, Mark's career was flourishing and he helped to establish the accounting firm Hacker, Rubens and Co. With the outbreak of the Second World War, Elektra and the children left London to live in a 'safer' location, while Mark remained at home and commuted to be with the family. Elektra and the boys first stayed in Brighton, then Cranleigh in Surrey, and on to Trefnant in North Wales. Finally, they settled in Letchworth, where they stayed for the duration of the war and several years afterwards. Here Elektra worked for the Women's Voluntary Service (WVS), and Mark was active as a sergeant in the Home Guard, often responsible for fire-watching in London.

After the war, Elektra began volunteering as a counsellor for the Marriage Guidance movement (MG). In 1951, she and Mark moved back to London, where they remained for the rest of their lives. Here she continued with her MG work and also became involved with the Children's Committee of London County Council, which aimed to improve the dire conditions children were subjected to in foster homes.

Through Marriage Guidance, Elektra lectured all over the country to various youth groups, schools and communities about relationships. She became Chairman of the Education Committee for National MG. In 1956, she wrote Telling the Teenagers, a book addressed to teachers, youth leaders and social workers explaining how to discuss sex, sexuality, love and relationships with *teenagers. Soon after, she adapted the book to speak directly to adolescents. This new version,* The Opposite Sex, *sold about a quarter of a million copies. The book was one of the first of its kind and Elektra was inundated with requests to give more lectures.*

Elektra wrote to the CCC in 1956 about one of the many times she was interviewed in her capacity as a Marriage Guidance Counsellor.

1956

Yesterday I went to Lime Grove to appear on TV. Did any of you see me? *Yes indeed! (Ad Astra)*

What a fuss and palaver for 2 speeches of precisely one minute each. The programme was in *Panorama*. Four of us and a chairman were to be discussing the recommendations in the Royal Commission's report on Marriage and Divorce. I had a phone call on the Thursday, about 6 p.m., I had just washed my hair and was drying it, a Miss Dove, she had my name from Colin Morris (a Marriage Counsellor who writes wonderful documentaries, *Strike*[*] and *The Unloved*[**] and *Woman Alone* etc.).

[*]*This was marvellous. (Ad Astra)*
[**]*This I thought less successful. (Ad Astra)*

We chatted about the MGC and arranged that I should come to Lime Grove at 5.15 p.m.

The studios are dreary and tumble down and depressing, so very different from Broadcasting House. Where did you go, Angharad? I did not see any flowers anywhere. The studio was a weird and nightmarish place. The cosy rooms you see on your TV screen are show screens with dummy windows, views of London and bookcases. In one corner was Richard Dimbleby, in another a Coster with his adorable pony 'Dolly' and his painted barrow. In another corner Lowry and two of his Manchester paintings, he's a darlin' man, the genuine article, a real primitive, nothing phoney at all.

He was mad at all the time wasted and never a decent cup of tea!

All over the Studio were great prehistoric beasts with enormous heads on long necks which went up and down in terrifying swoops. Riding on the neck were fancy camera men, and technicians rode behind on the beasts' hind legs! Strong batteries of light, rows of TV screens up in little compartments suspended high on the walls where more technicians or producers called instructions matily to Christian names.

Our party consisted of a delightful chairman Robert Mackenzie, really a Sociology lecturer from LSE who is often on TV, Robert Pollard of the Marriage Law Reform Society and Frank Dawtry of the Probation Service, Joe Brayshaw Secretary of the National MGC and myself. We were told that Pollard and Dawtry would attack MG and we were to be prepared to defend. We (Joe B and I) had a preliminary discussion with a producer, who asked us what points we'd like to make if we got the chance. Then we had to have a spirited conversation as a rehearsal, but were told *not* to discuss the 'topic' we should really be discussing at 8.30. Three of the Camera beasts are trained on you at close quarters, you must not look at them, or at any of the TV screens, tho' you are dying to see what you look like! The three pictures are scrutinised and the best selected by 'Vision Mixers' and assembled in split-seconds for transmission.

Apparently our voices and postures were OK and we had to sit silent while the Artist was interviewed and his paintings shewn. Then the segue in on houses, partly film and partly the Coster and his Dolly, then film, of Pepe making Paella. *Lovely Stuff! I've had it and made by Pepe himself. (Ad Astra)*

Then we were led to the hospitality room, through the cafeteria for staff only, Gin and Whiskey were offered, Coster and

Lowry asked for tea, and got it. Dainty plates of salad appeared, scorned by Coster and Mr Lowry!

I had to eat quickly and find the basement with the help of a friendly guide for the make-up department. The men were all made up in an anteroom on the studio. The purpose of male make-up is to lessen the hollows round the eyes and brows are well powdered as the heat of the lights would otherwise produce unbecoming beads of sweat!

A charming young girl had me sit back in a chair like a dentist's for half an hour while she applied brownish grease paint, blue eye shadow, white to hide the bags under my eyes, plenty of mascara and powder, lipstick I was told to apply myself.

You looked lovely.
(Ad Astra)

Then back to the Studio to take our places for the discussion. Mackenzie whispered that Joe was to start off and could make a statement about what MGC tried to do, then Pollard would attack and I was to reply. Then it would be Dawtry's turn, then see what happened, and only 8 minutes for the lot!

I tried to relax and remember not to look at the 'monitor' TV screen or the frightening beasts. My heart was thumping so madly I felt it must be visible!

It was all over so quickly, I hardly realised that I had spoken twice and of course had not been able to think fast enough, and all I knew was that I had not made one of the points I had been so eager to express! We had again to remain silent and tried to tiptoe our escape. This lay through another studio where J. B. Priestley was being filmed for his book talks, so we had to return to our studio till the end of the programme. Goodbye to the performers, producers, technicians, kind words of reassurance and encouragement, 'Dolly', easily the most assured, composed and confident of all the performers, calmly emptying her bowels on the studio floor at the height of Dimbleby's patter. Viewers did not see this part of the show, nor the neat little man armed with brush and pan and sawdust!

On the way out, a girl at the desk called 'Miss Rose Hacker'. Amazed, I nearly said, 'Present!' and she gave me a slip of paper with name and telephone number. 'Please phone at your convenience. It is a viewer.' The viewer proved to be a lady in distress and I was able to offer her an appointment with a counsellor in her district. Home in the rain, windscreen wiper packed up, mentally kicking myself for opportunities missed, speeches not made, regretting half-remembered phrases. Home to an admiring family, full of sweet praise, cup of chocolate and bed, phone calls from friends, awake at 4.30 a.m., unable to sleep again for wishing I had said this, that, the other!

Mark joined me in the kitchen for a cuppa at 6 a.m.!

Now it is Mother's day and she has heard all about it. Have to act as chauffeur for Mark because of his plastered leg.

Day of Glamour over. Back to earth with a bump. Flat after all the excitement. Quite an experience.

I wish I could have seen you – I'm sure you looked lovely and that you will be around again and then you can get over what you missed. (Sirod)
I saw the programme, I thought you looked lovely and sounded perfectly self-possessed, it only goes to show! and what a nice voice you have. The maddening thing is, I never read the second half of the list on the first page, and didn't know till <u>now</u> that Mrs Rose Hacker was Elektra! (Angharad)
How I'd loved to have seen you! (Michaelmas)
Damn! No TV. (Yonire)

Elektra was also actively involved with the London hospital system and the National Association for Mental Health, which would later become MIND. One of her most time-consuming commitments was her voluntary work at Friern Mental Hospital and the smaller therapeutic community hospital Halliwick, which was opened on the Friern grounds. For over thirty years, Elektra worked to improve the patients' quality of life.

In the late 1960s, Elektra shifted her attention to mental health in her local area, Camden. Along with her husband and a few friends, she worked to establish the Camden Association for Mental Health. Through the association, she and Mark helped to turn derelict houses, donated by the council, into liveable homes for patients who had been discharged from mental hospitals and were trying to reintegrate into the community.

Due to mandatory retirement at the age of sixty-five, Elektra 'officially' retired from Marriage Guidance in 1971. However, although she was no longer counselling, she was still busy with lecturing and teaching. She wrote the following article when she was en route to Grantham to lecture to a group of new recruits in the WRAF about sexuality and relationships.

1972

Diary of a Madwoman

This summer was to be one of leisure. I had dreamed of lying in the garden in the sun reading and re-reading loved books, or listening to music, or just spending time with beloved friends, alas getting fewer as we grow old.

What compels me to do the opposite to what I plan? Restlessness, conscience or just plain Schizophrenia?

Having retired from Marriage Guidance I seem to be doing a Nellie Melba, repeated farewell performances, although no longer counselling. I still travel about giving occasional lectures and I am starting one more 'final' series of group discussions for counsellors in training.

Having retired from Friern-Halliwick hospitals I am working almost every day for the Camden Association for Mental Health, especially on the wearing and frustrating task of negotiating with the gas, electricity, builders, council departments, volunteers, furniture donors and removers etc. etc.

Having decided that I would serve on fewer committees without responsibility so that I need not attend so regularly I allowed my name to be sent forward to the general management committee of the local Labour Party as a sort of act of loyalty to the ward group and because they did not seem enthusiastic about nominating anyone else, and then on Tuesday I found myself at a Selection Conference where I was adopted as the candidate for the St Pancras North Constituency for the elections in May to the Greater London Council.

I have never fought an election in my life and thought I would be considered too old anyway. As a co-opted member of the Children's Committee I enjoyed life at County Hall, so there is the attraction, if I get in, of being a member again of a very fine club and of feeling part of a great organisation. One hopes that one might be able to play some small part in cutting down the amount of red tape and bureaucracy and of furthering what I consider to be progress in the field of education.

Today I am writing this on the train en route for Grantham, where I take part in a whole day of lectures and films and discussions for the WRAF recruits at Spitalgate. My partner in this exercise is the Dr Morris whom I encouraged to write to Yonire.* She is a most interesting person and her hobbies include driving a variety of old-fashioned carts and carriages about the countryside.

*I had a long letter from her yesterday. We correspond regularly. (Yonire)

As I am away from my desk I have no notes of the last mag and could probably not find them among the heaped-up chaos of papers. *Ah, but you did. (Ad Astra)*

My office is another obvious sign of my lunacy!

In 1973, at the age of sixty-seven, Elektra won her campaign and became an elected member of the Greater London Council for St Pancras North. Her term finished in 1977, at which point she and Mark continued working with the Camden Association for Mental Health. They were instrumental in opening a day centre in 1980. Much to their surprise, it was named the 'Rose and Mark Hacker Centre' to honour the pair for all of their hard work and dedication.

Unfortunately, Mark's health was failing and, in 1980, a stroke left him paralysed. Elektra nursed him for the next two years until his death in 1982.

Elektra moved out of the house that she and Mark had lived in since 1951 into her own flat in Highgate. She had taken up sculpting during Mark's illness and became quite involved with this once he was gone. She also started travelling, with trips to China and India. She visited California every year because she had reconnected with Moira, the daughter of an old friend, who lived there. The two unofficially adopted one another as mother and daughter. Through Moira, an art historian at Berkeley, Elektra was introduced to feminist art, archaeology and the goddess culture, all interests that she continues to pursue.

In 2002, at the age of ninety-six, she won the award for the Oldest Active Artist in the UK. In the same year she was declared the Honorary Lifetime President of the Highgate Labour Party.

Elektra is still going strong at the age of 100. She is extremely energetic, practising t'ai chi weekly, writing a fortnightly article for the Camden New Journal, and attending operas and concerts. She is insightful, open, reflective and exceptionally well read. She is an incredibly generous woman, willing to share all her experiences with the next ready listener.

6

Hard Times

No Second Chance

A month ago, on November 20th, my mother died suddenly at the age of 67. My father 'phoned me, earlier in the week, to say that she had had a heart attack and had been ordered by the specialist to stay in bed for a month. I was undecided whether to make the long journey south to see her then, or to wait until she was a little better and more able to stand conversation without tiring. Fool that I was! My father seemed to think that there was no urgency for my visit and, faced with the difficulty of farming out the family and worried, too, about John who has been at home since the beginning of November suffering from nervous exhaustion (manifested at first in trigeminal neuralgia of an acute type), I stayed at home and worried, haunted too by frequent mental pictures of events in my childhood that I had long half-forgotten. That alone should have warned me as I am not a psychic (or whatever one must call this type of experience) type. All day of the 20th I was desperately worried and had it been possible should have left everything and set off on the 300 mile journey; by evening I had it definitely in my mind to go the following day, but my father 'phoned at about 8·00 pm and seemed so cheerful that my anxieties began to appear as morbid imaginings and I once again decided, mentally, to wait another week before going to Dorset. Alas, the 'phone rang just as I had got into bed at 10·45 pm; Daddy again, to say that my mother had had another attack a few minutes before, and was dead. By 9·00 next morning I was on my way, leaving John to cope as best he could with the children and, thanks to the kindness of a cousin who met me at Bristol, I was at the little Dorset village of Netherbury soon after 6·00 pm. The trip was an example of bitter irony — arriving a day too late at this cottage, once a weekend cottage which for reasons too complicated to enter into here, I had never liked and had avoided

Written by Accidia in 1956 when her mother died.

We all have reason to be grateful for CCC and never more than when in trouble. The feeling of warm friendship and mutual support flow from the dear pages.

Elektra, 1953

The CCC women relied upon the magazine when they were struggling through difficult times, particularly family troubles. When family members passed away, the women often felt the need to present 'a stiff upper lip', but the intimacy of the magazine gave them the opportunity to share their fears and pain, to grieve, and to admit to the strain that they often felt as caregivers.

Glen Heather, Cornelia and Sirod all wrote about their struggles with, and experiences of, loss.

Glen Heather

Glen Heather was born in 1903 in Winchester but grew up in Southampton. Her father was a merchant seaman who was, to all intents and purposes, absent and barely provided for the family. Glen Heather and her mother survived on the meagre wages that her mother was able to earn from dressmaking. After attending Southampton Girls' Grammar School, at the age of sixteen Glen Heather found employment as a clerk.

Her future husband, Don, lived in Southampton and worked as a clerk at a local grammar school. The pair met, fell deeply in love and married in 1928. After Glen Heather's difficult childhood, she felt Don was her saviour. Once married, they had Marilyn in 1930, Coral in 1933 and Ralph in 1934.

The family was separated for some of the war when Glen Heather and the children were evacuated. For part of this period Glen Heather worked as a billeting officer for Marilyn's school in Somerset. Don remained in Southampton for the duration and was employed as a government officer.

Following the war, Glen Heather found work as a school secretary and Don became chief clerk of the Southampton Education Department. They occasionally took groups of young people on camping trips to the New Forest, as they shared a passion for exploring the countryside. Eventually the family moved to the New Forest, where both Don and Glen Heather spent much of their spare time gardening and walking.

Glen Heather was one of the least formally educated members of the CCC, but she was well liked by the other women for her warm personality. It is possible that when writing to the CCC she romanticised parts of

*her life. She was best known amongst the women in the
group for the passionate love that she shared with Don,
a love that perhaps came at the expense of her relationship with her children.*

*Glen Heather sent this article to the group in July
1958, immediately after Don had been diagnosed with
terminal cancer. At the time, their children Marilyn
(nicknamed Bunty), Coral and Ralph were twenty-
eight, twenty-six and twenty-three, respectively.
Marilyn had already married David and Coral had
recently married Tex.*

July 13, 1958

My Dear AA,

I remember starting a letter to you but I was removed
to bed or something in the middle of it. Now, however, I've been doped to sleep and have far better com-
mand.

The Staff nurse on Don's ward fobbed me off with
some technical information which was true but incom-
prehensible to me, she hoped. So she told Ralph, but
they don't realise that the layman is not so ignorant
on these things nowadays.

When Ralph went to see the hospital doctor he told
me that they wanted it to dawn on Don slowly to
avoid adding to the post-operative shock, so that he
would recover enough to be sent to a 'convalescent'
home or even home. He would, therefore, not be told
unless I wished differently.

I knew very well I could never keep up a pretence of
lies etc. for a fortnight. Besides it is not our way of
meeting catastrophe. I decided to tell him. The children agreed. It *was* hard, but I managed to do it and
he was absolutely wonderful and has decided to do all
he can to keep calm and get ready for home.

The doctor does not give him long. It's advanced in

stomach and liver and he's awfully tired. But he's determined to beat it as long as possible, he says. I don't think he realises it's only months. His only worry is the pain and whether I can bear to see him in it, but the doctor assured Ralph that the drugs will be available, so I am longing to get him home.

Coral is packing to begin her new life with Tex in London. It seems incredible that mine with Don is ending, it only seems five minutes ago we began.

I know you'll be thinking of me. GH.

We are indeed thinking of you, Glen Heather
dear, and hoping that things will be as easy
as possible for you. All love. (Barnie)

1958

Dear CCC,

I seem to have written to you more in the past fort-night than for ages. Don is asleep and I can't settle to anything and as you are my solace I write to you.

Yesterday turned out to be a bad day but the early morning was beautiful, tho' the tax it made on my heart strings was more than I could bear.

I didn't know what date it was, hardly the day, but when I went into Don's room at 6 a.m. he said, 'Darling, there's just a little parcel for you in that drawer. Of course, I've had to have accomplices.' I found it and, puzzled, opened the note. I can't disclose to you now what was in it but it was our wedding anniversary and there were little roses and lace hand-kerchiefs and perfume. How could I bear it. The tears rolled down my face and for the first time Don cov-ered his face and wept. The arduous task of nursing I seem to manage and I stay with him every minute pos-sible, but the pain in my heart seems unendurable. It's indeed a high price to pay for our closeness all these years but I wouldn't have it otherwise.

Poor CCC, I ought not to torment you too. The

children have been truly wonderful, but Coral now has joined Tex in London and there is only Ralph, who is away all day. Coral and Tex were always here. Coral living and Tex from Friday to Monday morning early. The house was full of young people at weekends and often evenings. I miss them all but even they don't understand quite the bond between Don and me as CCC does.

Bunty has been coming down at weekends and Coral and Tex will take a turn I know when they return from Spain, where they've gone for a belated honeymoon. Don insisted that they go having arranged and paid for everything in advance. They were dubious but he persuaded them. It's such a pity this should have happened just now to cloud their happiness when they are starting their own home in London. But they're young and it's bound surely to leave their minds for quite appreciable periods. I hope so.

Thank you *so* much those of you who have written to me. I know just how you feel. Whether to or not, and whatever to say. But I did find something in receiving them and I am grateful from the bottom of my heart for your allowing me to share my pain with you, for I can't seem to see any hope in the future just now. All I can do is to get thro' the present. At night I worry about the future, but at that time it's probably all exaggerated and unreal. If only I could reach out and find normality somehow or another for just a little while. Ralph is very strong-minded and *makes* me behave normally when he's here. But there's a difference in going thro' the motions and actually feeling stable. I've talked about myself and nothing about the others' sorrow or Don's troubles. Oh dear, it's dreadful to think that my nursing, however devoted and expert, can do absolutely nothing. Well, not nothing because he is comforted, but there's no point in talking of his trouble.

I wish I could come and cry in each of your arms! Here I have to be constantly dry eyed and brave for the sake of Ralph and Don and to repay the kindness of my friends, but dear CCC doesn't call for such control.

Thank you all again for writing to me. I seem to have no faith in anything, nor see any purpose in anything. Then a letter comes and somehow it takes the place of my 'safety valve' a little (which is just one of the hundred things Don has been to me).

Agony to read this. (Roberta)

August 20, 1958

Dearest AA,

I feel that probably at the end I may not be capable of writing all I would wish to CCC so I will do it now.

Everyone has been so good to me with their thoughts and letters that I would like them to know that as far as Don has been concerned the path of his illness has not been *too* nightmarish. There have been times and one day especially when pain did get the upper hand, but it wasn't too awful even then. The repercussions from the drugs were sometimes a bit alarming when he would get out of bed and be delirious but there was nothing to hurt him in that. The fruitless operation accelerated things, of course, and altho' it's hardly six weeks he has now virtually gone from me. He reached the stage yesterday when dope has to be administered every few hours so that time, etc. means nothing to him. He has opened his eyes (which have recovered their dark-blue colour of his youth) and murmured my name and tried to raise his hand to my face but mostly now just murmurs what appears to be gibberish.

He has been a wonderful patient throughout. Never a 'Why should this happen to me?' In fact he said, 'There's only one consolation in this. If it's me it isn't somebody else.' I've nursed, fed and bathed him every day until yesterday. I really felt I was exhausting him too much with my amateur lifting so gave in and had a nurse. And her ministrations were nearly fatal. Apparently the wretched disease has now reached a lung too and in moving him on to his side she sapped what strength he had. It was touch and go but today his pulse is a little stronger and the doctor thinks he may hang on for days as he was wiry. So now there is nothing I can do but administer a little drink and tea-spoonsful of medicine. I long to go in and caress him but it would only disturb a state which is to him now of greater benefit.

His hair is black and soft and curly still in spite of a poor ravaged face. We have had some wonderful moments as you said we should. In one he said, 'This is worth all the illness and pain.' But I couldn't echo his words. Just to have him until he at least could see the result of our work and joy in the garden. Just to – but what's the use! It has come and must be faced.

Thank you again for your thoughts and letters. The days would have been longer still without them.

The agony to read this. (Roberta)
Glen Heather. You are so brave and sweet. I do admire
you. (Waveney)
There is so little one can say or do – I only hope I shall be
as brave if/when my turn comes. Bless you GH. (Yonire)
Dearest GH – My love and thoughts. (Janna)
And mine, GH, are so often with you. (Robina)

August 24, 1958

Dearest AA,

Don died early yesterday morning and altho' we were prepared the finality is bearing down upon me and I don't feel that I'll ever get attuned to living without him. But surely it'll come, it must do. In the meantime the children are doing everything possible. Ralph has, it seems to me, developed into a responsible man in a few weeks. He's only twenty-three but he has done absolutely everything.

Don said one day, 'I wonder if all this can be for the purpose of helping Ralph to really reach manhood or something like that.' I feel that price was terribly high but I listened. And last night Ralph and Bunty were talking to me and Ralph explained what this experience has done to him. It was profound and more involved than Don's explanation but I was struck by it all and I just wondered whether I may be wrong in thinking it all so purposeless. It would be easier to bear.

CG [Cotton Goods] asked me to go there to stay and Ralph is sending me next weekend right away from anything to remind me. Wasn't it thoughtful of her? I only hope I get some spirit with which to return. With Love. GH

Dear AA, I think Cornelia is my oldest friend in CCC but I really can't write any more. Would it be asking too much if I asked you to tell her for me?

After losing Don, Glen Heather found being alone very difficult. She longed for a companion and in around 1961 married an ex-naval officer named Robert, who worked for a manufacturer of sweets. They lived in the Norfolk area until he died from heart problems in 1967. In 1973, she married Bill, a man whom she had known when she was younger. He worked for a horticultural firm. The pair moved to Cornwall, where Glen Heather spent her later years exploring the countryside, gardening and reading. She died in 1979 after a stroke.

Cornelia

Cornelia was born in 1894 in Woodford Green, which was a little village in Essex and is now a part of Greater London. When she was five years old, her father, a joiner, died after a work-related accident. Fortunately, the family was well provided for, as her mother's family was wealthy. Cornelia attended school until the age of sixteen, when she left to work in a cocoa importer's office. She loved this job, earned a very good wage and developed a great relationship with her employer, who treated her like a daughter. It was here that she met her future husband, Pat. He was six years younger than Cornelia and later confessed that he spent his evenings pining for the 'top dog in the office'. After they had finally established a relationship, Pat had to leave to serve in the army. When he returned, Cornelia was able to secure him a job at the Westminster Bank, since one of the directors was a family friend.

The couple planned to marry but had to wait for the bank's approval since, at that time, permission was dependent upon income. The bank also attempted to influence them when they wanted to buy a house. They offered Pat a 4 per cent mortgage, contingent upon three factors: that he had come from a public school (which he had), that he would promise never to speak from a public platform, and that he would never buy anything on hire purchase. Pat would not agree to the stipulations and arranged a private 5 per cent mortgage instead. The bank also refused to allow employees' wives to work, so when the pair finally married in March 1924, despite the fact that Cornelia had a higher salary and loved working at the cocoa importer's, she was forced to leave her job. As a parting gift, her boss gave her a piano, enough money for their honeymoon and two years' supply of Terry's Bitter Chocolate, which Pat took to work every day in a half-pound slice.

As Cornelia had been reluctant to leave her job, she was later delighted to join the CCC and find companions who had also been forced to give up work prematurely. However, unlike many of the other women in the club, Cornelia enjoyed life as a homemaker. She was a skilled craftswoman, who was involved in pottery, marquetry and pewter work. She joined both the Women's Institute and Townswomen's Guild, depending on where she was living. Although she wasn't the best chef, her craftsmanship was evident in her baking and she was famous for her elegant cakes. In spite of her interests, Cornelia was known to go into seclusion for a day when the CCC magazine arrived at her door.

After Cornelia and Pat married, they lived in Woodford and then Ilford. They had Michael in 1926, Peter in 1929 and Ted in 1934. Cornelia was a very loving and generous mother and explained to the women in the CCC:

If God made me with any great desire it was for children. I was a plain, squat figure, but probably because, although fatherless, I had had only brothers who probably knocked me into shape. How dearly I would have loved a 'Daddy', a sister or a daughter! So before I would marry Pat, and after 60 years neither of us care to be apart for long, I made him promise that if I had no children, he would allow me to adopt one. (I had no idea then how difficult it is to do so!) and it is not so morbid as it seems as out of my mother's family (7) she, only, produced offspring. I knew I could not be happy without a child.

It was with this mindset that Cornelia chose her nom de plume from the Roman story of Cornelia and her jewels. One version of the story is that the Roman lady Cornelia, daughter of legendary war hero Scipio Africanus, was captured by barbarians and told to pro-

duce her jewels. Another version suggests that a wealthy lady visited Cornelia and, after displaying her own jewels, asked Cornelia to display hers. In both cases, Cornelia produced her two sons, Tiberius and Gaius Gracchus, and said, 'These are my jewels.'

Aside from the war years in Oxfordshire, they lived most of their lives in Ilford, where Pat worked for the Westminster Bank until he retired. On his limited salary, they were only able to send Michael and Peter to university. Ted was able to get state funding and pursued a career in teaching. Michael became a GP and moved to Saskatchewan in Canada. Peter graduated in entomology and specialised in tropical agriculture. He was Chief Entomologist in Kenya until it achieved independence in 1963. Peter then returned to England with his Kenyan wife, Susan, and worked at a large government research laboratory as Director of the Tropical Products Institute. They had three children, Malcolm, Alan and Kitty, and they lived in Farnham Common in Buckinghamshire. In Kenya, Susan had been raised in a privileged household with servants and had a difficult time making the transition to life in England. She struggled because Peter frequently travelled due to work, and she did not get along with many people in his family, including his mother. This was particularly difficult for Cornelia as she loved her son so dearly. It was common knowledge that Peter was her favourite, and she was devastated when he was diagnosed with a malignant brain tumour in 1974, at the age of forty-five. She wrote to the women of the CCC to express her despair.

1974

Open Letter

Dear CCC, If you are feeling down in the dumps, skip this as it is not a happy letter, and *I* shan't know, but in true CCC fashion I am trying to ease my pain by

sharing it with you. Selfish perhaps! First of all, if you
could know the kindness, the loving kindness I have
received from AA this past fortnight! Some of you

So little. We'd all have done
the same. (Ad Astra)
True C, I have been in your
shoes ever since, and imag-
ined how I'd feel if it was
one of my boys. (Roberta)

must know her aptness of saying
just the right thing and her prompt-
ness in trying to alleviate the pain,
might *yet* be surprised, and I can
NEVER be grateful enough to her.

As I have read her letters to Pat, the tears streaming
down my face; the balm and comfort of genuineness!
And then dear Roberta! I had to ring her last Saturday
about mags coming, and somehow it all came out and
her words! and just before I left on Monday morning
early, a letter of sympathy. She knew just HOW I felt,
I'm sure. And I thought back to something she said to
us when her divorce was pending, 'Here I am in a little mountain train – saying it CAN'T be true!' And
that is HOW you feel. It MUST be a nightmare!

It was generous of you to think of this, but my
pain was <u>nothing</u> compared to Peter, but Nightmare
is so true! (Roberta)

I forget what I have written so I'll start and tell all.
When Peter was here last September after their Spain
holiday, he told us he had been to his dentist who said
he had an abscess under his wisdom tooth and sent
him (I think) to his GP for antibiotics. And he said,
'The pain goes up my left side to the eye.' The antibiotics he said on the phone did ease the pain a bit,
but he had to go off to USA and said to me as I rang
to say 'Bye, Bye', 'Oh it's not too bad' (the abscess). I
don't know whether he came home early or not but he
flew back 13/14 Oct. and was due to do a big safari in
Africa on 2 Nov. *I* was not told anything until when I
was just about to ring up on the 1st to say 'God
speed,' Susan rang, talked a little to me and then said,
'Peter wants to speak to Pat' . . . Pat returned to me

and said, 'There's bad news and Peter has to have a head X-ray as they are afraid there is something which might eventually cause brain trouble.' I knew afterwards that Peter was very much against us knowing until later and Susan thought this all wrong. Anyhow I rang up Monday night and went cold as Susan said, 'The brain X-ray shows a small tumour, in a good place, so the hospital thinks it's benign. There is some silly trouble with the theatre and Peter is being sent home for six days.' Naturally I *had* wondered if it was a brain X-ray, but I didn't mention my fears to Pat, as I am not an optimist and I realised they were trying to let me down lightly, but as Susan said BRAIN X-ray, I went cold. Later Peter rang and said, 'I've just been out with the dog, don't WORRY. I'm fine and am going to dig the allotment tomorrow!' Ted was away for the half term at his old friend's at Ramsey, so I wrote off Sunday to Michael by air. I rang Ted Monday evening and he said, 'Don't you think you ought to *phone* Mike?' And I told him we were suffering so much, waiting, that Mike could do nothing and there was no point in his having a long wait to suffer. Apparently Peter also wrote the same day as I did. Alas! It was a strike of technicians and all immediate ops had to be cancelled! This was at the Central Middlesex Hospital in Acton. I did not know until afterwards but on receipt of either mine or Peter's letters, Mike rang up Peter, asked the name of the surgeon and said would he mind if he, M, rang him. 'Don't be a clot,' said Peter. 'I have every confidence I am having the best brain surgeon and all is under way.'

Later I learned that when Peter returned from USA, he saw his GP and said as he was to leave on Safari on 2nd, would it not be better to go on privately. The GP said, I think *not*, as being a government scientist he would get every priority and he thought best to leave it as it was and he would send him to a specialist ophthalmologist. This man said, 'I can see no problem with your eyes AT ALL. They seem in PERFECT CONDITION.' The GP, on getting this report, said, 'That's funny! I'll do a little examination myself!' and said, 'You have a blind spot which could be serious, so you must have a brain scan at the Nuffield Clinic at Slough. It was at once (because of priority), and what they found, it had to be a brain X-ray.* They put in dye and found a small tumour – they thought – at the base of the brain. There had been brain haemorrhage which had caused half sight in each eye. By the position they felt the tumour would prove to be benign. Michael meanwhile had rung up his old pal, Ewart Jepson, and found he was a consultant at Central Middlesex! (I'm sure I've told you this!) and Ewart rang Mike and Mike rang Peter, who came on the phone Saturday night and said to *me*, 'Mike has just rung up! Ewart has phoned him and he feels VERY optimistic. I drove the car today *very* carefully to the allotment (7 miles) and found it not at all difficult, and spent the morning digging the allotment. I go back to hospital tomorrow for the op. early Tuesday!' Alas there was a nearby accident and the op. did not take place until afternoon. Susan said, 'Mother, I will ring you as soon as I have news.' The day wore on. Pat listened to the Budget until I felt I could scream but propped a newspaper in front of me and waited for that phone call. At 6 p.m. I said to Pat, 'I'm going to ring the hospital,' but he begged me not to, and I didn't. At 7 p.m. the phone went and it was *Ted*! He had rung at 2.30 p.m. and they said Peter was still in the theatre. His secretary is ex-nurse and she said, 'Don't worry, these brain ops sometimes take 6 hours.' He rang at 7 and they said Peter was back in

*This is where we heard. (Cornelia)

the ward but they could say nothing until they had
seen his wife, who had been expected earlier. (I am
sure Susan was there when she was told to be.) They
said nothing to Ted about the op. being delayed
because of accident op. I could bear it no longer and I
rang Susan at 9 p.m. She flew off the deep end about
Ted ringing the hospital, said he was only a brother!
And to my mild, 'Susan, we are a *loving* family and
Ted dearly loves and is worried over Peter! But I will
tell him not to ring at all! I will act as intermediary,'
Susan said, 'Yes, you do *that*! If you think it's fun to
sit an hour and watch a man with tubes out of his
head, rambling on about things in the past, I can tell
you it isn't. Good night, Mother!' I wept for a long
time! It seemed so dreadful, even making allowances
for her anguish. I rang Ted and warned him not to
ring *her* and that I'd do it. Half an hour later the
phone went – and I said to Pat, 'That's Susan to apologise,' but it was Ted to say Susan had rung him, had
been very nice and he thought I should not let her
know I had repeated the message. I said, 'I won't mention it but if she asks if I *did* ring you, I'll say briefly,
Yes.' She has never mentioned it. She rang Wednesday
night, said she had seen a surgeon who had said matters were graver than expected. The path. report
would be through Monday and she thought we should
be '*en famille*' to hear it, but she didn't want Ted
there. As she did not see Peter Monday afternoon or
until 6.45 p.m., she would come down for us. 'There's
no need for that, but when I ring tomorrow I will
arrange things with you.' When I rang I said that we
would come up on Monday and we could easily get
the late train back here without putting her to the
trouble of putting up beds. 'No,' she said, 'I'll need
your moral support and I want to talk to Pat about
finance! Arrange to be prepared to stay longer than a

night.' (I might add Peter always fetches us and brings us back, quite unnecessary but he hasn't believed that!)

On Monday we went up to town and as I wanted badly to take Peter some mangoes, took a taxi to Soho for some. I went into several shops and then the most luxurious-looking one to be told, 'If there were mangoes in London, we should have them,' so settled for a melon that I felt must be nice as it was £1.25! Pat said we MUST have a lunch as we anyhow shouldn't get anything much, later. Well, our favourites in Soho and Charlotte Street are too remembered by happy family parties, so we went into Schmidt's, I remember recommended by Amelia,* years ago. Pat had a lunch; I had some very nice consommé and a coffee and he had a carafe of red wine, and back to Victoria for our luggage. And on to North Acton to meet Susan, at 5 p.m. Of course, we were there very early and she was there by 4.45 p.m. I must add that I had taken the precaution to put a flask of brandy in my handbag. Had a swig – and a sweet to hide – before meeting Susan.

*And by Ad Astra years before Amelia joined CCC! (Ad Astra)

And so to the hospital. We went into the lounge, where Pat got coffees and cakes and we could talk as we were not due to see Peter until 6.45 p.m. Susan said he was to hear from the Surgeon on the path. report that afternoon, but she knew that the cancer was deep seated and far worse than they had expected. Peter had said on the phone to me, 'I have been warned that I may not get my half-sight back, but *really* that won't worry me much.' Susan had already learned from her interview last Wednesday the worst, I *think*. We went up to the ward, which has – (in fact each ward has in this immense hospital) – a small lounge close by, where patients able to move freely can smoke or sit or have friends in visiting hours. Susan said, 'I will go in and fetch him and see if he is in a fit state for you.' To my dying day I shall NEVER forget Peter as he came through that door! Of course, shorn head in place of his wavy mop, with a curious open knitted skullcap on; in the dressing gown I had made him YEARS ago in cotton material for the tropics, *beaming all over his face* and arms outstretched to embrace me and kiss me again and again. He looked SO WELL! We sat and he held my hand and pressed it all the time, with Susan on the other side. He told us his surgeon had said that he had gone as deep as he dare, and thought all cancerous cells taken away, but he was to have deep ray treatment for some time – which he could get at the Nuffield Clinic in Slough – only 10 miles, so easy for Susan, but they might cause him discomfort. He could attend a conference abroad but not go on a safari therefore putting himself out of quick touch if immediate surgery became necessary. That he could never drive a car again. He was *so* cheerful and GAY!

Peter is marvel- Another lovely hug and it was time for him
lous. (Isis) to return to the ward, and we went in to see his bed, and left him. Susan said she would not go in the next *afternoon,* as he was to return Wednesday morning, as she wanted to get some veg. from the allotment and I guess because of us. Going home I said I thought our best plan was for Susan to drop us about 11 a.m. at Acton St. on Wednesday, go on for Peter, and she agreed. While we were there Malcolm had slept in Peter's bed and as there are always two beds in Malcolm's room, we had that room. Usually Kitty is turned out of her bedroom for us and a second bed put in – all somewhat work-taking. Kitty has a carpet-covered bedroom and the two boys' rooms are plastic covering – gosh! cold.

We got home at 8.30. The hospital was a good

$3/4$-hour ride. In the dining room the children had not attempted to remove the remains of their supper – which only meant loading into dishwasher, which I could not help noticing! Susan got us something . . . We had supper and retired. Next day Susan left for her Spanish class – I advised her to go – and left me cutting up ingredients for some chutney. I always think their house so cold altho' CH. So I said to Susan as we were setting out for the allotment, 'I think Peter is going to miss the great heat in hospital, would you mind me buying him a sort of fishing cap?' She thought it a good idea and ran me to a sports shop. Nothing as good as I wanted but no choice. I forgot to say Michael rang up Monday even, talked with Susan and then to me, when he said, 'Mother, it seems incredible that this could happen to one of us!' And Diane: 'Mother, darling, I've tried five times to write you and can't!' And told Susan that he had got a flight for next week and would be here for a fortnight . . .

To get back to my story . . . Next night we got to the hospital and the same darling *happy* face greeted me. There was a middle-aged[*] man sitting in the corner of the lounge – a small one, as only 8 beds in ward. And soon after Susan and Peter came in, procedure as before, Peter said, 'Oh, as I am leaving tomorrow, let's have some sweets,' and went back to his locker and as the door swung back after him, the patient on my right said to the lounge at large, 'That is the most courageous lad I think it has ever been my pleasure to meet!' Susan said I said, 'Thank you – he is my son!' I don't really remember, this was afterwards when I said I didn't know how I started to talk to him. But Susan started off at once to Peter with a whole tirade about 'Alan was sure he had failed his exam, the kids were simply AWFUL! and etc.' In fact I had never known them so peaceful. I felt

[*] *Spine case not brain. (Cornelia)*

I couldn't *bear* it! So I turned and chatted to my solitary patient, in case I wept! Each time I was having swigs* in loos before moments of stress and my God HOW they helped.** I hate brandy but not quite as much as whiskey!

Peter and Pat and I said our last farewells for a bit and

*How sensible of you, only wish at times I liked it, or it me! (Roberta)

**And, dear God, how you *needed* help. (Roberta)

returned to Farnham Common. I must say that Peter DID NOT seem distressed by Susan's catalogue of complaints and I am sure they have a great fondness for each other. She *did* say in my hearing, 'I DO love you so much, Peter,' which I shall remember. When we got in, the children were listening in, in the lounge. They have their own room and TV, but this did not upset Susan at all, it seemed to me. The table was as last night, not cleared. And I'm sure she is used to that. Alan seems to have lost his 'sloppyness' towards me and is quite casual, but knowing this was my only opportunity to speak to him, I sat on the sofa next to him and, putting my hand on his knee, said softly, 'I am sorry to talk while you are listening, but last year when Mummy was to come to me after her op. you wrote and asked me to be good to her as you loved her dearly. Now I am ASKING *you* to be kind to Daddy, who is a desperately sick man and will need great care and peace and to try and not to have quarrels.' 'Yes, I will, Gran,* but shut up now.' After a little while I went via the hall, where I changed my shoes into slippers, but only gone

*This rings such a bell. (Michaelmas)

surely not 3 minutes. Can I do anything, Susan? *NO!* and shrieking at the top of her voice, 'Next time Peter has to go into hospital these bloody kids are going into lodgings, I WON'T look after them.' I quietly went back to my place next to Alan, and had no idea anything had happened. Pat said Malcolm had come in via a different way, kitchen/dining room/lounge, and said, 'Alan, Mummy wants you,' and he said, 'After I see this!' Pat thinks that he was annoyed that I had spoken and then his mother wanted him and Pat says he went. But the whole incident could not have lasted four minutes! I knew it was *my* only chance as he was going out after the film, and we were going to have supper, and I didn't particularly want Susan to know! I am wondering how Mike will cope or if his presence will affect this turbulent family!

And now to a really *lovely* incident that even now I can hardly believe happened. I got down next morning after the kids had left for school and Pat was still upstairs. There was a paperback on the table and Susan said to me that over the back, behind their 8ft hedge, there is a house where a lab. assistant from Peter's lives. A few days earlier she went there with news, and his/her mother was staying with them. This lady had written to Susan from Harrogate, sending the Christian Science book with a letter which roughly said, 'Dear Susan, Forgive an old woman you hardly know sending you this book, but I DO feel you might get comfort from Chap. 32 on prayer' . . . I said, putting my hand on the book, 'Susan, dear, I have read that book twice but years ago and it didn't DO anything for me, but would you mind very much if I wrote to this lady?' and she said, 'I would like you to very much, mother,' and wrote down her address for me. ME! I DO believe there is a vast reservoir, God, or anything you like to give it a name to, from which one can draw strength. I call it praying but it HAS helped me during this past fortnight as it has in many sorrows in my life. For me, alas! it does not stem my tears and I can't always connect, but sometimes I can and it gives me peace! Susan said, 'I shall read that chapter!' Pat came downstairs and our intimacy finished. But I still can't believe it happened and it has made me SO happy. I think Susan is, as Ted always maintains, a very sick-emotional woman. She went off the deep one night when she said, 'I nearly threw something at the TV when I heard that the government were bringing in ? number of Egyptians for medical treatment and MY husband is sent home because some technicians won't work! I wouldn't mind betting the accidents brought in that delayed Peter's operation for hours were Asians!' Yet she is a BSc! She just has no logic at all! Actually I didn't see a great many coloured people in the hospital, which is a large one. Peter said, because of the noise of trolleys passing the few private rooms, they had to bring one patient into the bed next to him for quietness! Ewart has visited him for 20 minutes or so every time he has been in the hospital. Because of this connection he has had rather special attention. Mike is of course seeing the surgeon.

His wound looks SO neat. It is horseshoe shape, dead centre, back from hair line about 3" at base and 4" high. They fear the deep rays may cause baldness. The 48 stitches are SO small and neat!

Oh, Cornelia, I hope all goes well – thank you for telling us all about this heavy & unexpected trouble. (Barnie)
Oh, dear Cornelia, I just sat & wept for you. (Sirod) (and so did Roberta, & still does)
Cornelia, I hope things will be much better for you all by the time you re-read all this. You are marvellous the way you cope with your none too easy daughter-in-law. They should BLESS you & probably do in their hearts. (Waveney)
You have truly been through hell, Cornelia – one's heart aches to read it – Peter's courage is wonderful. (Isis)
Cornelia, I just know the utter hell you must be going through. How brave of Peter to welcome you so. He's a real poppet. (Michaelmas)
It is so difficult to know what to say that might help you. All we can do is to sympathise. (Cotton Goods)

Peter lived another two years, knowing that his condition was terminal. He celebrated life to the fullest and died in 1976 at the age of forty-seven. The family suffered another tragic loss when Michael developed a

heart condition and died the following year. After los-
ing two sons, two of her 'jewels', Cornelia never quite
recovered.

She and Pat had retired to Seaford in 1963, and they
lived there for the next twenty years. Cornelia contin-
ued to pursue marquetry and her other hobbies. They
had eleven grandchildren, six of whom were in Canada.
Their relationship with Ted and his wife Carole was
extremely close and, after Cornelia fractured her hip,
she and Pat moved to East Bergholt, Suffolk, to live
with them. Cornelia died in 1993 at the age of ninety-
nine.

Sirod

Sirod spent much of the 1970s working with the National Association of Flower Arrangement Societies, as well as dedicating herself to her flower books and her artwork. She also pursued ontology, a type of scientific religion that focuses on living through experience. Through her involvement with ontology she visited Colorado twice to work on a commune. During these trips to the US she managed to travel to visit Accidia in Canada.

Though Sirod was busy with her various activities, she spent some of her time with her grandchildren, particularly James, who suffered from a genetic disorder called tuberous sclerosis (TS). James was the child of Sirod's son John, who was to become a professor at Oxford University. He and his wife Ann lived in Oxfordshire with their three children: David, born in 1966, Helena, born in 1968, and James, born in August 1971. James was diagnosed with TS in the spring of 1972 after suffering from seizures. At this stage he was placed on a steroid to control the epileptic attacks, but unfortunately it inhibited his development. Sirod frequently wrote to the women in the CCC about James and the time she spent with him. It was shortly after he began taking the steroid medication that Sirod sent the following article.

1972

That Baby

It's really very good news, which makes one wonder what it means. About three weeks ago (four now) he started to smile and then quite quickly began to move his legs, in a week he was crawling, and this last week he was trying to stand and even drinking out of a cup.

He doesn't try to talk, but to do the other actions is not all that retarded at 13 months. *No, it's hopeful. Very good news. (Barnie)*

He looks abnormal, and before he went into hospital he was beautiful. He has a tiny mouth between two huge pendulous cheeks. His body is large and his hands and feet normal. You can't help wondering how he can possibly stand with all that weight on such tiny feet. His head is almost $\frac{1}{3}$ his body and legs, which is the proportion for a newborn baby. This is all caused by the steroids he has been given to cure the fits. Why give them? Because in an infant each fit causes some brain damage. *And in some adults too. (Yonire)*

Ann hopes that as the steroids wear off he will become more normal in looks. She appreciates he will be retarded but wonders now if it will be much. They are very good at it. Not one murmur of distress and I think a closer family rela- *I hope it will be little – any retardation is* tionship. It always astounds me how *enough. (Ad Astra)* good my sons are with babies. One expects it from daughters, but when I hear John talking so encourag- ingly and so lovingly to James I get a silly lump in my throat.

I was thinking about the situation the other day and I couldn't help appreciating that if someone in my family had to have a retarded child it should best be Ann. She is intelligent enough not to blame herself. She needs more occupation than she gets from cook- ing and caring for children and could perhaps enjoy caring or forming a local parents' association. She and John are not short of money and do not need to long for some apparatus or special food as perhaps Gill would have had to do. They have a lovely home and plenty of room, and great interest in the garden. So there is no longing at present to travel abroad or to take special holidays. She did say that it was a great relief when he could sit up and so they could use the push chair for shopping etc.

In August 1972, James stopped taking the steroids and his speech and movement began to improve. However, in the spring of 1974, when he was almost three, he had a severe epileptic attack that left him with significant brain damage. He lost the ability to walk and speak. Sirod wrote the following excerpt after this attack.

1974

About James

The day after John returned from his lecture tour in Japan, the lad, James, had a setback. John said a little pathetically, 'I was welcomed home by such a happy little boy.' Whether the excitement was too much I don't know. John thinks he reacted badly to one of the drugs he was given for some minor ailment a few days before. He just had fits every few minutes for hours.   *Truly sad, and terrible, poor Ann, and John. (Roberta)*

They got him to hospital and he was drugged for three days and then returned to them unable to move his arms or legs – only his eyes. They did not know if he had a three-month's mentality in a three-year body . . . or if he had merely the baby ability and knew he could not move. And he had been talking well and attending Nursery School!

One naturally wonders and one naturally hopes he might die to save the distress of his parents. That seems to me the natural reaction, but whether it is right or wrong, I haven't worked out and don't intend to. I maintain that I have no right to judge right or wrong in such a situation. It is something to experi-ence and whether the experience becomes an avenue of opportunity depends on the person and the only person I can influence is myself. Opportunity for what? That again I have no need to anticipate. A bit involved but something dear AA wrote in a comforting letter made me try to work it out thus.

How many 'comforting' letters that woman writes in a year! It must be a great number – thank you AA.

Well, to continue about James. He went back to hospital for observation as a man was over from the States who was an authority on his disease.[*] Nothing much came of this but Ann has to inject 'soneril' (I think) with the first sign of future attack.

Oh no. (Ad Astra)
I agree! (Roberta)
Me Too! (Cornelia)

But <u>what disease</u>, S? (Roberta)
Tuberous sclerosis. (Sirod)

Meanwhile he is improving, just as the last time. He can now crawl and pull himself up on the furniture but does not attempt to talk. I have not seen him. I have not been needed as Ann's mother now lives in the village, having retired from schoolteaching. She was head of a Primary School in Upminster, and does a little relief work in the village and is v. good with David and Helena.

Also Ann has made herself so popular in the village, helping other mothers by minding their children at times, that they have had more offers of help than they can use.

John brought the two older ones down to me for a brief holiday and change for them. They play well together (6 and $7\frac{1}{2}$ y.) . . .

I will keep you informed as I know how sympathetic you all are.[*] I did not write it up at the time for I felt there would be some further news to add, one way or the other, and I thought it would be easier to add the latest at the same time – as now (and he still progresses – now just walking).

Oh yes, more than that even. (Roberta)

After several months, James regained the ability to walk and slowly started to speak again. His development dif-

fered somewhat from when he was a baby. He had been right-handed before, now he was left-handed, and he was more artistic. Sirod reported on his progress to the CCC in October 1974, during the UK's second general election of that year.

October 1974

Mostly James

This morning I am minding James, so as you have all been so kindly interested I may as well write about him – if I can. I mean, if he lets me.

Ann is scrubbing the floor of the shop 'next to the Co-op' which the Labour Party are using as committee rooms, I assume in Witney, but I'm not sure . . . Ann is secretary for the constituency but as no one else seems to bother about the cleanliness of the place and she will be taking James along later she felt she would at least start with the place clean for him to run around . . .

James has just managed to pull down the red Labour poster in the window of the next room. I can't believe he really reached it – I've just measured the height from the window seat on which he had climbed and it is 50 inches! I tried him on the seat and he must have been well on his toes.

Ann has just rung up to give me the number as the phone has just been installed, and she has to take Lionel (member, I think) into Oxford so won't be home till about 3. 'Is James all right? If he gets grotty take him up to his cot or his room and leave him. He will just play around till lunch time. Make sure the window and door are shut.' Such are my instructions. He has the run of the downstairs part of the house. It is raining outside. Everything is up – out of his 50-ins reach . . .

The house appeared clean but oddly bare when I arrived, no copper or brass in the hearths, no ornaments or flowers on tables, and no personal belongings, handbags, etc. left anywhere in reach – no books or letters in particular – he eats them!

He does understand a limited amount of 'no', which includes the television, telephone and kitchen drawers. The latter are fortunately handleless and not simple for him to pull open. He is learning words, in fact he talks all the time – 'up', 'down', 'bang'. He definitely calls Ann 'Der', which may be a copy of 'there' or 'dear' from her. He seems to call me 'bug-ah' but Ann assures me that she did not say that 'b. . . . .ring Ma' is coming! As he applies it to my suitcase (carefully closed) and also the cleaning woman, Mrs W, I am not sure whether it means an attempt at 'Granny-ma', the other children's name for me, or 'good-boy', another frequent word he hears.

Ann says he is learning quite different words this time. He started with 'hot' and 'mum' last time.

She blames the very strong dosage of Mogadon he had *after* the last attack. She thinks when he came from hospital he could still remember, for he was saying the last word of a nursery rhyme then and came in with 'day' after 'see-saw . . . penny a . . .' But Mogadon produces amnesia, so beware you insomnia sufferers.

Ann quite sensibly said, 'He is educationable to a certain extent but what he will be after the next attack I don't know,' thus appreciating there will be another.

He is so pleasant to look at. He has fair hair and blue eyes, no apparent abnormality except in the unsteadiness of his walk (as a learner). He has a ready smile, likes anything to eat, and is really *a happy little boy* – and very loving – in a messy sort of way as he usually needs a nose wipe – or clean pants. Sad because he was dry and asking for the pot before Easter. He plays round the garden very happily, eating leaves, fallen apples and chicken food if he can get the bin open. It's too wet today and I am not sorry for there are more places for him to disappear into . . .

The result of the check-up at a retarded children's hospital the other side of Oxford was unexpected. It appears that concern is more now to the retarded child's family than for the child. The latter is much easier to deal with.

The child was taken away and Ann had searching questions to answer about the other children, her relationship with John and her hobbies – what they do in the evenings . . . 'go out separately!' The Dr said that sometime it would be good to leave James there for a weekend and he said quite definitely that Ann would not be able to manage him and he would be there permanently in the future. Ann cried all the way home, and then on my shoulder . . .

Poor Ann. It *is* a strain. I have just spent ten minutes trying to change his underpants and long trousers. First he won't stand up, and then he will only stand and he wriggles off your lap. You get one leg in, and then when any other child would lift the other foot his weight is still on it having lifted for the first leg. He is heavy to lift, so you have to heave him over to get the other leg in – quite exhausting!

The other children are awfully good with him, but children are adaptable. They always go straight to him when they come in, so does John. Just a word, usually 'And what have you been doing today?' and they seldom grumble if he gets at their toys. They know to keep their things up out of reach and appreciate that James gets his meal put out first or he will make a noise.

David is rather a solemn little boy, good average intelligence, and probably the sort of child at school to be given responsibility.

Helena is a real live wire, very clever and intelligent with loads of character, an impish sense of humour, impetuous and mischievous. Both would be quite enjoyable to teach in school.

This is exactly the impression of them that I had. But oh, <u>poor</u> Ann and John <u>and</u> Sirod. (Isis)

James continued to improve and was enrolled at Springfield School in Witney, a place for children with severe learning disabilities. He still had many physical and behavioural problems.

For several years Ann corresponded with other parents of children with TS via a 'round robin' magazine similar to the CCC. In 1977, through Ann's initiative, they met to discuss their concerns. From this meeting the families formed a mutual support charity, the Tuberous Sclerosis Association, with Ann as secretary because she had a typewriter!

After progressing well for a number of years, James suffered a serious setback. He developed a benign brain tumour and, after consulting with specialists, Ann and John decided that it was in James's best interests to have it removed. Sirod informed the CCC shortly after the surgery.

May 1978

. . . I very much doubt if *this* experience will be repeated. I am sitting in the garden minding a retarded child who is newly blind.

Oh Sirod – how dreadful. (Yonire)

Oh Sirod – Poor poor child and all of you! (Elektra)

Yes, James, and if I was not being observant and writing I would be weeping.

This made <u>me</u> weep, anyway. (Waveney)

He had a brain scan with that new apparatus they use now – at the Radcliffe, Oxford, because he was obviously suffering – why, oh why not sooner? They found an operable growth in a ventricle of the brain but it had already affected the optic nerve.

And me. (Janna)

And me. (Roberta)

Oh yes, he might have <u>had</u> some sight saved. (Ad Astra)

To their relief his memory is OK and he has even learnt a new word or two. He had a second operation to insert a pipe from his brain to his heart – inside! It drains something! They evidently expect him to live, for they say as this pipe will not grow with him it will need lengthening at six-month intervals – oh dear!

Too ghastly – poor child and parents. (Roberta)

So we have a little boy – very thin now, and with a shaven head with all sorts of healed scars – with memory of being able to see. (He came out of hospital yesterday.)

For instance there was a cry of 'church' when eleven o'clock struck, and 'brmm-brmm' for a plane, and on both occasions a hand pointing upwards in the garden. He sits fairly immobile on the grass but when a toy is turned over so that he can turn the wheel he chants 'ch-ch-ch-oooo' (i.e. train sounds).

I wonder how much the memory will work when it has to be used for something new like finding his way round the house, avoiding obstacles?

As Ann says about other problems, 'We'll meet them as they arrive.' She will bear the brunt of this. Thank goodness she has

She is courageous. (Isis) Brave girl. (Roberta)

her friends of the Association with similar children, but with such dissimilar symptoms. Naturally she hopes this may help others. Already three others have had their brain scans, and some who have been considered inoperable are now being reconsidered. James, sadly, keeps saying, 'No, Mummy,' but 'Funny, Daddy.' I think because Ann visited him more in hospital and John has been amusing him.

3 Days Later

He is really adapting very well. The 'no' or a long wailing 'oh' is when he wishes he could see or perhaps because he cannot understand why he cannot see and thinks Mummy could make it right – as mummies usually do. To me it seems a pity to remind him what he cannot do, such as looking at books or giving him a torch, an old toy, to play with, but they think he must be encouraged to remember. But I found all this morning no 'wail' when hearing and feeling were within his ability.

He already is learning to feel along the furniture but needs to be reminded to put out his hand. He can manage to climb two steps with help. He can build bricks to about four or five and enjoys large-size Lego. But it is the tape-cassette recorder that is the best of all. He will sit in a chair for a whole tape, getting up sometimes to do actions of the songs he knows or to beat time if the tune has a good rhythm. He loved my Greek dancing tape from Corfu. He remembers the songs he had been taught, hums them well in tune. They remarked in hospital that he was singing even when all bandaged up. He will sing a tune on request and his repertoire goes from nursery rhymes, carols, to 'God Save the Queen'.

A Day Later
He has nearly ceased that pathetic wail of not under-standing but he is not easy, he still needs one person with him all the time. His other granny has returned from a holiday at Paignton, where she took David (11) and Helena (9) for their half-term week. She is very good with him and he loves her. While we (John and Ann and I) think she excites him too much, never-theless it is her interest and enthusiasm that has taught him so much.

He now feels his way along the table to his seat or to his boxes of toys and today he came up the two steps from the kitchen by himself. He can also walk quite a distance (with no obstacle of course) to a voice calling him – he didn't orientate himself to a voice at all at first.

He has several times pointed and said, 'What's that?' and then lost interest. It was a bright window, a shaft of sunlight and once a solitary buttercup in the grass. So we wonder if there is some sight. Today he played with the torch he was disappointed with yesterday, holding it to one eye. His eyes are quite normal looking and it seems impossible to think they cannot see when he appears to look at one. His hair is growing well but the scars on his head are large with huge curves.

He is liable to have small epileptic fits – not much more than a quiver of his lips, a stare, a pause, and then he carries on with what he was doing. This can be controlled by pills and is as he was before – no different.

Later Still
I write now at home with a more distant view. I am sorry if I appeared to write incoherently but I was being observant and wanting to write so I think I will still post it to you. **Thank you for doing so. (Roberta)**

Of course you will be thinking as I did, 'Why couldn't they let him go?' John said that when the Dr asked them if they wished him to operate they did not really understand what he meant and of course they said, 'Yes,' wouldn't you? Loss of sight was not anticipated then.

The operation to remove the growth was successful and the growth was benign but it had pressed on the optic nerve too long. The tube is to regulate the flow of spinal fluid by means of a valve and goes from the brain to the jugular vein and then to the heart. It does not appear to trouble him. All the scars have healed well and his body looks so fit and his hair visibly growing. If the valve should clog up Ann has to press a spot on his head to clear it, but she wonders if she dare do as instructed.

She has discussed frankly the difficulties, the possibilities. She says she is not the type of person to be able to devote herself to one child however demanding, she must have other interests to keep sane (remember why CCC started). She has the *Of course. (Isis)* Tuberous Sclerosis Association, with requests *Yes. (Roberta)* for more information leaflets at every post. She has her job (9.30–12) with computers, which finishes in a month, and she has her political interests, which are in abeyance just now.

Fortunately John's other interests are connected with the home, i.e. he is building a stone wall with Cotswold stone and proper old technique – in order to redesign the vegetable garden. So he is often available at home. He does not have university vacations as he does research. He has had three professorships offered to him but has refused as they really cannot consider moving elsewhere.

The special school are very keen to have him back daily. The teacher visited him in hospital and since he returned home, and they made him a tape (which he loves) of the children singing at school and they each in turn said, 'Hello, James,' and 'Goodbye' at the *What a* end. They have got permission to employ another *lovely idea!* teacher especially for him. The wardens at the *(Janna)* holiday home will take him but at first only if they have quiet sighted children with him.

Ann says, 'How could I insist on a place in a residential home with everyone leaning over to help?' This because the GP had asked if they were considering this. I would say 'no' even more now while he is in a way less trouble to mind as he stays put, and when he needs to learn to adapt with the confidence of familiar voices.

He is still such a happy little boy and, even in distress, if you say 'funny' (almost his favourite word) he will smile and repeat the word. He is still obsessed with 'chimney', pronounced 'imeny', and will balance a brick or a toy on his head. Ann even wondered if he thought the operation involved making a chimney on his head – how can you get inside a child's thoughts? Also apropos of sending him away, 'How could anyone else understand his language?'

She also asked if I thought the other two (now 11 and 9 yrs) suffered. I remarked that I thought they had gained by learning, earlier than most, that consideration and compassion for others was the accepted thing. Also I reminded her that she had found a book for some reference for David's homework that evening, and that Helena had come in with a moth and they had together looked up its name. They both go to riding lessons, Helena is learning the piano and David plays the trombone. Other children come in and out to play and they have fields and trees besides large gardens to play in . . . No, I don't think they suffer at all. I think James may be a blessing. Is that the value of such children? *Perhaps – but poor poor children. (Ad Astra)*

Sirod, my love and thoughts and prayers for you all. (Yonire)
Sirod, the important factors, I think, for Ann, does he <u>sleep</u> well? (Roberta) No. (Sirod) Also, can he indicate when he needs the lavatory. (Roberta) No. (Sirod)
This is one of the saddest things in CCC – yet Sirod and Ann are so Brave. (Janna)
Dear Sirod, Thank you for all of this. What a marvellous family you are. (Elektra)
Yes indeed. (Roberta)
Love and Many thoughts to you, Sirod. <u>This</u> is sad to read. (Accidia)

After James lost his sight, it became increasingly difficult to care for him because he became hyperactive as well, so he couldn't be left alone for even a minute. The strain was too much on the family and they began looking for alternative care.

More James

I am sitting here with mixed feelings and as I do this – as usual – I write to CCC to help clarify my thoughts.

Last week Ann and James spent in residence at the big Mental Hospital, Borocourt, near Reading. It is a *I think Isis once* special place for Oxon, Bucks and Berks, *mentioned it to* and her special man, Dr Taylor, of the *me. (Sirod)* 'Parks' part of the Radcliffe made special *Yes. (Isis)* application to get them there. *It has a wonderful reputation. (Isis)*

Sorry about all the 'specials' but Ann always speaks of him as one in authority.

I thought it was to assess James but it was to assess the situation. At first they didn't even have James's case history. She slept in a sort of flat – a room off the night nursery for 23 children. She heard James start up as usual at 5 a.m. and turned over with relief as there was a night nurse. I asked what she did with him and Ann said took him into the big room to play.

Ann was a little upset at the disturbed state of the five other blind children – not violent, more non-cooperative. None were as over-active as James.

On the Friday they had a case conference and the result was they offered James a place in the unit, Monday to Friday. In other words he comes home each week Friday afternoon until Sunday evening.

One's pretty-soon-reaction is to think that releases Ann to do the work she is doing and plans to do. She is hard put now to get the correspondence in connection with the Tuberous Sclerosis society and she does research with another woman's thesis on senile geriatrics and she has been accepted to take teacher training in Oxford for handicapped children . . .

Then they considered the fact that John cannot accept a professorship (offered more than once) as he cannot move. I'm not sure if he wants to, having rebuilt home and garden, but at least he might be a weekly himself. You cannot move up in your own University, the one you are already in – seems silly to me.

Then they considered the other two normal children. But, oh dear! He is so happy at his daily school and they have this special teacher. Will he be happy there? Will he mind the other difficult children? Will he learn as well as he was developing at home?

I have so often thought of them. (Waveney)
Me too. (Roberta)

This would have been debated during the stay there? (Isis)

It goes through my mind, what do John and Ann feel? They were asked, 'Do you wish me to operate?' though they didn't realise the implications of 'or else' then. And having agreed, they have accepted the responsibility – now they are handing it over. Many folks would say 'rightly so' but they say it with very mixed feelings.

It has been decided, for today, Sunday, he goes back to Borocourt and 'they' assume future responsibility for him.

Can understand your feelings about this – sympathise. Such a difficult decision. (Isis)

It takes some getting used to the idea. I really don't know why it has left me more disturbed than the original news that he would be blind.

Oh, by the way, there is some hope that his one eye might improve. Now on the sensible way of looking at it, all common sense says this is right. They are very very lucky for to get him even in a temporary home for a holiday costs £70 a week . . . Also they have not lost touch. There will be the weekend visits to assess his progress. Oh dear, I hope they will give him the pills that

Yes – these weekends are v. important. (Ad Astra)

keep his epileptic fits so small – she will of course tell them, but she will worry when he is not so fit.

He will go to school there – and be in a unit of six blind children, with two attendants, and of course the schooling will be mostly with sound, geared to hearing and not seeing. I hope they will understand his words.

I asked Ann if there were any others with his complaint but she said no, not in that unit. But she quoted an enquiry into autistic children there, which included three Tuberous Sclerosis and there was a suggestion that autism, as epilepsy, might be only a symptom – but of what?

Ann's TS Society is very flourishing. They have enquiries for information from all over the country and the questionnaires the doctors asked for are beginning to come in. They even had one from New Zealand. Esther, the chairman (Ann is sec.), wrote optimistically to 'The Society for the Handicapped, New Zealand', and presumably other countries, and got answers!

It is just foolish of me to have mixed feelings, I know, and probably by the time I come to read this I will smile at myself – time having passed – and as time does, it will heal.

No! Very understandable. I would be the same. (Waveney)

Hang on to fact that James goes home for weekends. Very important this, I think. (Roberta)

July 1984

Sad Story

It has taken me a long time to be able to write about this bit of news. About six months ago Ann and John were told that as a result of a brain scan on James there was a new frontal growth which was not operable. The Drs suggested he had about a year of life.

Naturally we were upset but said to each other, 'Well, we have had him for twelve years to enjoy his being.' I thought most of Ann, whose life has been wrapped round the case of James and how she would react when it comes. Granted she has other interests when he is at school Mon–Fri. She lectures to voluntary helpers at homes for the mentally retarded,[*] has her work for the Tuberous Sclerosis Parents' Society, and she is a JP in Witney. But when James is home she has to help him dress – though he is very able to feed himself, amuse himself, and is lavatory trained. But he is still overactive and needs someone to be at hand all the time. He can always be calmed and quietened by a fond piece of music on the tape recorder, often pop or 'Pat the Postman'. He can draw but his efforts are about a 3-yr-old, IQ I should think 6 yr. Speech OK.

[*]*Suzanne does V.W. 3 times a week at small schools offshoot of Gt. Ormond St. Hospital. (Roberta)*

They brought him down to me one weekend but unfortunately it was cold, but we did paddle, both of us. Then they took him to a small place in S. West Wales, where he was able to enjoy lovely weather and lots of sea. Fortunately John was able to be there some of the time – Ann's mother was there and she is so good with him.

It was a strange sensation to look across to the boy and think, 'You are going to die,' but a somewhat silly thought for it's about the only thing we are all sure of.

How will he go? I asked my Dr, who said one of three ways: (1) bronchial infection (2) gradually getting weaker (3) sudden attack. One hopes the last.

What can one say? The poor parents! (Ad Astra)
Yes. Terribly sad indeed. (Isis)
Oh Sirod, I am so terribly sorry for you all. (Janna)

James 1971–1984

I write at John and Ann's on the eve of James's
funeral. Everyone else is out, about necessary jobs and
the house is clean and tidy for visitors. I think there
will be many at the crematorium as he was popular
with all the school and the social services, and of
course the village and the Tuberous Soc. which Ann
has helped to organise.

I came here Sunday, John fetched me, and I go to
the postponed holiday in Cornwall on Thursday – to
my brother and Joan in this Helford Estuary Cottage.
They planned to come up and fetch me but Douglas
wasn't well at the weekend, and I am quite able to
take a coach from here.

When James came to me for the weekend 2–3
months ago he complained of a headache. Ann said he
was asking for the seaside. Unfortunately it was cold
and we could only paddle. She had wondered if he
would last for their planned holiday in Pembroke, but
he did and they had a lovely two sunny weeks on the
beach near Haverford West, where they have taken
him for years – staying at the same understanding
people who have a handicapped child themselves.

John and Ann plan to take the ashes to scatter there
(St Bride's Bay) this next weekend, as they have no
connection with churches and don't like cemeteries.
He also lasted to enjoy his 13th birthday.

Then he started vomiting with screaming headaches.
It was distressing as the hospital was not interested
until the brain-scan unit was available in four days'
time. Fortunately Ann has some pull at Radcliffe – she
has a 'desk' there and he was admitted. The brain
scan showed the growth had caused the 'shunt' to fail.

For the uninitiated this is a plastic tube inserted
below the skin to take the liquid preserve from the

brain to the jugular vein which he had worn for years. They were able to insert another on the other side and he had three days at home and then the acute pain came again and one was inserted between brain and stomach. This gave him peace and he died in his sleep Friday 7th. Ann had washed him and put him to bed in hospital as usual, she read him *Postman Pat* and left his favourite tape running as usual, *Bridge over Troubled Water*.

Of course, Ann wishes she had held his hand to the end and that it had been at home, and that he need not have suffered. But as I pointed out to her, if he had not been ill he would not have been in hospital, and they would not have been able to set up the removal of the tumour to be frozen and sent to the TS research doctor at Nottingham – which was done without fuss. It is ironic that Ann was one of the people who organised this research project and this is the first one to be sent in time – the others which had been sent were too late.

Later. I write now in Cornwall and somehow all this seems another world. The funeral was OK – just. Some of the impersonal routine jarred a little (sorry if that upsets anyone). I made two bunches of flowers from the garden for myself and Joan and Doug. Which were on the coffin with theirs and other Gran's. Then there were lots of flowers, bunches, posies and pots, including a hebe called James in the vestibule, and I gathered lots of cheques for TSA . . .

My heart aches for [Ann], but trust she will find herself busy. She is a JP–parish councillor, and gives a course of lectures – I think for volunteers who wish to help with the mentally retarded. And she has her TSA correspondence.

She was typing away at copy for *SCAN*, their magazine, when I started this. She showed me this:

James 1971–1984
We gave you a blade of grass.
And you gave us back roses.

Oh Sirod – So much sadness for her
and John – and for you. (Accidia)

Ann continues to work with the Tuberous Sclerosis Association. It is now a mid-sized charity with chapters in many countries. The organisation provides support to families and promotes further research into the disorder.

Sirod remained physically active until 1988, when she fell and broke her hip. At this point she moved from her flat in Weymouth to a residential home. Here she spent her time reading, writing to the CCC and visiting her family. She died in 1996.

7

Growing Old

Going home at last

1

I am HOME *Cornelia* after two disappointments which made me feel rather hopeless. Sister came & see me in the ambulance — there was already a woman my age going to another hospital. & we went there first. It was odd the ambulance men did not know — & c

Bergholt and we stopped five times to ask where Aldous Close was before we got here and even at the top of the Close I said "It's not here" but they went down it and I recognised it at last

Ted had seen the ambulance from school so was here to welcome me

Carole has been helpful and has come twice to lunch — I think she enjoys lunching with us & while we were having our coffee today a social worker called with a chair which is easier to get out of. There is no doubt there is help for the sick once you get your name on their books. They have fitted a contraption over the loo and over the bath but a nurse will blanket bath me for the present. If only the pain ceased a little it would be fine but "they" say Its early days yet and I suppose its just grinning & bearing it for the time being — (This makes me mad, C, because there are pain killers Codeine, Aspirin, etc. & I would use them. Can't understand Dan not helping you at this time — poor Sarah)R

Thank you all so much for letters received

[margin note top left] Hope pain is better somehow & that you are not bored out of your mind — At least there are events in hospital MC

[margin note middle left] I hope with the bed bumps on cooked at for Jun? Poor love, do hope pain is easing, & that you feel stronger or might. (Pds)

[margin note lower left] Oh, poor you! Do hope pain has eased now.

[margin note bottom left] (I did write — did you get it? Earlyon. Tos)

I found myself depressed after reading CCC . . . If only one could help! I own to a slight frisson each time I open a mag. There is a sensation of 'what now?' which mars the former anticipation of interest and pleasure. And I do feel a bit guilty to be hale and hearty when others clearly are not, even though I know my turn will come.

Accidia, 1979

The final years of the magazine were difficult ones. As the women aged, they faced the unavoidable hardships inherent in deteriorating physical and mental health, for both themselves and their loved ones.

Many of them assumed the role of long-term care-givers for their partners, and several of these women became widowed. The CCC helped them to endure their burdens and their grief. Losing a member was one of the most distressing parts of this new, harsh reality. Between 1975 and 1980, seven women in the CCC died, and it became increasingly painful for surviving members to carry on with the magazine. As Janna wrote in 1980:

One feels almost as if we in CCC were the cast of some ghastly Agatha Christie play in which one after another is struck down and we have no idea who will be taken next – and who left until the bitter end.

However, it was important for those who remained that the magazine should continue to exist, because it was their main source of support and friendship. It was also their antidote to the loneliness and boredom that ensued as they lost their husbands and left their communities to live and die in nursing homes.

A Priori, Ad Astra and Cotton Goods all wrote to the women about their heartbreaking experiences of growing old.

A Priori

At the end of the Second World War, A Priori's husband Lough was offered a commission from Sir Ernest Debenham, who had an estate in Dorset at Affpuddle. Sir Ernest wanted a war memorial built for the Affpuddle church, and following this project he became Lough's patron and commissioned him to refurbish much of the interior of the church. The family enjoyed economic stability for a few years and Lough was able briefly to give up teaching and focus on his art, which was in the style of medieval church sculpture.

When Sir Ernest passed away, Lough hoped to return to teaching, but the school authorities were reluctant to reappoint him because they knew that he would leave if he found sculpting work. The family faced financial difficulties and the house in Swaffham Bulbeck started to deteriorate. In 1950, Lough and A Priori decided to sell and move to Cambridge.

They bought a tall Victorian house and let rooms to students as a way to supplement their income. The house was a gauge of the family's economic situation, as the harder times were, the more rooms they had to let. A Priori worked in Cambridge first as a private secretary to a senior consultant at Addenbrooke's Hospital and then as a transcriber for J. H. Plumb, the Cambridge historian and author. Lough was hired as a woodwork teacher at Cambridge High School for Boys and he remained there until he retired. During this time he also became one of the founding members of the Cambridge Designer Craftsmen. He continued to sculpt and received many commissions for work in and around Cambridge, most notably, the Madonna and Child *in the entrance of the University Church of Great*

St Mary's and the Pelican in her Piety in the Great Court of Corpus Christi.

In the mid-1960s, they moved to Milton, about three miles outside Cambridge, but continued to be involved in Cambridge life. They both participated in local drama courses and productions, with Lough producing and creating the props for the shows and A Priori performing. A Priori was also the president of the Townswomen's Guild.

Generally Lough worked in isolation and basically lived for the love of his wife. The intensity of their relationship was evident to every CCC member. Even today the remaining women and children of the CCC refer to their union as the 'best marriage of the CCC'. Yet, to some extent, this image of a perfect marriage may have been misleading, created by A Priori through her persona of writer. Never one to hold back her thoughts, A Priori was one of the most dynamic writers in the magazine. She was constantly challenging the others intellectually and established herself as a straightforward, no-nonsense, self-assured woman. Her lively spirit and sense of humour made her one of the most likeable members of the group. She wrote to the others how much she valued the magazine: 'I could never have anticipated how much CCC could enrich my life, not only in friendship, but in enlarging my outlook and knowledge of life. Blessed CCC!' Yet the confidence and clarity that she radiated throughout the pages of the CCC threw a veil over some of the insecurities that she had in her daily life. A Priori struggled with emotional honesty and often found it difficult to communicate intimately with Lough.

In 1977, when A Priori was preparing to look after her granddaughter Rachel while her daughter Sally had a hysterectomy, she herself fell ill and had to be rushed to hospital. Lough had been diagnosed with melanoma *on his leg the year before, and now A Priori had bowel cancer. She was unable to give Lough the news and informed her younger daughter Vicky that she would have to be the one to tell him.*

February 2, 1977

Well, of course no crisis ever happens to us without its ludicrous side. Here have I been since before Christmas fussing about Sally and her hysterectomy and being told how we must all appreciate how hard and difficult her situation is and how it's our duty to rally round and how she was too busy to come to Yorkshire for Christmas and the children didn't mind because they appreciated that she had to rest and prepare for her operation. So she went into hospital on Thursday Feb. 3 and I spent the day down at her house clearing things out and cleaning the fridge and stripping Rachel's bed and collecting the cat, etc. etc. Her op. was fixed for Friday afternoon. So I developed what appeared to be a classic acute appendix and was rushed in and operated on the same night. So there was poor old Lough frantically ringing two hospitals trying to find out how we were doing. Sally was in the old hospital in the town and I went to the grand new one on the outskirts. Funny how life in hospital develops a rhythm of its own and life outside it seems unreal. *Yes. (Yonire)*

I was thankful I wasn't in a separate ward. There were six[*] of us, mostly dental cases. The dental clinic there is doing some of the most advanced work in the county, orthodontology, I think it's called, and there were short-stay people having impacted wisdom teeth removed.

[*]*Nice number – Tony's ward had 15 beds! (Roberta)*

Jane and Vicky have been so marvellous, coming here and staying to help Lough and now to help me. Rachel has been here and has been so super, such a help and companion to Lough. Sally was in a big ward at the old hospital, a very jolly show and everyone in lively and crashing form, a real Butlins camp of a place. Sally, they said, seemed to be enjoying herself no end and everything went well and she has made a very good recovery. They sent her off to Hunstanton, their home of recovery, what a grim place at this time of the year, but of course Lough and I couldn't cope with her here. She comes back next Tuesday and dear Jane is coming down again to see her settled in. Lough used to drive over to see me, about seven miles from Milton, and then go down to pick Rachel up from school and take her in to see Sally. It was all rather much for him and naturally he got very tired and it was anxious for him too. When they told me the ulcer was malignant I was anxious to keep it from him, but then we all realised it is much better to face it together as a family.[*] They have all been so wonderful and he has supported them too.   [*]*Yes FAR better. (Yonire)*

They have removed all the infected parts of the bowel, so they don't seem to think it's likely to spread. Naturally I'm as likely to get secondaries as anyone, but I'm not much concerned. It's funny how unreal these situations seem when you're involved in   *Yes. (Yonire)* them. The snag is that when they take a chunk out of the bowel the rest of it isn't very keen to go on working and also food tastes filthy for ages. Well, they give you a drip feed for days and days, there isn't much to that or the drainage. What is nasty is the tube they put down the nose into the stomach and that really is a form of torture. However, one recovers. Everyone has been so kind to me and the nurses were so nice to me. It was lovely to see *Rosa*, such a long way to come from No. 34. Many thanks to all of you who have written and sent cards. I try to do a bit more every day, but I don't really care much about food.

However, I'm determined to get going again as soon as possible.

The family is now anxious for us to think of moving this summer. What with Lough last spring and now me, we have really been such a bother to them, and of course cancer-wise we are both in the same boat. So as soon as I'm fit we'll go and have a prowl round Merton and see if we can see anything we could afford and bear to live in. I think it will be all rather exciting.

Sorry none of this is madly coherent, I'm not feeling very bright. I feel so thankful we've had such fun lately, seen the Greek Islands and Yugo-Slavia and Majorca. When I came home I thought how super our home was with all the things that Lough has done. We've never had any money, nor any proper pride or cared a damn about the cost of things or keeping up appearances and yet here we are surrounded by a loving family and lots of friends dropping in and enjoying life and mean to go on looking our last on all things lovely and living from day to day.

This is the way to be happy. (Janna)

Us too. (Roberta)

Long may it last! (Ad Astra)

And we have each other, how lucky.

Oh yes! (Roberta)

We all think this has clarified our ideas as a family about how we feel towards each other. So silly really that it should be me – when I'm never ill and usually rushing round after somebody or something – should cause all this to-do. I'd actually lent my dressing gown and only two decent nighties to Sally, so Lough and Jane had to go to Mitchams and buy one! All so ridiculous!

Just what would happen! (Isis)

Thank God, say I, for the Welfare State and the National Health service, from which I

Yes. (Yonire)

have had such wonderful care and attention and such kindness from the nurses, who are so young and you'd think would be fed up with old women like me with their drainage pipes feeding into plastic bags of disgusting liquid. When the wound broke down and there was a hell of a mess I said I was sorry to be such a pest, and they kept saying, 'Don't worry, it doesn't matter!' I had to stay in a few days longer to get rid of the infection and now the district nurse comes in to dress it, but it doesn't hurt any more, or not to speak of. I went over to the Impington Art exhibition this afternoon! You can't keep this tough old bird down. I hope to get up to the lunch if things go all right.

Oh yes, and brave, AP (The tube has been removed?) what can you eat? Poor love. (Roberta)
Very sorry about all this and while admiring your toughness, hope you are taking care. (Accidia)
AP – Did you ever have pain before? Ulcer must have been hard at it silently for ages – cruel cancer. (Roberta)

A Priori wrote the following excerpt on the day of the CCC luncheon in March. Elektra was hosting the event, as she often did, but A Priori was unable to attend because of her cancer treatment.

March 17, 1977

From A Priori with Regret

Today I thought I should be in London, enjoying Elektra's fabulous lunch party. I don't think I have ever missed one before (sometimes to the Prune's fury) and here is a big thank-you to E for all the super times and super food she has given us both at West Hill and at County Hall. Happy memories!

I have radio-therapy on Monday, Tuesday and Thursday, and the last is obligatory (I could have asked to change one of the other two) because the doctor sees one then. I would have had a bash, but both Carol, who was here on Sunday, and Lough were adamant that I could never have made it, so it saved argument! Also the reaction from radio-therapy set in today, I suppose the effect is cumulative, I have been very lucky to get away with no side-effects until now, and indeed since I left hospital a month ago I have almost led a normal life since Vicky and Jane left. Bless their hearts, they were here for nearly a month between them, looking after Lough and Rachel whilst I was in hospital and then coping with me when I got home. But today has been a bad day, with a lot of pain and sickness, so I'm glad I wasn't in the train to Liverpool St. Our cheerful medics, as usual, totally unperturbed, gave me some pain-killers, which I promptly lost, however the pain disappeared too and now, 6 p.m., I am more or less back to normal. It says in the *Guardian* today that radio-therapy units cost millions of pounds, that the 'cobalt bomb' (which I am to have next week), one machine alone costs £400,000. As we all sit round in our hospital gowns, waiting our turn, we are a real 'Cancer Ward', but pretty cheerful on the whole, swapping news of our side-effects. And also a great deal cleaner and kinder than Solsinitzon's grim hospital. Well, I hope it does us all some good, as I look at some of the patients obviously a great deal worse than me, I sometimes doubt it.

Sorry this made me cry. I still can't believe it's our AP to suffer so. (Roberta)

I have often thought in the past how different our set-up is from Yonire's; how impossible it would be for me to take to my bed, even for a day or two, and leave the cooking and housework to Lough. I have been lucky enough to be almost never ill.*

*Yes, that is why your op. plus is such a shock. (Roberta)

I have nursed Lough through his gall-bladder complications, hiatus hernia, to say nothing of his melanoma last year and numerous minor ailments. I have also, of course, stuck by the girls in all sorts of ailments, particularly Sally. And it has never occurred to me or anyone else that Ma would not always be on her feet, who ever else went down. The last seven weeks have been a decided eye-opener. Lough has been prepared to cope with everything, as well as these tiresome journeys and hanging about at the hospital. I have managed to pack him off to the workshop, whilst I do the shopping (in the village – ancient bike), cooking and a bit of washing, but as soon as I flag he is on the job. And both Jane and Vicky said what a tower of strength he was to them all when things were rather grim. Even when Vicky told him (at my request) that the ulcer was malignant, he was naturally very upset, but he supported them, there was none of this 'O poor me' stuff.[*]

[*]*But there wouldn't be with him. (Sirod)*

They said they had never realised what hidden reserves of strength he had. And at the same time he was sweet to Rachel, they were laughing joking and teasing each other. No wonder all the grandchildren love him, young and old.

Of course! (Ad Astra)
Well understand this. (Roberta)
Yes indeed. (Isis)

April 18, 1977

Today I went down to the town on my moped for the first time for nearly three months. It started like a bird and took me down to the nearest petrol pump (it runs on a mixture, so any old garage won't do) where I observed that it had done 68 miles since I last filled it in early January, and of course I must have run it nearly dry before packing it in after I came back on it from Sally's in the pouring rain that fatal Thursday night, January 27th.

Roberta says she would like the details of 'my operation' – well, I've always thought that however much one is delighted to talk about such things, *Not mine! (Ad Astra)* it bores the pants off everyone else. *Nor mine. (Roberta)*

However, skip, if that's how you feel. *Or mine. (Yonire)*

It is quite true that I felt no pain or discomfort at all, until the early hours of that Friday, and even then I snoozed a bit and said to myself, 'Silly old fool, worrying about Sally. Pain is all in the mind.' And even when I got up and it didn't go away, I got myself a cup of coffee, fed the cats and did the dustbins before telling Lough. I did take my temperature but the thermometer, being very seldom used, didn't work very well and registered about 86, so I abandoned that. In fact, it was quite high, I believe. I have had long talks with the hospital and radio-therapy doctors as well as with our own, who is a friend, and they do seem at Addenbrooke's to be extremely forthcoming, and they are always saying, 'Any questions? Anything you want to know?' I was surprised that they told me, as I have known people who were never told. Piers insisted on seeing the registrar, as he did with Lough, and they told him in both cases. One of the registrars then told me. Anyway I would have to know since it is obvious that all the dozens of people who go to radio-therapy clinic have had cancer in one of its many forms, so you'd have to be pretty daft if you didn't guess. The fact is that cancer is not *in itself* painful.*   *This is the evilness of it. (Roberta)

A tumour has to impinge on a vital organ or an ulcer touch a nerve before the trouble starts. There are no nerves in the gut, so mine worked its way till it got stuck to the abdominal wall, and this set up the peritonitis. In the surgical emergency dept they were a bit doubtful about appendicitis, which in general gets much younger people. But it had all the classic symptoms. I was much more concerned about Sally and was quite convinced they'd do it, if not as an outpatient (!), at any rate only keep me a day or two and I could skip off home and look after Rachel. They in fact removed the secum, if you know what that is, I don't. I thought it was a plant, no, that's sedum, but the stick-up is what they are directing the radio-therapy at, in case there is any cancer floating about there, 'Which might,' he said, 'give you trouble in years to come.' 'Years?' I said. 'Yes, years,' said he. Anyway, I think one should be open about cancer, realising that heaps of people have it in various forms and still live to be very old,[*] which anyway I've no desire to do. Radio-therapy is nothing at the time, you don't feel it, but the cumulative effect of a month's treat-

[*] *I read somewhere that almost all the very old have a carcinoma of one sort or another. (Ad Astra) Yes. I've heard of several. (Isis)*

ment is to make you feel rather queasy and very tired. I suppose it's a sort of radiation sickness. The girls who work the machines shove it in position, then skip off and watch it on a television screen. Now I have a month off and then have chemo-therapy, which reduces the blood-count, whatever that may mean.

I read a book at Jane's about nature cures and health and all that which said that cancer of the bowel[*] is caused by people taking no exercise and eating all the wrong foods and taking drugs and so on. And ulcers there are caused by worry. Well, I

[*] *Bowel – 'They' always say change in motions heralds trouble (but not in your case?) (Roberta)*

should have thought I was just the wrong person, for I think I take life's ups and downs pretty philosophi-cally. It is true I have been worried about Sally lately . . . but in general I'm not a worrier. Also I take lots of exercise, I walk, I bicycle, I garden, I swim when I get the chance and until recently I have done keep fit and country dancing. And although I'm not a vegetarian, I eat lots of fruit and vegeta-bles, which I like. I have never had any trouble with my 'works' and I never take drugs, not even aspirin, not so much that I'm against them,

Must you diet in some way? And how long? Where is scar? (Roberta)

but I have no need of them. Well, you never know
when life is going to smack you in the eye.

May all go well now. (Ad Astra)
Please Lord yes. (Roberta)
Yes – I hope things improve a bit now. (Yonire)
Thank you for this, <u>brave</u> you, but details?
No! A) Did removal of tubes hurt? B) What
were you fed on after that? Etc. (Roberta)

> *In the summer of that year, Lough and A Priori moved*
> *back to Cambridge, as everyone felt it would be easier*
> *for them to be right in town. A Priori sent this article to*
> *the women in the CCC in 1978, after she had been*
> *admitted to hospital for more tests.*

1978

. . . I had another one of my ludicrous days at the hospital the other day. I have probably said I've been having a spot of bother* with my back, so they decided I
should have a 'bone scan'. I had to be

*Oh AP dear. What an understatement – You are so brave. (Janna)

there at 9.30 a.m. and dear old Sally, who,
like her parents, is no early riser, actually
got me there in time. She offered to come up to the
Nuclear Clinic with me, but I knew she had a lot of
jobs to do, so I sent her off again. Well, the procedure
is that they inject the blood stream with some sub-
stance or other and then ask you to wait or come
back in *four* hours* – having by that time drunk
two pints of liquid.** As I have told you, the new
Addenbrooke's Hospital is miles
from the town and to add to the com-
plication there was a bus strike on!

*Oh, what hell. (Roberta)

**Drinkable, or foul? And <u>HOW</u> does one get down 2 pints of liquid on demand? (Roberta)

Lough didn't want me to go on my
moped, as I usually do, because these drugs often
make you feel a bit queer.* So I rang him
up to ask him his suggestions. 'I'll come
and keep you company,' he said, and he got

*This is an under-statement, I'll bet. (Roberta)

on to my moped and came along. Fortunately it was a lovely day and although there are no nice gardens round the hospital, which is still being built, there are some nice trees turning to autumn colours and we found a wall to sit upon and amused ourselves doing the *Guardian*'s easy cross-word (not bright enough for the difficult one) . . .

I've told John that you did this as he was rather scornful when I became an addict! (Accidia)

In due course I got back to my department of nuclear medicine, where they have a scanning machine which goes backwards and forwards taking lots and lots of photographs. And of course nobody tells you any-thing and I don't suppose they ever will, except that you've 'got to learn to live with it'. Ha! Ha! . . .

Oh AP, can't one force them to tell you something? You are truly brave and I do admire you more than I can express. Marvellous writer and reporter. (Roberta)

A week today and no news of the bone scan of course. But if it was serious we would have heard because they always jump on cancer like lightning. The girls keep ringing up and coming down, and Lough gets in a tizz and I say, 'What do you bet me that Keith (doctor) comes breezing in and says, "Nothing the matter – take an aspirin!"?'

I trust no news is good news. (Janna)
I admire your courage enormously and hope it will not be stretched too far. (Accidia)
I send you genuine admiration and love, AP. (Roberta)

Fortunately, the results of A Priori's bone scan were good and she remained in remission for another year. She and Lough took advantage of this time, spending it with their eleven grandchildren and travelling. How-ever, by 1979, A Priori's health rapidly started to decline due to a recurrence of bowel cancer. The couple moved to London to live with Vicky, and A Priori was treated at the Royal Marsden cancer hospital.

A Priori struggled with emotional honesty and she found herself incapable of talking to Lough about dying, even though she was organising her affairs. She asked her daughter Vicky to tell her father and help him to prepare. Though Vicky tried to convince her otherwise, A Priori said, 'I can't do it, you'll have to.' Lough was also unable to approach her about it, as his life had revolved around his love for her and he couldn't bear to face the truth about her illness. In the end, they never acknowledged to one another that she was dying.

On January 10, 1980, A Priori passed away in a hospice at the age of seventy-two. Though she had hoped Lough would stay in London with Vicky, he did not feel comfortable around her husband and chose to move to Yorkshire with Jane. He lived there for about six months, but kept to himself and was obviously struggling. A Priori had sheltered him so much during their life together that he had never needed anyone else. He now felt completely alone and wasn't able to cope without her. He decided to move back to London and get his own flat near Vicky's house.

After she died, Lough sculpted a beautiful memorial for his wife, an angel that is displayed at St Mary's Church in Merton Park, London. On the morning of October 30, 1980, Vicky and Lough went to visit the angel. Lough said to Vicky, 'I've decided that I'm going to move on. I know she's waiting for me, she's waiting for me just outside a door, and I've got to find that door,' but, he added, 'in the meantime, I'm going to start my life again.' He and Vicky parted and arranged to meet in the afternoon to look at a house that Lough had decided to buy. He never arrived as his heart had stopped and he was gone.

Ad Astra

Ad Astra was undeniably the heart of the CCC. She was meticulous in her organisation and coordination of the magazine. She sent out each edition like clockwork, on the 1st and the 15th of the month, and took great care in embroidering and pressing the linen covers before circulation. More importantly, she kept the momentum going because she truly cared about the CCC and each individual member. Even though some women were less connected to the group than others, everyone seemed to have a special connection to Ad Astra.

Ad Astra was born in 1903 and grew up in Kensington. She came from a working-class family and her father was employed by Barker's department store in the packing department. During her childhood she was a voracious reader and was awarded a grant to attend the county secondary school and then a scholarship to University College London. From 1922 to 1925 she studied English and French and graduated with a First Class degree. The following year she took a diploma course in Pedagogy.

After her studies, Ad Astra moved to Lancashire and taught in a grammar school near Bolton for two years. In 1927, she met her future husband, John, on a crowded train in France. He thought she was French and tried to offer her his seat, but he didn't speak French, while she thought he was German and she couldn't speak German. After struggling to communicate, John said in frustration, 'Oh, I do wish you spoke English!' and she said, 'Oh, I do!' Then they discovered that they were actually both from Kensington!

John was a timber importer and veneer merchant and ran a business in the East End of London. A year after meeting him, Ad Astra moved back to Kensington and taught at Ealing County Grammar School. They were engaged for three years before they finally married, in 1930, because Ad Astra was reluctant to give up her teaching job due to the marriage bar. Once they did marry, they moved to Harrow because John didn't want them to be too close to either of their families.

In 1933, Ad Astra gave birth to Clare, and then had her son, Christopher, in 1934. When the war started, John kept his job, which was a reserved occupation because he supplied timber for the big liners. Regrettably, he was separated from his family, as he was required to fire-watch nightly at his business in Shoreditch. He and the nightwatchman would stay awake at night so that when a bomb fell they could smother it with sandbags before it could explode and burn down the building. He only came home for a few hours on Sundays throughout the entire war. In 1940, Ad Astra sent Christopher and Clare to A. S. Neill's progressive school, Summerhill, which was temporarily located in Wales. The children stayed for six months, along with Elektra's two boys, but then Ad Astra and Elektra removed them. They realised that their children were not being properly cared for or educated. Ad Astra spent the next year tutoring Christopher and Clare.

In 1947, Ad Astra and John moved to Essex. They found a large mansion on six acres of land, 'Down Hall', which had nearly thirty rooms, including over ten bedrooms and a chauffeur's quarters. They decided to share the space with Ad Astra's brother and his family and her father, who had recently retired.

Once they moved to Down Hall, John continued to work in London, where he stayed four nights a week, returning home on Friday evenings. Christopher and Clare were away most of the time at boarding school. Ad Astra was kept very busy renovating the house as it had been occupied by the Air Ministry during the war and was then left empty and in disrepair for two years. Her day-to-day involvement with the CCC was also enormously time-consuming, and she often hosted the CCC's yearly meeting, as she had room for the out-of-town members to stay overnight. In 1951, John rented a flat in London to be used by him and the two children, who were studying. Ad Astra frequently spent time there socialising.

After retiring in 1959, John decided to grow and sell organic vegetables. Ad Astra had severe arthritis by this time but helped John by preparing the vegetables for market. In 1972, they moved temporarily to a village outside Norwich because a nuclear power plant had been built near Down Hall. After three years they moved again, to 'Greshams', a house in Carleton Rode, sixteen miles from Norwich. Around this time John started to experience health problems. Unfortunately, his condition deteriorated rapidly. He had been a heavy smoker all his life but had stopped in the mid-1950s prior to surgery for a detached retina. The doctors had warned him that if he coughed, he would ruin the operation and the chance to recover his sight, so he never had another cigarette. Despite this, John developed trouble with his lungs in 1974. A few years later, Ad Astra shared the details of his illness with the women.

July 19, 1976

'Us'

I suppose I ought to be able to write something worthy as a record of our forty-six years of marriage, but nothing elevating springs to mind.

Here we are 'surprised by time' in these last few years, remarking with Ulysses that 'we are not that strength which once we were' but essentially our same selves who married on July 26th, 1930. I must admit we don't look the same! John is two stone lighter and I am two stone heavier than in 1930 for a start! And the usual penalties of age haven't been spared us, so we have fewer teeth and thinner hair and our backs are not so straight and our steps not so quick. (In fact my arthritic hips make mine *slow*, though I note with amusement that I still use the old vocabulary and speak of just nipping upstairs for this or that, just *So do I. (Yonire)* dashing here or running there.) And John is in a rather bad way just now.

It has been rather sudden, this change of state from the never-ill, strong-as-an-ox man to the man now in hospital with a mask and an oxygen cylinder to help him breathe. It was in December 1974 that he had first had a day in bed. He and our neighbour at Wood Green had been working on the surface of the track to the cottages on the 17th and the wind had been high and the work hard and I supposed he had overdone things. On the 19th he had only liquids but was up in the afternoon, but by the 21st our good Dr Hill came out to him and said he had influenza. He was up for parts of the 22nd and 23rd and for all Christmas, but was not very bright and went to see Dr Hill on the 30th at the Health Centre. However, he went for a weekend to Clare in London Jan. 3rd to 6th of the new year and on Jan. 10th cheerfully had his chest X-rayed in Norwich to please the doctor. By Jan. 22nd he was in West Norwich hospital for two days and by Feb. 4th 'a spot of bother' in his chest had been diagnosed. Even so, on the 5th he went to London and gave Neil and his bank manager lunch, returning the same day, quite a journey, and on the 6th had a bonfire in the sunny afternoon. The visit to Brompton Hospital had been arranged and (another day return) took place on Feb. 11th. The two hospitals, W. Norwich and Brompton, seemed to disagree about

John's lung, the former saying it was not operable, the latter that it was, and by Feb. 25th poor Dr Hill at last said the word 'cancer', and if you think John was an invalid then you're wrong for he promptly did a lot of pruning and bonfiring and bought some new shirts before the week was out. At the end of February he did his income tax returns and gave me £50 'to carry on with' for the short time he'd be in Brompton. On March 3rd he departed, on the 4th and 5th he had tests and a bronchoscope, on the 8th he phoned that he was coming home, on the 11th I visited him in London and on the 12th he had a lung removed.

So you see in less than three months he went from strength to weakness and whether that operation was the best way to treat his condition or not we shall never know. See *The Doctor's Dilemma* and you will see the arguments of different doctors for different treatments. A surgeon naturally wants to cut it out; a physician to treat it by other methods, a naturopath to believe that it is curable by still other means. One simply can't help oneself, Clare and Jo were much against the operation, John trusted the surgeon. I honestly don't know even now if we did right, for the operation was in itself at the time far more devastating than the cancer. But one doesn't know how fast the thing would have developed, and developed secondaries, if it had been left alone. When John came home on April 1st he was undoubtedly ill, weak and exhausted. Dr Hill, who visited him on the 4th, said he should rest more, he was typing and 'catching up' with letters! Was he *thin*! I called him Belsen for he was skeletal, but he ate fairly well and spent most of his time sitting by the fire in his dressing-gown and within a fortnight was able to go to Long Stratton and even to Diss by car. Before the end of April he was walking all round the Green and had been to London for a weekend and a check-up at

Brompton. We were still having fires when May came in but he got a walk most days in the good patches, but when he attempted a longer effort on May 16th in Norwich (preparing for our move) he came home very tired and rather out of temper, having walked too far to no purpose about vinyl and carpets. The following week he went over to Carleton Rode twice and by the end of May he was at Clare's again for a weekend. On June 10th we moved to Carleton Rode and I took care that John neither lifted nor pulled or pushed things but even so a journey into Norwich by June-end could leave him too exhausted to eat after he came home. I suppose by July he was as well as he will ever be post-operation.

Now what's gone wrong when a year ago he was able to trip off to Chelmsford or Norwich or London and only sometimes find it a bit much? He didn't do any heavy gardening for we had the front laid out, the back made into hay, and the patio was put down by two men who specialised in that sort of thing. He weeded, he sifted soil, he cleaned up a ditch, he bonfired, over months you understand, nothing rushed, and this May (as you all know!) we were both tackling the flowerbeds and lawn that were suddenly full of weeds. So I think it was as recently as June 4th when things changed. John went to Brompton for a check on a chest pain on the unoperated side and they wanted him back for a bronchoscope (I notice some doctors put in the 'i' – bronchioscope – and some don't) which he had on June 16th followed by the disastrous return home on the 17th. After that John just got worse and worse in spite of all Dr Hill or I could do with pills, medicine, a steam-tent and kettles and so on. John could not breathe lying down so passed the nights in an armchair in his bedroom and I could hear him trying to breathe though I was in another room. It was like Vesuvius but there was no eruption so no clearance, and because he couldn't breathe he couldn't eat and lost rapidly the stone he'd put on, Belsen again. Finally Dr Hill got him into a single room in West Norwich hospital and that's where he is now. In a bed, but with a back rest and six pillows keeping him up and an oxygen cylinder and a mask helping him to breathe.

I can't tell you how glad I am John is so well looked after as he is in West Norwich. It's a little hospital (the Norfolk and Norwich one is the big one) and the Mancroft Ward is the chest-specialising part and it's a separate building across the road from the rest of the hospital. It has its own staff and dietician and kitchens etc. John wouldn't *look* at Brompton's food nor Nfk and Nch's when he was there for a day, but this is different. I enclose diet sheet showing what he manages so far. You never met a more devoted staff nor a lovelier bevy of young nurses with their blue eye shadow matching their uniforms and their useless little white hats jauntily topping their untidy hair. They wash him, cream his 'seat', shave his face, chivvy him along and coax him to another spoonful of ice-cream. I have been introduced to his favourite, a beauty from Ceylon, and of course to George, who is a Ghanaian who wanted to know me. They're all invited to Greshams *when he's better*. 'I should be so happy!' as the doubtful put it, a Jewish idiom I believe?

Well, I set out to write about us and all you've had is a blow by blow account of an illness whose outcome is doubtful. Happy anniversary it will be if all goes well till July 26th . . .

A Century later the same day.

It was at that point that the telephone went. 'Your husband's condition is deteriorating rapidly. Would

you come?' The formula that gives the mind a short
time to switch from 'No, no, no' to 'Brace yourself',
for of course he was dead and I knew it. I think he
must have been alone and collapsed sideways and hit
his head on the corner of his trolley-cupboard. He had
a small cut above his left eyebrow and a bruise length-
ways out towards the ear from his left eye.[*] It was
quick I hope.

[*]*Oh! Ad Astra! How nasty. I'm sorry about this.
(Yes – It must have been quick.) (Yonire)
This was terribly poignant to read. (Isis)
Oh! Indeed it is. (Sirod)*

I expect you all know Cory's 'Heraclitus'? It came
to my mind today, so here it is whether or no.

> They told me, Heraclitus, they told me you were dead,
> They brought me bitter news to hear and bitter tears to
> shed.
> I wept as I remember'd how often you and I
> Had tired the sun with talking and sent him down the sky.
>
> And now that thou art lying, my dear old Carian guest,
> A handful of grey ashes, long long ago at rest,
> Still are thy pleasant voices, thy nightingales, awake;
> For Death, he taketh all away, but them he cannot take.

And last night I was rereading *Akenfield* and came
on this which pleased me.

I remember one cold November, I couldn't tell you how long
ago, and a woman came to me and said, 'My Billy has passed,
Sam. Ring the bell!' I said, 'How can I do that, Ma'am? The
tower has all been scaffolded for the repairs.' So off she went
sorrowful. Then I had an idea. I climbed up into the bell-
chamber, sat on the frame and banged the passing-bell with
my hammer! I thought, old Billy won't mind. It was that
bloody cold. But all could hear of the passing and take note.

*Almost a year later, Ad Astra sent this entry to the
women in response to an enquiry about life as a widow.*

You want to know about being widowed, Accidia.
Honesty, at all costs on all fronts? I'll try.

Anyone will tell you the obvious things you already
know. You are alone and whether you love or hate
that condition depends on a) your temperament b)
your previous married life, its condition and its length
and c) the length of time since the death of your husband. So you know or can easily imagine the silence
and how one tackles it. If you are like me you will
think 48 hours with no word spoken to or heard from
a living person bearable but not enviable, if you're like
some folks not given to reading, writing or introspection you'll either go mad and smash things, get out
and do something very active, or you'll become miser-
ably self-pitying and probably ask your doctor for
anti-depressants, valium so you sleep etc. or you take
to the bottle. I suppose for most people under 70 and
still active some sort of outside interest, a paid job, a
voluntary work, a study of some sort or a family
responsibility will fit the bill. For the handicapped
loneliness must be more of a problem, especially if
some of the handicapping involves loss of sight or
hearing. The radio, TV, records and tapes, knitting,
sewing, embroidery, pot plants, pet animals or birds,
one needs one's senses to help out and if one is widowed, is widowed at, say, 70, one has the double difficulty of physical deterioration and the longer than
average period of marriage behind one to make for
difficulty. I suppose it does become easier if one lives
on beyond the allotted span? If you've bloody well got
to do things you do them. But I am supposing. John
hasn't been a year dead yet. Why I always thought he
would outlive me I'm not sure. He came of a long
lived family, the *youngest* of the aunts was 85 at
death, but I think there was something else too, an

emotional (not mental) inability to imagine such a loss. Even in his last week I was sure he would recover and come back home. Even he thought that he would live, though 'not better'. I literally could not, with him, go through tax returns, his will, any business he had in hand, and if he sat quietly and then began, 'You have this house, my insurance . . .' I never let him finish. 'Stop it, stop it. I don't want anything except for you to get better. You'll see, you'll be all right and you'll do all that as you always have done.' Or if he said, 'Will you stay here if . . .?' I'd say 'We'll stay here. Stop it.' When the hospital people phoned their stupid 'deteriorating rapidly' and I knew their silly lie meant he had died I literally couldn't speak. Thank God I was alone. I remember staggering with the phone in my hand and I believe I may have been more conscious of the gap than they were at the other end because I said I would come at once and did.

Now eleven months later when, in what John would think a very haphazard way, I have seen to the bank and the expenditures and taxes, and claims, remade my will, got a man to do a scrap of digging and mowing, in fact somehow staggered on, even making meals, writing stories and letters, sowing seeds and 'potting on' this and that. I do not feel I am a scrap nearer 'adjustment', nearer living a life that is based on widowhood. And this is an odd thing but true and you must make what you like of it, but I'd have guessed that I was if anything likely to adjust to a life that involves a few women and no men inti-mately (I'm not meaning sexually, I'm meaning in close friendship), and I find I'm not. I quite definitely miss the male reaction to anything I do or say. I fear I may by writing this make more of it than it is. It is not that I don't enjoy the company and conversation of women. I do. My friends are women and have always been women and I think I would say that I admire many women and of the men I have known do not admire as many.

But I am definitely heterosexual in my make-up, I guess. I put it on record only because it is unexpected and makes things harder, but I should be horrified if you thought I could dream of remarriage or even of a man's living in the house so that I *had* to talk to him or cook for him. No, but I would like an occasional evening to talk books, politics, ideas – something a little more satisfying than *employing* a painter, carpenter, gardener and tradesman.

I can WELL understand all this. (Elektra)

Another thing I have discovered is that the death of one's partner reinforces the sorrow of other losses, revivifies losses of years past. One feels not only raw with the new wound but sore with the older ones that open up again. And then like an animal one is glad to have a hiding place and to be alone to suffer. This sounds so ungrateful to people who, like Samaritans, would be ready to 'pour in oil and wine' and cart you off somewhere where you'd be cared for. That's not what *I* want, not most of the time anyway, not when I feel most raw. If I can talk with a steady voice and laugh at jokes and behave with normality in company, then others can think me as hard as nails if they like, but I must have my hiding place when I need it. And it's the silly things that catch you unawares.

I mean, if for example you go through letters in the handwriting of the dead who was dear to you, you brace yourself because you know you're asking for it, but if suddenly you come upon a letter where you didn't look to see it you can be floored in a second. A coincidence, a quotation, a piece of music, a bookmarker, a hair even, can suddenly put you back to the beginning, make you realise afresh that he's gone forever and things will never be the same again, that they may in fact get worse and worse till life releases its hold on you too.

I think in fairness, Accidia, you should get the reactions of other widows now. We have in CCC widows of long standing, widows who after a time have made a new life for themselves alone or with another, women who are much better at adjusting to a new condition than I am, I guess. *It does take 2/3 years. (Robina)*

See what they are doing and hear what they think. Perhaps they weren't married as long as John and I were, perhaps they felt the *burden* of marriage more than I did; probably they are better, more adaptable people, or women who can find consolation in religion, good works, social activities; people who are extroverts, people who weren't 'looked after' as much as I always felt I was by John. *Me too. (Robina)*

We are all different in widowhood as in everything else.

This is beautifully written AA – but so terribly sad
– as how should it not be? (Janna)
Yes indeed. (Isis)
AA. Thank you for writing this – I appreciate, and
feel deeply for you in the great sadness and
loneliness. (Accidia)
Oh yes, oh yes (and, believe me, divorce holds
the same pains and horrors. This sounds
impertinent to say so, alas, it is true), but of course
now I am lucky, grateful and happy. (Roberta)
Dear Dear AA. I know only too well. (Robina)

Ad Astra adjusted as well as possible to widowhood and lived another fifteen years without John. She remained at Greshams because the thought of moving was too daunting. As a result she was quite isolated, which eventually presented a problem because her health was failing. She had several strokes and was diagnosed with osteoporosis and severe arthritis. She underwent a hip replacement in 1984, but remained in constant pain and had great difficulty walking as a result of her bone deterioration.

After ten years alone, she moved into a nursing home, refusing several offers to stay with her children or with Elektra. She spent her last three and a half years there and became quite depressed. She was unable to find a kindred spirit in the home and she could not write due to a stroke. She could no longer connect with people in the special way that she always had. Her last few years with the CCC were strained as she was suffering so much physically and emotionally. The CCC had always been a lifeline for Ad Astra, and the remaining women did their best to support her. They continued to write to her even when she couldn't reply. She died in 1991 at the age of eighty-eight.

Cotton Goods

*After Cotton Goods left Albert, she remained in Derby
living with her son Jim for the rest of her life. Jim had
designed and built a house with two large separate living areas, joined by a long corridor. Cotton Goods lived
on one side and Jim on the other. Late in her life she
wrote this touching article to the CCC when she was
experiencing many health problems and was being
cared for mainly by Jim.*

1979

This is the strangest contribution I've ever made to
CCC. Sometimes I feel light-headed but on the whole
I'm sane and in my right mind. I feel to be a great
responsibility to Jim but he is always thoughtful and
kind. We decided that some weeks ago he should take
me to stay with Betty while he had a long-weekend
with Roy, his climbing companion. He got a wheelchair to take me from my bed to the car (his new
Volvo). All went well. He taped a recording of my
favourite Gilbert and Sullivan to entertain us on the
way and Betty and John welcomed us heartily. They
had a new settee which made a comfortable bed (with
all mod con. available on the ground floor). When getting back into bed after relieving my bladder I fell. I
was dazed and thought I was at home. My light was
reflected but I thought it was the light in Jim's room at
home. I called and called but got no reply, then I collapsed and lay on the floor till Betty got up to make
breakfast. All that day I rested but the next night the
very same thing happened again. It was due to no neg-
ligence, for Betty and John were kindness itself. The

third night I took my usual sleeping tablets but soon awoke, thinking I was at home. Again I called and called thinking the reflected light was in Jim's bedroom. I felt I must get to him, so wriggled and rolled and bumped into walls etc. till I lost consciousness. The next morning Betty found me in the hall behind the front door. Betty fetched the village doctor, who gave me a prescription but I don't know what for. The rest of the week passed fairly well but I was light-headed and not aware of where I was. Jim got me home safely and, as the Easter holidays had started, he could care for me.

I seem to have regained my right mind to some extent but the Dr's Surgery is closed except for emergencies.

It's jolly hard on Jim and I sincerely hope these conditions won't last long. I've felt better these last few days for I seem to have had rounds of children visitors. Nancy has brought Nial and Josie, of course. Dora, my best friend in Derby, is away as her adopted daughter has just had a third baby and always leans on Dora, but her son in Derby brought his two toddlers (aged 2 and 4) to cheer me up. Another day who should come but my nephew, Peter, with his two children . . . I had a lovely chat with the little girl of 4, Maria. They call me Grandma, though I'm their Great-Aunt.

Maria: 'Grandma, why do you stay in bed?'

Me: 'Well, you see, my legs won't walk.'

Maria: 'You should make them do as you tell them.'

Later, 'All grandmas are good but some are stupid. You are stupid, Grandma, because you don't make your legs walk.'

Then came a beautiful smile.

Maria: 'You are not stupid really. We are only playing a teasing game, aren't we?'

They are two lovely children and a great tonic better than medicine . . .

No children have turned up today so far . . .

I have not read anything for weeks. I can't concentrate. I asked Jim to fetch me a book from my bookcase. He picked up quite casually Howard Spring's *The Sunset Touch* which roused my master failing (the scribbling of doggerel).

The Sunset Touch (MY VERSION)

We are born at sunrise to this world
Innocent, loved and sweet
Nature's mystery how we got here
Such a wonderful feat!
The sun then rises in the sky
And hour follows hour
And so the baby follows too
Learning human power
The sun then rises in the sky
And hours develop to years
Experiences happenings
And often many cares
At last 'The Sunset Touch' appears
Life comes to an end
What we have done either good or bad
It's now too late to mend
But thanks for all the 'Fun and Games'
Life's not been all that bad
To some of us life's puzzling
It just seems *simply* mad.

It's 3 a.m. and all is so quiet
Am I dead or alive or simply just dying?
The pain has departed – at least for a time -
Or is it the pain-killing pills leaving me lying?
I'm back in the past, live again in my youth
Meet relations and friends of old who help to
Ward off return of the pain with their memories
Enjoying myself until this peace ends
I wish that everyone could die quite quick

It would be easier for them and their relations and
Less suffering for all while waiting for death
Less fretting and other complications
I had a chat with my bath-lady once
About suicides, euthanasia and such
Said she, 'Oh never, never think of suicide
'Tis cruel, for those who love you in life would think
They'd failed you or not thought of you over much.'

This may be all a lot of rubbish for the mag.

Whether I'm being over-sentimental (in Jim's word
SOPPY), exhibitionist or whatever, please excuse me,
put it down to drugs (my pain-killing drugs). *What is
TRUE* is that CCC has been a big part of my life and
I'm grateful. May CCC go on flourishing. I'm sorry if
my writing is so hard to read. Anyhow, if it's not legi-
ble, you have not missed much.

I think my first contribution to CCC was an anec-
dote about my false teeth, so I'll end up with another
(if it *is* the end).

My nephew Peter wanted to take a photo of the
children and me. When he said, 'Smile please,' I took
out my dentures just for fun. Maria started and stared
and spent much of the day trying to get her teeth out.
She said, 'Can you do that because you don't clean
them?'

Again, love to you all. CG.

*Within days of that article, Cotton Goods had a heart
attack and died, at the age of eighty-six. Ad Astra
received the following poignant farewell two days later.
By the time the women read Cotton Goods' last entry,
they already knew that she had passed away.*

1979

Dear AA (and all CCC)
Thanks for your letter. I will try to add a bit to my

last letter. I don't remember how much I told you except that I was home again.

The 24 hours of the days seem to be in three phases.

No. 1 phase: I wake up with excruciating pain and grab my tablets at once. After $\frac{1}{2}$ hour or so the tablets take the edge off and the pain stretches across my thighs and gradually leaves me fairly comfortable and I sleep.

Morphia, I guess. (Roberta)

No. 2 phase: I always have vivid dreams during which I am on the Moors or up and down the Dales, always with children. We are happy until the children get lost and I search for them for hours and hours. I always find them at last and we are happy again.

No. 3 phase: After that I always find myself in a sort of Fairyland made up of incidents in my past. Last night I was back in the Infant School. It was home-time and we were singing:

> 'Now the day is over, night is drawing nigh
> Shadows of the evening steal across the sky.'

So apt! (Waveney)

It was beautiful. It was beautiful. I always love to hear small children singing.

End of Phase 3 and another day starts with the stabbing pain.

After I came home I had another fall. These falls always occur after I have got up to use the commode and am trying to get back into bed. This time Jim found me in 'a bloody mess', with cut forehead, the blackest eye of the century and one knee like a multi-coloured football. He got me back to bed and sent for the doctor, who said, 'Now what have you been up to?' I replied, 'Had a scrap in a pub.' Goodness knows *Lovely! (Roberta)* what made me say that, for I've never been in a pub in my life except for a cup of coffee some-where in the countryside. The doctor said jovially,

'Well, let this be a lesson to you.' Now I'm utterly immobile but Jim has got a wheelchair and takes me into the living-room for the evening. I am to go to hospital when there is a bed for complete examination. I don't like the idea of hospital but poor Jim can't go on with so much responsibility . . .

Now for a rest. I won't ask to have CCC sent to me, for I may be in hospital any day. I hope you can read this scribble. Love to you all. CG.

How game she was even at the end and there were loving children and grandchildren all the time. She had a good innings and really counted her blessings. We shall miss her. (Elektra)

Yes, it is amazing that she could still write so clearly, and be <u>ABLE</u> to write, when so near to death. (Roberta)

Quite amazing – she was 'herself' right to the end. (Janna)

Epilogue

Part of the sadness of growing older is to see one's friends becoming fewer; this happens in families and CCC is a kind of family. Probably one has to accept that it will follow a family pattern, with members dying, those left drawing closer, until eventually it all becomes just too much trouble and the survivors live with their memories of times past.

Accidia, 1976

The Cooperative Correspondence Club came to an end in 1990, just as Accidia predicted. The last decade of writing was particularly difficult for the women as they continued to lose members. As editor, Ad Astra especially seemed to bear the weight of this. In 1984, she wrote,

Nessun Maggior Dolore
Che ricordarsi del tempo felice
Nella miseria.

Inferno by Dante Alighieri.

So said Francesca da Rimini in answer to Dante's question about her presence in the Inferno. Putting it into plain English she said, 'There is no greater sorrow than to recall a happy time in one's misery,' or in poetic phrase, 'Sorrow's crown of sorrow is remembering happier days.'

Why am I quoting the *Inferno*? It is because I have spent the morning sorting old CCC entries – in fact I can't go to bed until I clear them all up. But how sad they are to re-read!

Facing widowhood and her own physical decline, it seems that, in addition to this, the decreasing momentum of the CCC was too much for her to cope with. In the late 1980s, after nearly fifty years as editor, Ad Astra retired. She wrote to the remaining women, 'Goodbye, CCC. It's best to acknowledge that old CCC is dead and you don't care enough to write for it.'

With Ad Astra clearly struggling, around this time Accidia suggested that the remaining women might have an easier time staying in touch if they sent round a notebook instead. This notebook, the last attempt to keep the CCC alive, ran for over a year but in the end sealed the fate of the group. After writing to each other for over half a century, in 1990, the seven remaining members, Elektra, Janna, Waveney, Roberta, Sirod, Accidia and Michaelmas decided to stop circulating the magazine.

Although the women no longer wrote to each other, the CCC was not to end here. Long before this, Ad Astra had recognised the richness and value of such an unprecedented and candid record of women's lives during the twentieth century and, in 1978, had suggested that the group consider going public with their story. Despite decades of secrecy, she felt that they should share their experiences and accomplishments. With a few exceptions, the majority of the others agreed, and they discussed their vision of the 'CCC book'.

Ad Astra had collected a significant number of CCC articles over the years that she edited the magazine. After circulation each edition was returned to her and she had diligently disassembled them and reused the linen covers. She returned many of the articles to their writers, but kept a considerable amount in her personal files. Despite group enthusiasm and Ad Astra's lifelong dedication to the club, she never quite managed to use these articles to write the book. When she was moving into a nursing home in 1987, she decided that the papers had become a burden. She told Elektra that she was going to burn them. Fortunately Elektra intervened, rescued the articles and decided to try to write the book herself. However, she was also unable to get it published, and nearly ten years later she donated the remaining CCC collection to the Mass Observation

Archive at the University of Sussex, where I would eventually come across it in 2003.

Since the 1930s women in the UK have been circulating correspondence magazines in almost exactly the same manner as the Cooperative Correspondence Club. There are over two hundred known magazines, but the CCC is one of the oldest on record. Due to the private and personal nature of the content, none of the others have ever been exposed to a public readership, making this collection particularly rare and valuable. It is hugely fortunate that these articles were kept over the years, not only because they make up possibly the only remaining example of a correspondence magazine but more so because they capture and preserve the lives of a remarkable group of women. And by making these papers available to the public and generously sharing their memories, the women and families of those in the magazine have made it possible for the story of the CCC to live on and to be shared with generations to come.

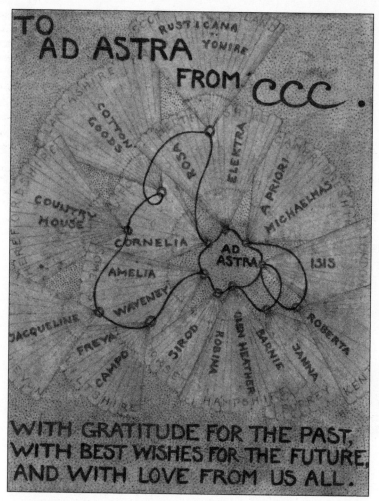

CCC cover.

Biographies of Members

Not all of the contributors appear in this book. Where their names have been mentioned and personal information was available, a biographical note has been included here for reference.

Accidia was born in Bristol in 1918. She entered Cambridge in 1937, studying first English and then Modern Languages. After graduating in 1940, she moved to Esthwaite Lodge, a home for conscientious objectors. Here she met John, whom she married in 1941. Soon afterwards, they moved to Lancashire, and Accidia became a full-time teacher. In 1943, she had Phyllida, the first of seven children. A year later, with John suffering from depression, the family moved to Cornwall. John found a job with the Workers' Educational Association. Adrian was born in 1946. Another change in John's career meant that the family moved to Yorkshire in 1947, where Accidia had Althea in 1947, Humfrey in 1949, Julian in 1951 and Lucilla in 1955. Due to John's depression, they decided that the family needed a change so they moved to Toronto, Canada, in 1956. Here Accidia had her last son, Benedict, in 1961. After several years in Toronto, John found a new job in Hamilton, so Accidia moved there with the four youngest children. Finally, in 1969, they returned to England. In 1972, Accidia began to work for Marriage Guidance as a counsellor and tutor, and continued until the age of eighty-two. In 1988, after John retired, they moved to a cottage in Dorset, where Accidia still lives today. She was widowed in 1996 and has lived alone ever since. She keeps herself very active, walking, reading and travelling.

Ad Astra was born in Kensington in 1903. She graduated from University College London with a degree in English and French. After graduating she taught at grammar schools, first in Lancashire and then London. In 1930, she married John. They moved to Harrow and had Clare and Christopher in 1933 and 1934 respectively. After the war the family moved to 'Down Hall', a large home in Essex.

John commuted to London for his timber business and came home for the weekends until he retired in 1959. Ad Astra tutored local children, wrote English-grammar books and readers and worked as editor for the CCC. John became ill after they moved in the mid-1960s and died in 1976. Ad Astra lived as a widow for fifteen years and struggled with many health problems during this time. She died in 1991 at the age of eighty-eight.

Amelia was born in what is now Pakistan in 1904. Her family moved to England when she was a young girl. They lived in several locations because of her father's various stations in the army. She attended finishing school in Switzerland at the age of seventeen. A year later, she became her father's escort, as her mother had died a few years earlier. In this capacity she met her husband Charles, who was also in the army. They married around 1928 and had four boys, Richard in 1929, Tony in 1933 and twins John and Peter in 1935. Throughout these years they moved frequently due to Charles's work. Once he retired in 1947, the family moved to Glazeley. In 1950, Amelia and Charles separated and Amelia moved to London, where she worked at Clean Walls as a secretary. She retired from the CCC in the 1960s. Amelia died in 1988.

Angharad was born in Hopkinstown, Wales, in 1920. At the age of seventeen she left to study English language and literature at Oxford. After graduating she moved to Norfolk and taught for the Workers' Educational Association. She met her future husband, Morien, while on holiday at home with her family in Wales. The pair married in 1945 and moved to Lancashire. Here Angharad had Dylan in 1946 and Gareth in 1949. Angharad and Morien then returned to Wales. At this point Angharad started to write television screenplays, something she would continue to do for the next thirty years. In 1960, she and Morien adopted a third son, Huw. She wrote two stage plays between 1963 and 1965, and in 1972 she published her first book, *The Descent of Woman*. Angharad went on to publish five more books on a variety of subjects. She is now widowed and lives in Wales.

A Priori was born in London in 1907. She went to work at the age of seventeen after her father died and left the family with little money. She started at Ginn's educational book firm and obtained her diploma in English literature at the same time. In 1930, she switched to a job at the *New Statesman*, which led to her working as John Maynard Keynes' personal assistant for a year. She left in 1932 because she met and married Lough, a wood sculptor. They had Jane in 1934 and then moved to Oxfordshire, where their second daughter, Sally, was born in 1935. Lough tried unsuccessfully to run a workshop and so, when he was offered a teaching job in Cambridgeshire in 1935, they decided to move again. Vicky was born in 1938. They spent the war years mostly in Cambridgeshire, with the exception of one year in Scotland, when Lough was an aircraft repairman. In 1943, their fourth child, Piers, was born. Lough alternated back and forth between sculpting work and teaching. Due to financial necessity they moved to Cambridge in 1950. A Priori worked for the Cambridge historian Professor John Plumb and Lough taught at Cambridge High School for Boys. Both she and Lough took an active interest in Cambridge amateur theatre, acting and helping to orchestrate the productions. They remained there until the mid-1960s, when they relocated to Milton, a village just outside Cambridge. Early in 1977, A Priori was diagnosed with bowel cancer, and that summer they moved back into town. During a period of remission, she spent her time travelling with Lough and visiting her family. The cancer returned in 1979 and she died in January 1980.

Auricula was born in Liverpool in 1927 and grew up mostly in Cheam. She graduated in 1944 with a diploma in teaching from Goldsmith's College, whose teacher-training programme was located at Nottingham University during the war. She returned to Cheam, where she taught until she met and married Phillip in 1949. She had five children: Mark in 1949, Elizabeth-Sarah in 1951, Paul in 1955, Helen-Jane in 1958 and Emma-Rachel in 1967. She and Phillip moved several times during their married life because Phillip was a seaman and then a pilot. Auricula had several different teaching jobs throughout her career. She taught at a secondary modern, a special-needs school and spent time working at a private reform school. She was one of the last to join the CCC, in the mid-1950s, and dropped out in the late 1970s. She developed a close relationship with Ad Astra but was not as connected to the magazine as many of the other women. Auricula was known as a bit of a rogue element in the magazine and believes that she left the CCC after a row with Cornelia over penny stamps! She is a lively character with a sharp wit and a great sense of humour, who enjoys socialising and spending time with her family. She currently lives in Felixstowe.

Barnie was born in Lowestoft in 1899. She went to Oxford in 1918 to study history. She had known her future husband John since childhood and eventually they had a romantic connection, but it would be several years before they married. John was a subaltern in the army and could not obtain permission to marry from his colonel until he received his captaincy. Barnie waited patiently for him, during which time he fought and was seriously wounded in the trenches of the First World War. During these years she taught history at Beverley High School in Yorkshire, Heathfield School, Ascot, and Norwich Teacher Training College. The pair eventually married in 1931 and shortly afterwards moved to India, where the Hampshire Regiment was stationed. They lived in North-West Frontier Province and Barnie gave birth to their first daughter, Anne, in 1933 in Nowshera (now part of Pakistan) and to John, in 1934, in Murree, also now in Pakistan. They returned to England in 1935 and eventually settled in Shawford. Here Barnie had their third child, Mary, in 1941. Barnie spent her time during the war raising the children and teaching history at St Swithun's School, Winchester. She also wrote many plays for the Women's Institute and for the local amateur dramatic society, the Heathcote Players. John retired as a lieutenant-colonel in the 1950s, but both he and Barnie remained very active.

Barnie was highly intelligent and a voracious reader. She had a genuine interest in people and was dedicated to her family and her community. She and John were members of the Church of England, regularly attending services and supporting many church functions. She was a true historian with a passion for learning, a passion that extended into every facet of her life. She was one of the original members of the CCC, joining around 1936 and contributing until shortly before her death. She loved the magazine as it provided a link with other similarly bright and dynamic women. She spent countless hours writing, often historical articles, much to the enjoyment of the other members. In January 1976, Barnie was diagnosed with bowel cancer and was admitted to hospital for emergency surgery. After this her health quickly deteriorated. She had been caring for John, who was showing the first signs of dementia, and so with her decline he moved into a nursing home. John died from a heart attack on August 12, 1976, and Barnie passed away six days later.

Cornelia was born in 1894 in Essex. At the age of sixteen she began working at a cocoa importer's office, where she met Pat, whom she married in 1924. They had Michael in 1926, Peter in 1929 and Ted in 1934. Cornelia immersed herself in various crafts, including pottery, marquetry and pewter work. She was a member of the Women's Institute and the Townswomen's Guild. She lost two of her sons prematurely, Peter in 1976 and Michael in 1977. After Pat retired, they moved to Seaford. Late in life, they moved to Suffolk to live with their youngest son Ted and his wife Carole. Cornelia died at the age of ninety-nine in 1993.

Cotton Goods was born in Oldham, Lancashire, in 1893. She trained as a teacher and taught in a village school in Lancashire. In the early 1920s, Cotton Goods married Albert, who worked in a cotton mill like her father. They lived in Accrington and area, and had Betty in 1923, Jim in 1925, Irene in 1930 and Nancy in 1935. Cotton Goods separated from Albert in 1955 and went to live with her son Jim in Derby for the rest of her life. She died in 1979.

Elektra was born in London in 1906. At seventeen she studied business at Regent Street Polytechnic. After graduation she worked in her father's clothing business. At the same time she attended St John's Wood Art School. In 1930, she married Mark, an accountant. They continued to live in London and had Lawrence in 1933 and Michael in 1936. Due to the war, the family moved to Letchworth, where they stayed until 1951, with Mark commuting from London at weekends. Elektra started volunteering as a counsellor for Marriage Guidance (MG). She was the author of *Telling the Teenagers* and *The Opposite Sex*, books for educators and teenagers on how to approach sexual and relationship issues. She also volunteered for various London hospital committees and helped to establish the Camden Association for Mental Health. From 1973–77, Elektra was a Councillor on the Greater London Council. She was widowed in 1982 but had remained active with her sculpting, travelling and socialising. She recently celebrated her hundredth birthday and is living in Highgate.

Glen Heather was born in 1903 in Winchester and grew up in Southampton. Out of financial necessity she did clerical work from the age of sixteen. She married Don in 1928 and they started their married life in Southampton. They had three children: Marilyn in 1930, Coral in 1933 and Ralph in 1934. They eventually moved to the New Forest, one of their favourite locations. She was widowed early when Don died of cancer in 1958. Around 1961, she married Robert, an ex-naval officer who died from heart problems in 1967. She married a third time, to Bill, in 1973. They moved to Cornwall and enjoyed gardening, reading and socialising. She died in the early 1970s after a stroke.

Isis was born in Edgbaston, Birmingham, in 1906. After graduating from Oxford with a degree in history, she taught in South Africa. She returned to England and married Alistair, also an Oxford graduate. They lived in the outskirts of London, where Alistair worked as a schoolmaster, teaching history. Isis gave birth to her first son, Thomas, in 1937 and then had Peter in 1940, David in 1942 and Matthew in 1946. She suffered from severe depression after Matthew was diagnosed with Down's Syndrome. In an effort to recover, she converted to Catholicism. She and Alistair retired to Oxfordshire, where she spent time reading and gardening. Isis died in 1989.

Janna was born in London in 1911. She attended boarding school on a scholarship, then moved to Mazamet, France, at the age of seventeen, where she worked as an au pair for a year. Upon her return she joined the London Junior Orchestra. Janna became a pacifist at an early age, and when she was twenty-one she fell in love with Max, who was also a pacifist. Once married, they moved to Surrey, where Max worked in an aluminium factory. The couple had Julian in 1935 and Tessa in 1938. Max was a conscientious objector (CO) during the war and left his job at the factory when they started to manufacture weapons. He found employment with the Fellowship of Reconciliation

(FOR), an organisation that provided emotional and practical support to COs. As part of the war effort, Janna and Max adopted a son, Jeremy, in 1941. They then moved to Yorkshire, where they lived on a commune with other COs, but didn't stay long as Janna found it difficult to adjust to life in that part of the country.

Janna and Max led an unconventional life in comparison to most CCC couples as they had an 'open marriage'. In 1942, Max and Janna returned to Surrey and agreed to house-share with another couple, Daphne and Tony (also COs). This arrangement eventually led to Max's affair with Daphne, and Janna's with Tony. As a result of this relationship, Janna had Miranda, in 1943. The other couple left and Max unofficially adopted Miranda. In 1947, Janna and Max had another daughter, Deborah. In 1949, they moved to Sussex, where both Janna and Max found jobs at Tylehurst, a progressive school for 'dysfunctional children'. A year later, they made their final move, to a cottage in Poundsbridge, near Tunbridge Wells. Their last child, Julia, was born in 1951.

Janna maintained her lifelong love for, and interest in, music by teaching violin and piano until around the age of eighty. Her other passions included gardening, walking, reading, theatre and the cinema. More recently, she also became involved in circle dancing and t'ai chi. In her later years she spent a great deal of time with her children and grandchildren and caring for Max, who had become quite introverted in his old age. She was widowed in 1997. The women in the CCC were some of her closest friends and they played an incredibly valuable part in her life. She submitted articles until the magazine ceased publication. Janna now lives in a home in Sevenoaks and has eleven grandchildren and fourteen great-grandchildren.

Michaelmas was born in 1903 in Great Yarmouth. She finished her schooling when she was seventeen and then worked as a governess. In 1928, she married Sydney, whom she had known for several years as both of their fathers, at different times, had served as the mayor of Great Yarmouth. Sydney ran a photography factory where he developed, printed and sold film wholesale. They moved to Gorleston-on-Sea in Great Yarmouth, where they had their only child, Pam, in 1933. Due to the war, they moved to Hunstanton,

Norfolk, and sent Pam to Yorkshire with her school. Michaelmas worked for Heinz and then for Marshall's Aerodrome in Cambridge, doing office work. In 1946, she and Sydney returned to their pre-war house, which had been commandeered by the WRNS, and remained there until 1988. They both worked to revitalise and maintain Sydney's wholesale photography business. Michaelmas was athletic and spent much of her time playing badminton or tennis and volunteering with the Guides. She was generally quiet and, although she was a faithful member of the CCC for nearly all of its existence, she never really integrated into the group. This was partly because she was so devoted to Sydney, who went blind later in life. In 1995, he passed away, and Michaelmas died in 2000.

Roberta was born in Kent in 1912. After graduation she taught at a secondary school until she met and married Walter in 1934. They lived in Kent, with the exception of one year in Cornwall, and had four children: Nicholas in 1935, Christopher in 1937, Guy in 1943 and Suzanne in 1945. In 1952, Walter was transferred to South Africa, and Roberta moved to Davos with the children prior to joining him. Soon afterwards, the couple divorced and Roberta chose to remain in Switzerland. In 1958, she married Tony and moved to England to live in Nottingham. They eventually retired to Kent, until Tony passed away in 1988. She spent the next eight years living in Surrey with her family. Roberta died in 1996.

Robina was born in London in 1907. After finishing school she earned some money writing theatre reviews and short articles for various periodicals. In 1931, she married Edward, known to everyone as 'Dicky', and they had Peter in 1931, Martin in 1935 and Adrian in 1937. At the beginning of the war they moved to Jamaica for a business opportunity, but quickly returned so that Dicky could join the army. Robina then had Vanessa in 1941 and Vivian in 1944. Dicky left the army around 1960 and he and Robina tried several different business ventures that all proved unsuccessful. In 1964, they moved to Australia. They had been there nearly ten years when Dicky passed away. Shortly afterwards Robina decided to return to England. Throughout her various moves she continued to write for the CCC. Though she was an avid gardener and enjoyed photography, the CCC was her main interest. She was one of the first to respond to Ubique's query in 1935 and she wrote avidly until she died. She came from a literary family and was best known amongst the women for her fervent belief that Shakespeare's works were actually written by Francis Bacon. Once she returned from Australia, Robina lived in Cornwall with her sister until her death from cervical cancer in around 1979.

Rosa (Dartle) was born in Burton-on-Trent in 1896. After leaving boarding school, she took a cookery course in London. During the Great War she worked at Coutts Bank. In 1920, she met and married Harold, whom she called KV in the CCC articles. They stayed in London, where KV worked for Bass brewers, and had three children: John in 1923, Katharine Margery in 1925 and Elizabeth in 1928. In 1929, they moved to St Albans. They remained there until KV retired in the mid-1950s, at which point they moved to Highgate. Rosa was widowed in 1964. She moved to Cambridge to be closer to her daughter Elizabeth and lived there until her death from cancer in 1977.

Sirod was born in 1903 in Evesham. In the early 1920s, she studied physics at Bedford College, London. After graduating, she worked in General Electric's research laboratories. She married Jack in 1930 and they moved to Cheltenham. Sirod had Daphne in 1932, Gillian in 1935, John in 1936 and Bill in 1944. During the last year of the war, Sirod and Jack bought a dairy farm in Dorset, where they lived and worked for nearly ten years. When they sold the farm they moved to Dorchester, where Sirod did supply teaching. She and her friend Mary established the National Association of Flower Arrangement Societies (NAFAS). Sirod was widowed in 1960 and moved to Weymouth. She remained actively involved with NAFAS and also volunteered for the Samaritans. Sirod died in 1996.

Waveney was born in Gosforth in 1909. In her youth she helped her father run his vicarage. Through parish connections she met her future husband Maurice, whom she married in 1929. He and Waveney moved to Surrey for his job at Sandhurst and then relocated to Kent, where they had Michael in 1931. A year later they moved again to Yorkshire, and Waveney gave birth to John in 1933. Finally they settled in Chew Magna near Bristol, and they had Ian in 1936 and Robin in 1938. Waveney lived with her father in Bourton-on-the-Water for the next five years after Maurice was captured and detained in a POW camp. Upon his return they moved back to Chew Magna and had their fifth child, Margaret, in 1947. When Maurice retired in 1952 they relocated to Exmouth. Waveney was widowed in 1965. She remained in Exmouth the rest of her life, working with the local parish and often travelling to the north to visit her family. She wrote for the CCC until the final issue. Waveney died in 1999.

Yonire was born in 1907 and raised in Edinburgh, where she attended finishing school. In 1934, she met and married Elliot, a sheep farmer. She moved to Elliot's farm on the Scottish borders and had their first son, Bill, in 1936. At the beginning of the war they relocated to an arable farm close to Edinburgh, where Yonire had Jock in 1940, Sandy in 1944, Adam in 1945 and Mike in 1947. They remained on the farm until 1961, when they moved to Herefordshire to run a local pub. Yonire spent much of her free time breeding, judging and showing dogs. She died quite suddenly from pneumonia in 1979 at the age of seventy-two.

Notes

Introduction: A Cry For Help

p. 7 'In the 1920s, marriage bars were implemented': for more information about marriage bars, specifically with regard to the teaching profession, see Alison Oram, *Women Teachers and Feminist Politics 1900–39*. Manchester: Manchester University Press, 1996.

p. 8 'birth control was not readily available for women': Hera Cook, *The Long Sexual Revolution: English Women, Sex, and Contraception 1800–1975*. Oxford: Oxford University Press, 2004.

— '"elaborate household routines and tasks"': quoted in Jane Lewis, *Women in England 1879–1950: Sexual Divisions and Social Change*, p. 116. Brighton: Wheatsheaf, 1984.

— 'greater stress and time commitments on mothers': quoted in Ann Dally, *Inventing Motherhood: The Consequences of an Ideal*, p. 82. London: Hutchinson, 1982.

p. 9 '"turned motherhood into a craft that could be learned and a baby into something that could be controlled"': quoted in *ibid.*, p. 82.

— '"child's character"': quoted in Lewis, *op. cit.*, p. 116.

p. 10 'familial support networks that past generations had relied upon': Cynthia White, *Women's Magazines 1693–1968*, p. 85. London: Michael Joseph Ltd, 1970.

— '"Woman Doctor", "Psychologist" and "Nursery Expert"': Deidre Beddoe, *Back to Home and Duty: Women Between the Wars 1918–1939*, p. 14. London: Pandora, 1989.

— 'a weekly periodical published for mothers and children's nurses': David Peck. 'Speaking Volumes', *Nursery World History 75th Edition* (Dec. 2, 2002), p. 4. *Nursery World* is still in print but it is now specifically aimed at childcare practitioners.

— '"publication which everybody read"': interview with Accidia, April, 2004.

p. 11 'provide the group with a different perspective': as there are few articles remaining from the first couple of years of the CCC, there is no evidence of anti-Semitic writing in the papers contained within the archive.

— '". . . a sort of guinea pig . . .'": interview with Elektra, August, 2003.

p. 17 'she would often attempt to facilitate a discussion about the submission': interview with Elektra, August, 2003.

p. 21 '"intellectual coffee morning"': interview with Accidia, April, 2004.

1. Nursery World

p. 28 'Phoney War': the term refers to the period between late 1939 and April 1940 when, after the attack on Poland in 1939, little military activity actually took place in western Europe, even though war had officially been declared.

p. 30 'Reby was up': Reby was Roberta's maid.

— 'fell into dear Hodge's arms': presumably a nurse known to her.

— 'Jennifer came to see me': Jennifer was Roberta's doctor.

p. 32 'the stock exchange going like mad owing to the Italian news': on July 25, 1943, an Italian coup drove Benito Mussolini from power and he was replaced by Marshal Pietro Badoglio, who opened negotiations for an armistice.

p. 33 'A Priori, even if Hariet IS Hariet': Roberta is referring to the child that A Priori was expecting. Evidently A Priori considered calling this child 'Hariet' if she was female. In the end she gave birth to a boy, Piers, in August, 1943.

— 'now Pat will have to have the girl': Pat is Roberta's younger sister. She actually had three boys and no girl!

— 'Autumn 1944': many of the CCC articles in the archive are undated as the date only appeared on the cover of the magazine. Therefore, dates of articles are typically only given in years and are often an educated guess.

p. 35 'David coming for tea': David was Roberta's nephew, son of her older sister Marjorie and her husband Roy, who had just returned from India.

p. 36 'They had M and B day and night': M and B refers to sulphonamide, an early antibiotic. The initials stand for May and Baker, the manufacturer.

p. 37 'entered the Ormiston at 5.30 p.m.': Ormiston nursing home.

p. 38 'I was worrying about Nether Fawke': Roberta's family home in Kent.

p. 40 'how *true* was Dick Read's book': in 1933, English

obstetrician Grantley Dick-Read published a book entitled *Childbirth without Fear*. Read believed that a woman's fear during childbirth caused blood to filter away from her uterus. He thought this process left the uterus without oxygen, which meant it could not function properly. This, he proposed, made childbirth particularly difficult and painful. He believed that nearly all labour pains were a result of the fear and anxiety felt by the mother.

p. 45 'based on Margaret Brady's book': Margaret Y. Brady, *Health for All Wartime Recipe Book*. London: Health for All Publishing, 1944.

— 'reflect with pleasure on the various stages of Julia's birth': Julia is Janna's sixth child.

p. 53 'pregnancies one to [five]': Accidia had originally written 'pregnancies one to six', which either refers to a miscarriage or was a typo, as she only had five children at this point.

2. Peace in Our Time?

p. 61 '"you could write minor irritations . . ."': interview with Elektra, August, 2003.

p. 66 'writing on the Marian Richardson methods': Marion Richardson was a London school inspector who created a cursive script that recommended joining most, but not all, letters. Her system was based on a series of writing patterns that she hoped would provide natural preparation for a handwriting style to be used throughout all school years.

p. 68 'Harold Nicolson's book *Diplomacy*': Harold Nicolson, *Diplomacy*. New York: Harcourt, Brace and Company, 1939.

p. 76 'she was referring to the Munich Crisis': the Munich Crisis was the week in September 1938 when Neville Chamberlain was in Germany to meet Adolf Hitler, Edouard Daladier of France and Benito Mussolini of Italy to discuss the status of the Sudetenland. Hitler had demanded the independence of the Sudetenland Germans in March and April of that year, and the Czechs had mobilised their army in preparation for conflict. The French, British and Italian leaders met Hitler in September to try to appease him and avoid a major conflict. The meetings ended on Thursday, September 29, with the 'Munich Agreement', which stated that Germany could have the Sudetenland in exchange for Hitler's promise to make no further territorial demands in Europe.

— 'more troops will be ordered to Palestine and Egypt': in April, 1936, riots broke out in Jaffa which led to a three-year period of violence and civil strife in Palestine known as the 'Arab Revolt'. Arab terrorists attacked Jewish villages and the British army and police forces. The conflict subsided for nearly a year between October, 1936, and September, 1937, but then the terrorism resumed and continued until early 1939.

p. 77 'I just don't want to write of the "war" week': she was referring to the Munich Crisis.

p. 82 'our jewel of a h. parlour maid': house parlourmaid.

— 'my ex-film photographer and now RNVR brother': RNVR stands for Royal Naval Volunteer Reserve.

p. 83 'explaining things to Nanny and Irene': Irene was the cook.

p. 84 'Olive, Irene and Mr Milton the verger': Olive was Waveney's father's housekeeper.

— 'like Epaminandos I became all solemn-like': Epaminondas was a Theban political leader in the war of Sparta against Thebes. He conveyed an image of calm and confidence in the battle and this is said to have inspired the Thebans to victory. It is also possible that Waveney is referring here to the character from a well-known children's book at the time, *Epaminondas and his Auntie*.

p. 87 'Julian has begun lessons in a little Froebel class': this is a reference to Friedrich Froebel, who invented the kindergarten.

— 'Daphne is a charming natural little girl': Daphne, Gili, John and Bill are Sirod's four children.

p. 93 'the attacks that have come to pass so far are the . . . .': a large portion of Rosa's letter was censored.

p. 94 'she has not yet returned': Rosa's sister Ella was on an extended holiday. She and her husband always took holidays separately.

— 'The three teachers are still here': only two teachers were billeted with Rosa at the time. Her children feel that Rosa was prone to exaggeration, but it could also have been a typing error.

3. A Day in the Life

p. 102 'the Moray Mclaren, James Bridie, Eric Linklater types': Moray McLaren was a Scottish author and critic.

James Bridie was a well-known Scottish playwright. Eric Linklater was a Scottish poet, novelist and historical writer. His wife Marjorie was a member of the CCC for a short time. Her nom de plume was 'Borealis'.

p. 103 'I wanted to hear Cortot': Alfred Cortot was a French pianist and conductor.

p. 104 'I began my singing career under Dr Greenhouse Alt': Dr Greenhouse Alt was a musicologist who took an interest in Yonire's singing.

— 'Sebastian worked out some Fugues': a Fugue is a piece of music consisting of three or more melodic lines played together.

p. 105 '"Jesu, Joy of Man's Desiring" – then "Sheep May Safely Graze"': both of these are piano arrangements of pieces by Bach.

p. 106 '"Release method No. 3" as taught by the RHS': it is likely that Yonire meant to write RLS, which stands for the Royal Lifesaving Society, of which she was a bronze-medal holder.

p. 107 'I thought Superintendent Merilees would be best': Superintendent Willy Merrilees was also a member of the CID, the Criminal Investigation Department, and was a friend of Yonire's.

p. 111 'According to Cocker': a popular English expression that meant 'quite correct'. The term came from Edward Cocker, who reputedly produced *Cocker's Arithmetic*, a book published in 1678.

p. 114 'I see it as something like "Mandelay" in *Rebecca*': Cotton Goods is referring to Manderley, which was the name of the house in Daphne du Maurier's novel *Rebecca*, published in 1938 (Alfred Hitchcock made *Rebecca* into a movie in 1940). In the book, the house haunts the family with memories of the husband's deceased first wife. Daphne du Maurier was the cousin of CCC member Robina.

p. 118 'It was while Micky (of Phoenix) was staying with us': Phoenix was the name of the correspondence magazine that was an offshoot of the CCC in the 1940s.

p. 123 'Poor Audrey had lost her voice': Audrey was Amelia's sister-in-law, married to Bruce.

p. 125 'I got in eventually to find Mrs Bish tearing her hair': Amelia is presumably referring to her landlady.

p. 126 'So I got Peter to send': Amelia is referring to her son Peter.

4. For Better, for Worse

p. 140 'more refined edition of Ernest Bevin': Ernest Bevin was the Foreign Secretary in the Labour government.

p. 158 'He then gave me a linctus': a medication used to suppress dry or painful coughs.

p. 164 'Matthew doesn't *look* like a Mongol': Mongol used to be the term employed for a person with Down's Syndrome.

p. 168 'treat me exactly like Mr Barrett of Wimpole St.': *The Barretts of Wimpole Street* was a movie produced in 1934 based on the true life story of Elizabeth Barrett Browning and her tyrannical father, who denied Elizabeth any freedom or opportunity to live her own life.

p. 169 'The person who perhaps helped me most to get through this time was Dorothy K': Dorothy K was a psychiatrist and family friend.

p. 175 'I took T to see *Monsieur Vincent*': a movie about the life of St Vincent de Paul, particularly focusing on his humanitarian and charitable work in seventeenth-century France.

p. 185 'known as the Indian Eskimo Association (IEA) of Canada': the Indian-Eskimo Association originated from the Canadian Association for Adult Education. It was created to study the problems of natives living in communities outside the reserves. To learn more, see: http://www.trentu.ca/library/archives/95-006.htm.

p. 193 'I had that awful feeling of disaster around Salt-wood': Saltwood was the house in Brasted, Kent, that Roberta and her family lived in from 1945–52 prior to the move to Switzerland.

— 'HATED my furnished white hospital-like room': as mentioned in the text, Roberta spent time in a convalescent-type home in Switzerland during parts of 1950 and 1951, prior to the family's move to Switzerland. Her children remember that she was away on and off over a period of two years, but not continuously. They also went to visit her.

p. 195 'spent a few days in Zurich with Vater': Vater is Walter's father, Guy's grandfather.

p. 197 'I thought to myself, keep your SA': SA refers to South Africa.

p. 199 'in Zurich one has to appear but not in the Grison': Davos is in the canton of Grisons or Graubünden.

5. 'Working' Mothers

p. 206 'working as a clerk in the Admiralty': the Admiralty is the government department responsible for the Navy.

p. 208 'the WAEC began to give orders for ploughing up': the WAEC is the War Agricultural Executive Committee. WAEC committees were established in every county during the Second World War to help boost food production.

p. 210 'Fred and Mrs W on the machines': Fred was the first dairy man on the farm and Mrs W was his wife.

— 'to run our reactors to the TT test there': the TT test checks cattle for bovine tuberculosis.

p. 212 'Syd tried to nail up sacks': Syd was a farmhand.

— 'Rhona and I cleared snow off cake bags in the barn': Rhona was one of Jack and Sirod's employees, hired mostly to take care of Bill when Sirod was working on the farm.

— 'Alf came down for spades': Alf was one of the main farmhands.

p. 214 'I'll post it in the hopes it gets to AA in time for 4a': 4a refers to the issue number of the upcoming CCC magazine. They produced two issues per month. These were labelled 1–12 depending on the month and 'a' or 'b' depending on whether it was the first or second magazine for that month. So issue 4a would be the first magazine for the month of April.

— 'drove himself into Dorchester to get ours and the Dorringtons' groceries': Alf, Syd and Percy Dorrington were the main farmhands.

p. 216 'we got her to the door of the loose box': the loose box is an area in a barn or shed where animals are allowed to be free rather than tethered.

p. 221 'the RSA exam, a lower standard than School Cert.': Royal Society of Arts exams are offered in a range of vocational subjects.

p. 222 'This star-studded cast included E. Arnot Robinson, Sir Compton Mackenzie, Richard Church, L. A. G. Strong, H. E. Bates, Eric Linklater, Marghanita Laski, Nancy Spain, Rupert Hart-Davies, Robert Henriques, old Uncle Gil Harding and all': E. Arnot Robinson and Richard Church were writers. Sir Compton Mackenzie was a Scottish novelist. L. A. G. Strong (Leonard Alfred George Strong) was a poet, novelist and journalist. H. E. Bates was a novelist and short story writer. Eric Linklater was a novelist. Marghanita Laski was a novelist and a critic. Nancy Spain was a popular journalist, novelist and feminist. Rupert Hart-Davies was a publisher, literary editor and man of letters. Robert Henriques was a broadcaster and writer. Gilbert Harding was a panellist, quizmaster and broadcaster.

— 'both BBC and commercial – Norman Collins and so on': Norman Collins was a radio and television executive. He played an influential role in establishing the ITV network in the UK.

p. 223 'The reporter from *The Stage*': *The Stage* is a newspaper for the performing arts.

p. 224 'their long-awaited third son, Huw': Huw is the Welsh version of Hugh.

— 'Somebody sent Ross of *The New Yorker* a cartoon of fencers': Harold Ross established *The New Yorker*.

p. 225 'Thurber's people don't bleed': James Thurber was an American writer and cartoonist who frequently drew for *The New Yorker*.

— 'it's dramatically far inferior to this *Finlay* I turned out': this refers to one of the episodes she wrote for *Dr Finlay's Casebook*.

— 'I'd like Harvey Unna's opinion': Harvey Unna was Angharad's agent.

— 'Harvey thinks it's good and has sent it to Michael Codron': Michael Codron produced and funded countless theatrical productions.

p. 226 'trying to get Hayley Mills to play the daughter': Hayley Mills is a British actress who had become particularly famous just a few years earlier with her film roles in *Pollyanna* and *The Parent Trap*.

p. 233 'she also joined the Workers' Educational Association, the Left Book Club and the Fabian Society': the Workers' Educational Association (WEA) was founded in 1903. It aimed to support the educational needs of all types of workers, men and women, with a particular focus on providing access to education for adult learners. It is now one of the UK's largest charitable organisations. For more information, see: www.wea.org.uk. The Left Book Club was started by Victor Gollancz in 1936 to promote left-wing thought. Gollancz published radical books cheaply so that they could be easily distributed, disseminating left-wing thought throughout the UK. It eventually grew from a small book club to a large political movement that held massive rallies. The Fabian Society was founded in 1884 with H. G. Wells, Beatrice and Sidney Webb, Bernard Shaw and Emmeline Pankhurst as some of its earliest members. It was a left-wing 'society committed to gradual rather than revolutionary reform'. It still exists as a left-of-centre think tank. For more information, see: www.fabian-society.org.uk.

— 'She became a member of the Progressive League': the Progressive League was formed in 1932 by H. G. Wells, C. E. M. Joad and others to unite progressive organisations against fascism. For more information, see: http://www.aim25.ac.uk/cgi-bin/search2?coll_id=5917-&inst_id=1.

— 'Aldous and Julian Huxley and C. E. M. Joad, to name a few': Aldous Huxley was an English novelist and critic and author of *Brave New World*. Julian was his brother, a biologist and author. C. E. M. Joad was a well-known left-wing British philosopher.

— 'he helped to establish the accounting firm Hacker, Rubens and Co.': this firm still exists today as UHY Hacker Young.

p. 234 'The programme was in *Panorama*': *Panorama* is a BBC current-affairs programme.

— 'In one corner was Richard Dimbleby': Richard Dimbleby was a BBC presenter and anchorman of *Panorama*.

— 'in another a Coster': this refers to a costermonger, an old-fashioned term for a person who sells fruits and vegetables from a barrow.

— 'In another corner Lowry': she is referring to L. S. Lowry, the well-known British artist.

p. 235 'Our party consisted of a delightful chairman Robert Mackenzie': McKenzie was a political scientist and broadcaster. He was essentially responsible for introducing political sociology at the LSE and in Britain.

p. 237 'the smaller therapeutic community hospital, Halliwick': Halliwick was a new kind of mental hospital that focused on psychotherapy. Both Friern and Halliwick have since been shut down.

p. 238 'I seem to be doing a Nellie Melba': Nellie Melba was an Australian opera singer.

p. 239 'the Dr Morris whom I encouraged to write to Yonire': Elektra connected Dr Morris and Yonire because they shared a love for horses.

p. 240 'the "Rose and Mark Hacker Centre"': the centre has since been closed. MIND in Camden moved to a larger central location.

6. Hard Times

p. 251 'top dog in the office': interview with TW, June, 2004.

p. 252 'who was involved in pottery, marquetry and pewter work': marquetry is a decorative form of woodwork that involves fixing thin sheets of wood of different colours on to the surface of a piece of furniture.

p. 253 'Tiberius and Gaius Gracchus': Tiberius and Gaius Gracchus went on to be prominent figures in Roman history.

p. 255 'Ted was away for the half term at his old friend's at Ramsey': Ted and his wife Carole had previously lived in Ramsey.

p. 260 'And Diane, "Mother, darling, I've tried five times"': Diane was Michael's wife.

p. 265 'James, who suffered from a genetic disorder called tuberous sclerosis (TS)': while the symptoms and severity of the disorder differ with the individual, people diagnosed with TS frequently develop benign tumours and suffer from seizures, mental retardation, behavioural problems and skin abnormalities.

p. 268 'Ann has to inject soneril': the drug Ann had to inject was actually Stesolid.

p. 270 'She blames the very strong dosage of Mogadon': Mogadon is a drug used for the short-term treatment of severe insomnia.

— 'he had *after* the last attack': this was an attack James had in March/April of 1974.

p. 273 'some who have been considered inoperable are now being reconsidered': James lost his vision due to the damage that the tumour had caused prior to his operation. The operation itself was a success, and that is why other children with TS were now being considered for the same surgery.

p. 278 'Dr Taylor, of the "Parks" part of the Radcliffe': the 'Parks' refers to the Child and Adolescent Psychiatry hospital in Oxford.

p. 280 'there was a new frontal growth which was not operable': James was diagnosed on February 14, 1984.

p. 281 'she is a JP in Witney' : a JP is a Justice of the Peace.

p. 282 'Douglas wasn't well at the weekend': Douglas is
   Sirod's brother and Joan is Douglas's wife.

p. 283 'the others which had been sent were too late': little
   was known at this time about how tumours in tuberous
   sclerosis differed from other tumours. Ann connected
   researchers with families of TS children who had died so
   that their tumours could be donated and examined.

7. Growing Old

p. 288 'one of the founding members of the Cambridge
   Designer Craftsmen': the Designer Craftsmen is a multi-
   craft society that supports and helps organise exhibitions
   for woodworkers, textile makers, calligraphers, sculptors,
   etc.

p. 291 'a real Butlins camp of a place': Butlins camps were
   all-inclusive holiday camps that were especially popular
   throughout Britain in the 1940s–70s.

— 'They sent her off to Hunstanton': Hunstanton is on the
   north Norfolk coast.

— 'such a long way to come from No. 34': no. 34 was the
   address of the home that Rosa lived in and wrote many
   stories about.

p. 293 'I went over to the Impington Art exhibition':
   Impington is a village just outside Cambridge.

— 'sometimes to the Prune's fury': 'the Prune' was the family's nickname for A Priori's employer.

— 'both Carol, who was here on Sunday': Carol is A
   Priori's daughter-in-law, married to Piers.

p. 294 'kinder than Solsinitzon's grim hospital': A Priori is
   referring to the hospital portrayed in Aleksandr
   Solzhenitsyn's book *Cancer Ward*, published in 1968. In
   the story, the patients suffer from different types of cancer,
   the disease being a metaphor for the totalitarian state.

p. 296 'they do seem at Addenbrooke's to be extremely
   forthcoming': Addenbrooke's is a hospital in Cambridge.

— 'this set up the peritonitis': peritonitis is a condition in
   which the abdomen becomes infected and, as a result,
   swollen and sore.

— 'They in fact removed the secum': the caecum is the
   name given to the part of the large intestine where it
   meets the small intestine. The appendix is attached to the
   caecum.

p. 300 'in the meantime, I'm going to start my life again':

interview with A Priori's daughter Vicky, July, 2004.

p. 304 'He and our neighbour at Wood Green': Wood Green was the village Ad Astra and John lived in after they left Down Hall.

— 'he went to London and gave Neil and his bank manager lunch': Neil was Ad Astra's daughter Clare's ex-husband.

— 'The visit to Brompton Hospital had been arranged': Brompton Hospital is in London, near Earl's Court.

p. 305 'Clare and Jo were much against the operation': Jo was Ad Astra's son Christopher's wife. She was a trained nurse.

— 'and even to Diss by car': Diss is the town nearest to Ad Astra and John's home, Gresham's.

p. 308 'I expect you all know Cory's "Heraclitus"?': William Johnson Cory, 'Heraclitus'. *Ionica*, 2nd edn, p. 7. London and Orpington: George Allen, 1891.

— 'And last night I was rereading *Akenfield*': Ronald Blythe, *Akenfield: Portrait of an English Village*. London: Allen Lane, 1969.

p. 315 'Nancy has brought Nial and Josie': Nial and Josie are Cotton Goods' grandchildren from her daughter Nancy.

p. 316 'He picked up quite casually Howard Spring's *The Sunset Touch*': Howard Spring, *A Sunset Touch*. London: Collins, 1953.

Epilogue

p. 323 '*Inferno* by Dante Alighieri': Dante Alighieri, *Inferno*, V. 121. Translated by Henry Wadsworth Longfellow. 3 vols. Boston: Ticknor & Fields, 1867.

p. 324 'she was also unable to get it published': a manuscript of the book that Elektra and Silva Simsova produced is available in the Mass Observation Archive.

Biographies of Members

p. 332 'He found employment with the Fellowship of Reconciliation (FOR)': the Fellowship of Reconciliation began in 1914 to give support and guidance to people who refused conscription. See www.for.org.uk for more information.

Editor's Note

The women of the CCC wrote their articles with the understanding that they would only be read by members of the club. Understandably, numerous privacy issues have arisen throughout the research for this book. After discussion with the women or their families, I have on occasion eliminated names, phrases, sentences or paragraphs in certain articles that might have infringed upon the privacy of the writer or her family. In a few cases I have changed family names and places. In these instances the original meaning of the text has not been altered. For the sake of readability, I have not always indicated where something has been eliminated or changed.

Personal articles often had punctuational, spelling or typographical errors. These have often been corrected to improve readability and square brackets have been used to add missing words.

The comments written by the women in the magazine also required a few editorial changes. Whenever possible, the remarks have been placed in the same position as they appeared in the articles. However, this sometimes proved difficult when a comment interrupted the text in a way that the original did not. Therefore, in a few instances, I have moved them or, when they did not influence the text, excluded them.

Unavoidably, there are details that have been lost forever thanks to articles that are missing and women who are no longer alive. Occasionally, the CCC children had a difference of opinion or were uncertain about what was 'true' in their mother's life. Ultimately I have let the women's words speak for themselves.

The Cooperative Correspondence Club Collection/Hacker Papers are held at the Mass Observation (MO) Archive. The Archive is a charitable trust in the care of the University of Sussex and is managed as part of the library's Special Collections department.

The MO Archive began with the papers from Mass

Observation, a British social research organisation formed in the late 1930s with the intention of accumulating a written record of the everyday life of ordinary people in the UK. Mass Observation ran from 1937 until the early 1950s and provides an especially rich historical resource on civilian life during the Second World War.

New collections relating to daily life in the UK in the twentieth and twenty-first century have been added to the original collection since the Archive was established at Sussex in 1970. One of these was the Cooperative Correspondence Club Collection, which was gifted to the Archive in 1998.

A major autobiographical project organised by the Archive is currently in progress. Hundreds of volunteers respond to regular requests to write in both diary form and in reports on themes concerning themselves, their families, work places and communities. This material has been gathered since 1981 and continues to the present day. The greater part of it is available for research and teaching.

The Mass Observation Archive is partly self-supporting and runs a Friends scheme to finance its work. Some of the funds earned by this scheme go towards conservation and preservation of collections like that of the CCC. To join the scheme, please see the website www.massobs.org.uk, email moa@sussex.ac.uk or write to:

The Mass Observation Archive
Special Collections
University of Sussex Library
Brighton BN1 9QL

Acknowledgements

First and foremost, I want to thank the women of the Cooperative Correspondence Club and their families. I am grateful that they generously made the CCC papers available in the Mass Observation Archive for public research. Even more so, I am thankful for the time and effort that everyone gave in helping me hunt down facts, proof-reading drafts and sharing and entrusting me with their personal stories. I would like to make particular note of Rose Hacker for her foresight in depositing the collection in the Mass Observation Archive and for the encouragement, help and friendship she has given me over the past three years. For the sake of privacy, I will not list the individual women or family members, but I am indebted to you all. This would not have been possible without your support and help, so thank you.

Next I would like to thank the trustees of the Mass Observation Archive at the University of Sussex for permission to use, and quote from, the Cooperative Correspondence Club Collection/Hacker Papers. I am particularly grateful to Dorothy Sheridan for originally granting me access to the papers and for her help and dedication with the initial stages of my research. This project would not have been possible without her and I am forever indebted. I would like to express my deepest thanks to the staff at Special Collections at the University of Sussex for all their hard work and support and for providing such a welcoming and friendly atmosphere to work in. Special mention goes to Joy Eldridge for her encouragement through the first half of the project and to Sandra Koa Wing for her endless support and advice. Many thanks as well to Fiona Courage, Karen Watson, Simon Homer, Helen Monk, Lucy Dean and Lucy Pearson for their tireless support, help and enthusiasm. With regard to the collection, I am also grateful to Hera Cook for her role in helping to bring the papers to the Mass Observation Archive and to Ann Hare for her work in establishing the initial copyrights. It is through their involvement and that of the staff of Special Collections that the CCC papers became accessible to researchers like myself.

Thank you to the members of the Centre for Life History Research in the Sussex Institute at the University of Sussex for granting me status as a Visiting Research Fellow throughout my research period. I owe a particular debt of gratitude to Al Thomson for encouraging me to do this book in the first place and helping me to get started. I am also incredibly grateful to Gerry Holloway and Claire Langhamer for reading drafts, helping with research queries, and for their enthusiasm and guidance.

I would like to make special mention of Robert Malcolmson from Queen's University, Canada. This book is very much a result of his tutelage and encouragement, and I am most grateful for all of the things that he has taught me. I am thankful to David Mills from the University of Alberta, Canada, for starting me along the way by giving me my first letter collection to explore.

A number of people were involved in the research process. I would like to thank Val Thompsett for her research and for leading me to the modern-day correspondence magazine network. Through her I was able to survey nearly a hundred other correspondence-magazine contributors, all of whom I am indebted to for replying to me and aiding me in my quest for knowledge about this once mysterious genre. In particular, I would like to thank Chris White, Janice Try, Margaret T, Carol Wake, Eilis Thorn, Richard Bowlby, Ann Ashby and Peggy Barnes.

Many thanks to the Western Mail and Echo Ltd for permission to use their photograph of Angharad, and to the *Scotsman* for permission to use their photograph of Yonire. Also, thank you to Jonathan Ring and Graham Jepson for their photographic contributions and to all of the CCC families who graciously lent me their special photos.

Many people offered their time and expertise out of the goodness of their hearts. I would like to thank: Margaretta Jolly and Nick Hubble for offering advice, Karen Tennant for her transcription work, Annette Rawstrone at *Nursery World* for helping with my research, Theresa Lawrence for her support and encouragement, Hera Cook for reading drafts of my thesis and giving useful feedback, Ann Hare for introducing me to Rose Hacker, Amanda Posey for her guidance and advice, Mary Cranitch and Emma Wakefield at Lambent Productions for their enthusiasm for the project, and Jill Frizzley and Tim Theroux for their legal advice. For their help and advice with regard to my contract, I would like to thank Camilla Hornby from Curtis Brown, and the Society of Authors, particularly Jo Hodder. I am indebted to Simon Garfield for having faith in my project and putting me in contact with Faber and Faber.

Special mention goes to Silva Simsova for all of her work in compiling and sorting through the CCC material before it was deposited in the Archive and for helping Rose to write her manuscript.

I would like to make particular note of the editorial work done by Ann Louise Bailey. She was a crucial part of the process, as she meticulously edited the entire text several times, working to very short deadlines. I am particularly thankful for her keen attention to detail and her unfailing dedication.

I am so thankful to the team at Faber and Faber for believing in the book and making it a reality. First of all I would like to thank the many people behind the scenes who worked hard to help shape the book into its final form. I am thankful to Camilla Smallwood for her help and patience with regard to the contract, to Henry Volans for his general support, to Bomi Odufunade for her help with promotion and, to name only a few, Joanna Ellis, David Watkins, Kate Beal and Susan Holmes for their work and encouragement. Many thanks to Ian Bahrami for his helpful editing, fact checking and design work. Finally, the whole experience was an immense pleasure particularly because of my two editors, Julian Loose and Hannah Griffiths. My warmest gratitude to Julian for giving me a chance, for editing and advising and being a great support. I am grateful to Hannah for her genuine enthusiasm, her investment in the book and all of her invaluable hard work and dedication.

So many other people have contributed to this project in various ways. I would like to thank: Manjula Alles, Lisa Benfield, Leocadio Bogata, Tara Borle, Todd and Joan Cassidy, Vicky Conry, Luke Dusza, Erika Erskine, Romaine Farquet, Pascal Keel, Michael McNair, Silvia Nardoni, Ramón Padilla, Dimitrios Patounas, María José Pedrosa Pardo, María Álvarez Reyes, Ivan Saldaña, Debbie Tremblay, Mikkel Vestergaard and Zoe Woods. I am so grateful and thankful to Sam Carroll, Jen Purcell and Krista Woodley for their kindness, editing, intellectual feedback and moral support. I owe particular thanks again to Sandra

Koa Wing, who was an integral part of the process and a mentor and friend to me in so many ways. Special mention goes to Nikki Anger, Anita Cassidy, Brandi Johnson, Genesta Mackay and Kathleen Wright for editing, listening and for being wonderful friends.

A Edgar Bermúdez Contreras, gracias por siempre estar ahí para mí, por ser un gran apoyo, por escucharme y por enseñarme tantas cosas valiosas.

My work is always the result of the efforts of my whole family. This was undoubtedly a group project. First I would like to thank Scott MacPhail for his passion for history and his enthusiasm. Thank you to my aunt Barbara Caffery and Art Caspary for their constant support and encouragement. To my brothers and sisters, James, Kate, Jim and Emma, I am so thankful for all of your hard work, for your editing, advising, listening and reading, and just for being there.

Few people are given the opportunity to pursue their dream. I was given this chance, and for this I will be forever thankful to my mom and dad. They gave me unending support and made this book possible.